Elliott Louis Gallery

June 21 – July 2

John Koerner spoke 6/24/11

A Brush with Life

A Brush with Life

John Koerner

Ronsdale Press

A Brush with Life

RONSDALE PRESS
3350 West 21 Avenue
Vancouver BC Canada V6S 1G7
www.ronsdalepress.com

Design and Typesetting: Michael Dymund and Paula Gustafson, Artichoke Publishing
Cover Design: Michael Dymund

Ronsdale Press wishes to thank the Canada Council for the Arts, the Government of Canada through the Book Publishing Industry Development Program (BPIDP), and the Province of British Columbia through the British Columbia Arts Council for their support of its publishing program.

Library and Archives Canada Cataloguing in Publication

Koerner, John, 1913–
A brush with life / John Koerner

Includes bibliographical references and index.
ISBN 1-55380-032-X

1. Koerner, John, 1913– 2. Painters—Canada—Biography. I. Title.

ND249.K557A2 2005 759.11 C2005-903387-8

Printed and bound in China

Contents

Acknowledgements

This book is gratefully dedicated to my wife, Lisa Birnie. It consisted of scattered notebook entries until her judgment, her writer's sensitivity, and her ingenious editing transformed it.

I would like to thank Gordon Snyder, who originally suggested this book and was a continual source of inspiration, and Paula Gustafson for her invaluable advice and professional assistance.

A vote of thanks is due to Raymond Lum and for his fine photography of a number of my paintings.

I am greatly indebted to David McLean and Eric Strauss of Berkeley for their continued and most valued support.

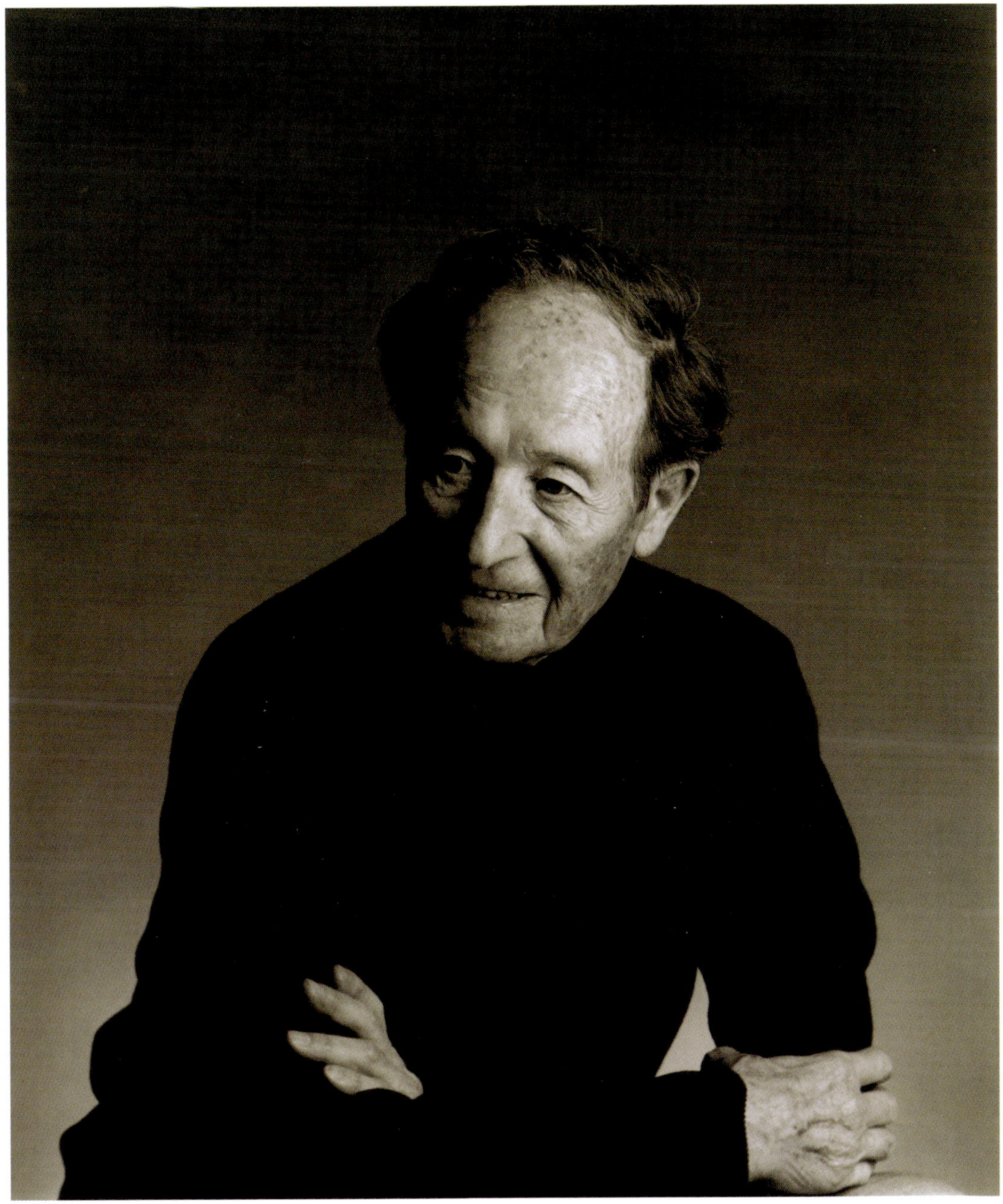

photo: Yukiko Onley

Introduction

To say I was thrilled to be asked to contribute this introduction would be an understatement. To add that I was also slightly daunted would be a fiction. I was thrilled because I have long felt it a privilege to live intimately with John Koerner's art. I have six of his paintings on my walls. They enrich every day of my life. But therein also lies the daunting constituent. In an age of speed, of the quick glance, of gobbling digestion, John's paintings don't so much invite as demand meditation, however foreshortened, however wrenched from the pressures of time. His is not the art of blaring headlines, of stark explosions of colour or dramatic statements designed to arrest the beholder and deliver an immediate message. These paintings don't radiate off the wall; rather, they irradiate and imbue — if the viewer is willing to slow down and calmly concentrate on the painting's visual values.

None of this should be surprising when one considers the nature of the man, the statements he has made about his work, or the palette he employs. Indeed, John's vocabulary of colour addresses the very core of painterly significance.

I have known John as a friend for nearly fifty years; that is, for the bulk of the time I have shared British Columbia with him. It is this fact that allows me to state with some assurance that the artist is the man and the man is the artist. In speech, in the cast of his mind, even in the ambiance of the several homes in which he has resided since we first met, there is a sense of place that connects directly with his paintings. The same pervasive calm of his home and the quietness of his demeanour is echoed in his canvases.

During those wonderful self-informing years when I was the art critic of the *Vancouver Sun* — a job that benefitted me as a writer more than any benisons I could bestow on my visual counterparts — I learned the necessity of approaching each artist with an individual perception, to submit to a proper passivity if I was to reach his or her inner essence: the signature in the pigment and form rather than the one written in the corner of the canvas. John Koerner's art, in spite of knowing him personally, proved to be amongst the most elusive. No, this painting was not a Gordon Smith, not a Don Jarvis, not a Toni Onley. Apart from the superficial regional sensibility these artists sometimes shared, John's paintings inhabited a different world, evoked a different aesthetic and philosophy, and ultimately spoke a different language.

I speak here of a time before the explosion in colour that issued from John's palette during and following his trip to Africa, before he began his extensive *Pacific Gateway* series, and also before he painted the singular mural inspired by Mozart's *Magic Flute* for David Lemon's classical record store in Kitsilano. All of these gave witness to a radical diversity in theme and colour spun from personal circumstance — the latter, in particular, to his profound empathy with classical music. I remember vividly the phone call when an uncharacteristically angry John Koerner sounded off at the philistine attitude of someone at CBC-Radio who had the temerity to air a blatant, cheap signature tune for a serious program he regularly enjoyed. Listener and viewer beware! This quiet-voiced man and author of calm canvases can erupt in moral indignation as well as painterly exuberance when the mood takes him.

I cannot conclude this brief commentary on an artist who holds such a significant niche in my life without reference to his extraordinary resilience and sustained artistic vision as he enjoys his tenth decade on Planet Earth. The mere invocation of age in association with his recent works, however, would be to besmirch and degrade the art *per se*. His paintings and drawings exist in their own insistent right and stand happily free of the sentimentality too many today accord to longevity. Assuredly, his latest paintings only shed further light on the extensive aesthetic and philosophical vision I believe has steadily developed as an intrinsic tool to his eyes and artistry ever since his enquiring youth in pre-war Europe.

Only a fool doesn't learn from his mistakes. The true artist is never quite satisfied, never stops feeding on both the temporal and moral experience. Such is John Koerner.

— *David Watmough*

The Magic Flute, mural installed in The Magic Flute music store, Vancouver, 1993; now in the collection of the Vancouver General Hospital

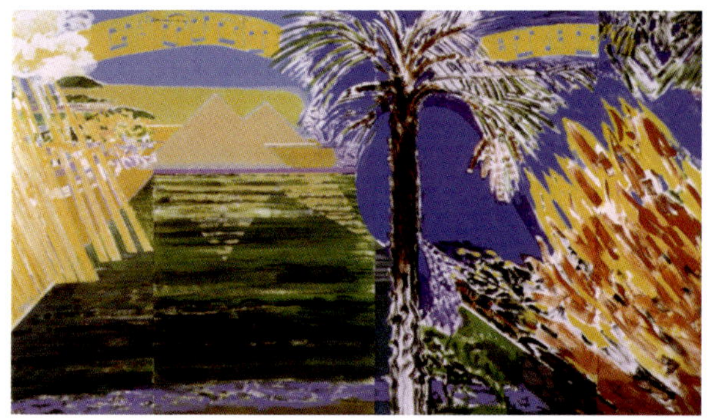

Work

Early in my career I decided that, despite the horrors and disasters in this world, my work would celebrate all positive values and leave negativity to those artists who perceive a nihilistic approach as being their best contribution.

The Japanese word *akirame* means acceptance without complaint, and the word *sosaku* means creation. I believe these concepts — the acceptance of our limitations and the determination to shape our life as best we can into a work of art — are of value to everyone. Even more so, they apply to the artist. For me, *akirame* and *sosaku* serve as a primary compass point to "never paint anything you cannot feel, never paint anything without emotion, never paint anything without passion."

In my work I try to produce images somewhat like a Japanese garden where, on a sand-raked surface, rocks, moss, and plants are sparingly but most effectively placed. Each aspect is to be contemplated and absorbed internally. Their meaning becomes clear through meditation.

As well, I have been guided for many years by the teachings of Bô Yin Râ, who counsels us to be caring in all actions, words, and thoughts. What Jesus of Nazareth taught in the form of parables, Bô Yin Râ teaches in a contemporary language that gives clear direction to be followed in life and in art. I try to metaphorically indicate this direction in my paintings. Working on a new painting to add to a series is like composing another verse to a favourite song.

In much of West Coast modernist painting, such as the work of Emily Carr, Jack Shadbolt, and Gordon Smith, we find ecstatic signs of natural rhythms and a joyous revelation of primal forces. My purpose is different. While I also admit an addiction to the beauty of British Columbia, I believe I am the only artist who uses these natural references while at the same time expressing a world view resulting from a study of the writings of Bô Yin Râ.

The formal characteristics of my paintings have been influenced by the Italian masters, such as Giorgione and Titian, which I studied very thoroughly in the Louvre during my youth in Paris. Amongst the modernist painters, I am much indebted to Bonnard and Matisse, whose use of spatial recession through the juxtaposition of colour — often in modulated, adjoining areas — enabled my design methods.

Actual observation has led me to introduce multiple horizons into my paintings. I have found that the eye can be deceived into seeing more than one horizon line, especially here on the West Coast where low clouds, effects of light, or the illusion of floating islands can easily lead to complex images. These mirages reinforce the notion that truth in nature sometimes reveals itself in a multiplicity of realities.

Similarly, in some of my paintings single horizon lines turn into clouds that transform into islands or the agitated surface of the sea. In other paintings flowers diffuse into geometric forms while still suggesting their organic shapes and structure. These overlapping, transformative relationships between the picture's various components declare my belief that spiritual consciousness and intuitive feeling offer keys to comprehend and accept the world around us.

Obviously, I am attached to the natural world that surrounds me and am continuously learning from it. At the same time, it does not prevent me from including abstract forms which can add opulence to a painting.

The painter's personality is inevitably stamped on a painting. It shows as clearly as his or her handwriting. Some artists, wishing to remain anonymous, avoid or erase all traces of individual touch. I find this impossible to do. I am fully committed to the work in progress and simply cannot avoid openly showing my involvement. This results in impulsive, idiosyncratic handling, rather than a finished appearance. To my mind, producing a finished painting would contradict the very nature of the work which — depending on the viewpoint — is either in a state of becoming or being reconstructed in the eye of the beholder.

Like the French Impressionists, whose work I admired during my first prolonged stay in Paris, I have been strongly influenced by seventeenth- and eighteenth-century *ukiyo-e* prints. During my visits to Japan I have had the pleasure of learning more about its culture. The Japanese aesthetic appeals to me enormously in many ways: the design of utensils and household tools, ceramics and weaving, as well as post-and-beam construction methods and garden architecture. Japan's all-embracing recognition of the arts and crafts seems to me far preferable to North America's grudging acceptance of visual art as an unessential embellishment.

The sand garden appears in many of my paintings. Its design clearly calls for contemplation, an essential approach to appreciating art. Another reason I use the garden motif is to juxtapose the coastline of British Columbia with the Japanese sea shore. There are also similarities between the appearance of our Gulf Islands in the ocean and the stones and azaleas in temple gardens.

In classical Japanese art, space recession is conveyed by a gradual mounting of far vision above a closer view. This sophisticated solution influenced much of modern art, replacing the Renaissance obsession with the depiction of deep space (which sometimes deteriorated into tunnel vision). Long before the Cubists sought to heed and preserve the flat surface of the canvas, Japanese pictorial space emphasized that a landscape was a paraphrase of nature, a celebration and an allusion. The pictorial space in my paintings is also flat with the composition rising upward, indicating distance only by variations in colour and not by perspectival recession.

I also owe my close colour relationships to historical Japanese art. Sharp colour contrasts produce a more immediate and more forceful impact — and tend to please the less visually literate — but they are not my aim. Rather, I choose colours that are the equivalents to inner calm, peace, and balance.

An element unknown to Japanese artists was the use of impasto. This technique of applying paint is a characteristic of oil painting. Heavy impasto used by European artists has often been considered a sign of passion. I have, instead, followed the Eastern approach, convinced that less can sometimes be more and that flat colour can be fully expressive.

Another lesson I've integrated into my work is the Japanese principle of restraint: a total opposition to the lavishness and extravagance of the Renaissance and the Baroque which have had such a long-lasting effect on Western art. A subtle work of art is more demanding of the viewer but it achieves its aim of involvement. In temple gardens and in many private gardens we can see the effective application of this principle, where the duality of nature and art is so subtly combined that it is difficult to decide where nature ends and art begins. Such a decision is not needed, however, because it is exactly this fusion that is intended. So close, in fact, were the Japanese to nature, and so indistinguishable was nature from art to them, that when Japan began to import foreign concepts during the Meiji era (1867–1912), the word *shizen* had to be invented to express the idea of nature.

An artist's statement often deteriorates into rhapsodic subjectivity, when what it should do is provide background information and clues that may be of assistance to the interested observer. This is a brief explanation of what I have been trying to achieve. There remains only a bit of advice to those who wish to devote themselves to art.

In my experience, waiting for inspiration is futile. I have found that ideas come to me in two ways. I may have had a theme on my mind for some time, then one morning I wake up with an almost fully formed idea and a sense of urgency to start painting to try to realize it. Other times, when work is not going well, it is useless to wait inactively for the "divine spark." Ideas sometimes lurk in the subconscious, or in dreams, so active work in the form of drawing, designing, or painting can often release them.

The word *inspiration* comes from the Latin *in spiritu*. I believe that true creation originates in the depths of the human spirit, a creative source that no psychological research has ever fully explained.

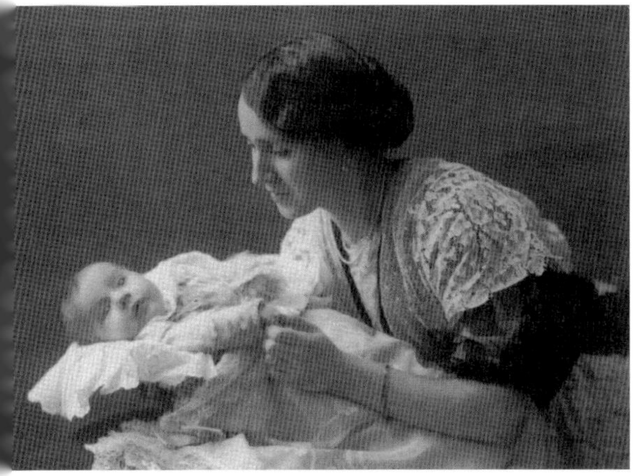

John Koerner and his mother, 1914

Being

In 1640 the army of the Hapsburgs defeated the Czech troops at the battle of the White Mountain (Bilá Hora) just outside Prague. That year the earliest reference to my family is made in the archives of the city. The House of Hapsburg originated in Austria and Spain in the twelfth century and for almost five hundred years ruled various regions of Europe. It's unclear whether my family arrived with the Spanish military, or whether they were established in the heart of Europe before that time; however, on my first trip to Spain in 1974, I had a powerful feeling that I had roots there, an emotional connection I have never experienced in my travels before or since.

Knowing about our ancestors, I believe, adds to the consciousness of ourselves and perhaps reinforces a sense of belonging and continuity. My paternal grandparents lived in Nový Jičín, about 150 miles southeast of Prague. Their large, comfortable house was set in several acres of land which included an orchard, an apiary, a duck pond, and a shed for geese and chickens.

My grandfather, Isidore, had four sons — all of whom later became engaged in the forest industry — and six daughters. The eldest child, my father Theodore, was born in 1881. He was given the name of the eighteenth-century poet Theodore Körner, the only known artist amongst my predecessors.

Grandfather Isidore was a genial man, well-read, well-educated, and possessed of great charm. He lit up a room when he entered it. I remember that every evening he would arrive home precisely as the clock's pendulum struck six o'clock. He would open the door wide and, with a smile and a twinkle, greet everyone with the words, "Your obedient servant."

My grandfather kept his own stable of four carriage horses. He was very fond of them. One day he took my brother Fred and me for a drive. It was late Fall, the weather was quite cold, and it had started to snow. On a left turn, the carriage wheels slipped off the edge of the road. As the carriage tipped, the coachman slid off his perch and the horses bolted. My grandfather jumped out and ran as fast as he could behind the runaway horses, trying to retrieve the reins trailing in the snow. Inside the careening carriage, my brother and I sat terrified and helpless. Fortunately, a passerby managed to seize the reins and bring the carriage to a halt.

My grandfather's interest in horses had developed during eight years of compulsory military service, a duty brought about because of a crisis in the Balkans. He was stationed on the Turkish border and later took part in the Austrian-Hungarian occupation of Bosnia and Herzegovina. His love of horses was shared by many family members, including my father who was a keen rider. He taught me to ride mainly, I suspect, so that I could exercise his horse, Agricola, while he was out of town. Agricola was very good at dressage, but refused to jump even the lowest fence or ditch.

My father kept Agricola at a local riding club located near the headquarters of a cavalry regiment which, I discovered, arranged tournaments or paper hunts for club members. This sounded like fun to me, so I joined the club. Fox hunting was never allowed, so we had paper trails, dropped by the Master of the Hunt, often leading to deliberately confusing dead ends. Nevertheless, to a blast of trumpets, the "hunters" would ride back to the starting point where trays of brandy were passed around. It was harmless, good fun and more of a challenge than it might seem, particularly since all of the mounts were provided by the cavalry regiment which went out of its way to choose the friskiest horses in their stables.

My grandmother, Maria, came from a farming family in the Moravian highlands. Her attachment to the land was deep, as was her pride in managing a household of ten children and several servants. If my grandfather met someone in need of a good meal, friend or stranger alike, he would bring him home for dinner. Like a magician, my grandmother would fill the extra plate.

If my grandmother was generous in her hospitality, she was equally strict in enforcing household rules, especially in the dining room. To this day, whenever I find my elbows touching the table, I can hear her brisk disapproval. She was equally careful about keeping track of the apples on the trees and the jars of honey in the pantry. If any was missing, she was quick to blame the inmates from a nearby minimum security prison who occasionally worked in the lumberyard or stables. Sometimes my brother Fred and I were at fault and our sense of guilt forced us to confess.

I did not know my maternal grandparents well because they lived some distance away in

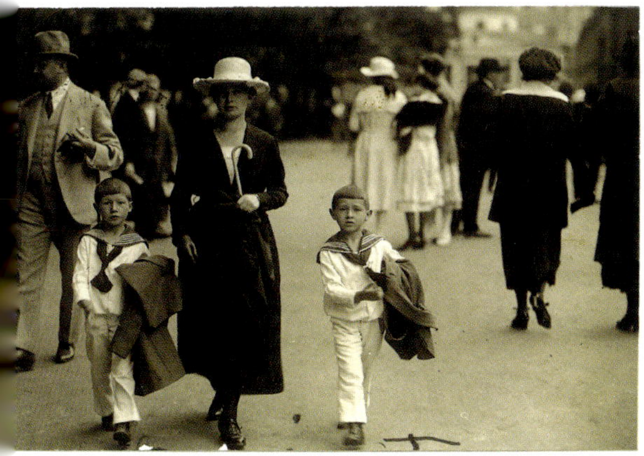

John Koerner and his brother Fred taking the waters at Mariánske Lázňe (Marienbad), Czechoslovakia, 1920

a small town in Moravia, where they owned a grocery business. Although my memories of visits to them are scanty, I was aware of the same welcoming love in their house as I felt in my paternal grandparents' home.

Even as a child I was visually active and I remember thinking that my maternal grandmother, Fanny, was a most beautiful woman. I later found out that this was not a very original observation. My admiration of her beauty was shared by many others. I also remember that my maternal grandfather always wore a bowler hat tipped at a slight angle, and that he kept a large barrel of sauerkraut in his basement where I went sometimes for a tasting.

When I was about seven years old my mother fell ill with tuberculosis and spent a year in hospital in Switzerland, leaving my brother Fred and me to be cared for by a variety of hired homemakers. My mother had always been an avid reader and during her recovery she immersed herself in the imaginative realm of literature. On her return home she introduced me to the richness of Czech literature, and many of the books she recommended are still important to me.

Czech is a Slavic language, derived from the same mainspring as Russian, Polish, and Yugoslav. With the possible exception of Lithuanian, Czech is today the most highly inflected language in Europe. It is full of affectionate expressions. Not only every proper name but also instruments, tools, furniture, animals, everything is called by an endearment, a pet word based on its formal nominative but enhanced by a loving ending. My Czech name is Jan (pronounced like Ian, only without emphasis on the I). As a boy I was called Jeníčku, and later, when grown up, Jendo.

When I was about twelve years old I was enrolled in what was then called a gymnasium, somewhat like a prep school. I was brought up speaking Czech and German, and had a natural and quite intense interest in languages, so I took classes in Latin and French. Later, I learned English, and still later acquired some knowledge of Italian, Dutch, Spanish, and Japanese. I regret not learning Chinese when I first came to Vancouver, but at that time no one anticipated the number of immigrants from Hong Kong, Taiwan, and the People's Republic of China. I tried later on to master the language, but without success. Too little, too late.

To improve my French, my parents sent me to Paris when I was fifteen years old. What an idea to send a boy that age to the City of Light! I had heard that the best way to learn

French was to have a French girlfriend. In my innocence I acted accordingly and became quite fluent. My main passion, however, was drawing and painting, and I spent weeks in the Louvre looking at works by the old masters and visiting galleries where I was equally thrilled by Cubist and Surrealist art. I also worked in the Montparnasse studio of Paul Colin and studied life drawing at the Academie de la Grande Chaumière. Othon Friesz, a prominent supporter of the Fauvist attack on traditional colour painting, would review our work. He was a man not disposed to being questioned or contradicted. After delivering a few cryptic comments on our efforts he would lecture us on using arbitrary combinations of colour.

Even before hearing these Fauvist statements I had become addicted to colour. In my visits to the Louvre I had wondered why the old masters applied warm colours to represent closeness in a landscape and cool atmospheric blues to convey distance. Should I be like Constable who departed from the rules of landscape painting by introducing local colours of green in the foreground? Why do our eyes register different colours? How did colours work together or against each other? At fifteen I longed to know the rules of the game so I could follow or depart from them.

Paul Colin's encouragement and wit were of immense help and his beautiful *amie* and model, Madelaine, was a most helpful mentor. Of all the French people I knew at the time she was the only one who gladly corrected any mistakes I made in the language. After a busy morning's work in Colin's studio, his students would gather at the lunch table in an adjoining room. Our meals would often erupt into wild discussions as we argued about art techniques and theories. Firmly yet gracefully, Madelaine would guide the conversation back to a courteous and civilized level. This was my introduction to French culture, politics, and social attitudes, and it could not have been more valuable.

After two months in Paris I returned to Prague to continue my high school education as well as my art training. By now I knew that all I ever wanted to do was paint. My parents were aware of my passion for art and had no objection to my wish to spend the next summer travelling throughout Italy with my school mate, Oldřich Blažíček, who later became an art historian.

That was a glorious summer! We hadn't a worry in the world and all the treasures of Italian art were spread before us. Together we went from one museum or gallery to another — Florence, Bologna, Pisa, Siena, Rome

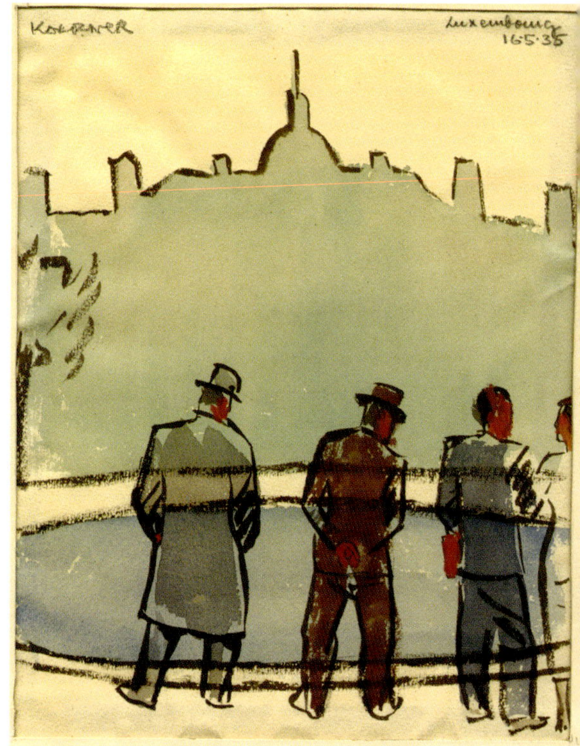

Men Watching Sailboats at Luxembourg Pool, crayon and watercolour on paper, 7 x 5.25 inches, dated 16-5-35 (1935), collection of the artist

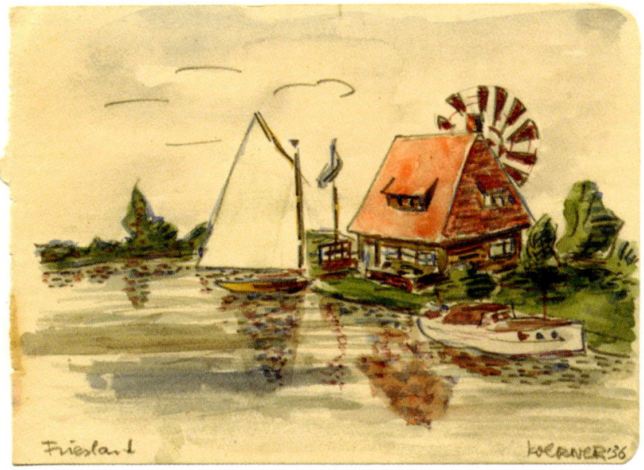

On a Sailing Trip to Friesland, watercolour on paper, 4.5 x 6 inches, dated 1936, collection of the artist

— studying, examining, reading, sketching. We would sit on the steps of a museum, waiting for the door to open in the morning. At closing time, they would ask us to leave. Of course, we sometimes behaved like the sixteen-year-olds we were. On one occasion a woman seated behind us on a bus said to her son, "I never want to hear you speaking like those two young men!" It never occurred to us that anyone in Italy spoke Czech.

During this Italian summer I fell in love with the glowing colours and luminosity of Giorgione, a love that continues to this day. I felt I had found in Giorgione a technique and attitude toward art that was in harmony with my own temperament. Years later it would prove to be the appropriate approach for the themes I chose to deal with.

Despite my passion for art, I had no confidence that I could succeed as a painter and I was uncertain about what I should do after completing my studies at the gymnasium. My father, for whom I had the highest regard, suggested I study law. I enrolled at the Charles University in Prague and, to my surprise, found the study of law very interesting, particularly after I discovered that attendance at lectures and seminars was not obligatory as long as I passed all the scheduled exams. With my time freed up, I began to travel, first to Geneva where I pursued the notion of doing my law studies in French. Geneva was a stodgy little town in those days, so I moved on to Paris where I sat in on the occasional lecture at the Sorbonne — and pursued my thirst for art.

By now I was nineteen and, despite my pleasant, untroubled existence, I was beginning to ask larger questions about life and its meaning — or if there was any meaning. I had been raised in a family of non-believers and non-joiners who nevertheless fully subscribed to a thoroughly moral and charitable way of life. This, however, did not satisfy me and I set out to try to find answers on my own. I was intrigued by Plato's statement that the world as we know it is only a reflection of the world of ideas, that true reality is beyond and above it. The distinction he made between the empirical world and the transcendent resonated with me, as did Socrates' awareness of the fundamental significance of the human soul. Such ways of thinking were new to me. I intuitively felt that these ideas were related to my love of painting, but I didn't know how. All I knew was that I had a very strong desire to learn more.

Socrates taught that the good life was achieved by conduct "as best serves the good of the human soul." One of the prerequisites was to know the nature and essence of "the good." I had already studied Descartes, Kant, and Hegel, but thought they all attributed too much to the intellect and far too little to intuition. Even Albert Einstein, whose five papers written in 1905 forever changed our understanding of nature, referred to his intuition as the origin of all his masterful findings. Nonetheless, all his intuitive leaps were later validated, although some were confirmed by evidence only many years later. I had also read many contemporary philosophers, including Jean-Paul Sartre and A.J. Ayer and his Oxford circle. They claimed that moral judgments are purely expressions of feeling and, being unverifiable, may be true or false. But I knew that feeling, intuition, and imagination are very real to those whose work is closely linked with art, even though, philosophically, all three may be deemed subjective. So although I did not totally dismiss philosophy, I recognized its limitations and refused to rely entirely on its findings. I also observed that true spiritual growth often was weakened when it was confined within insititutionalized religions with their dogmatic man-made rules.

I came to distinguish between the true meaning of the "glad tidings," and the mythology that was added later. I also realized that the Old and New Testaments, as well as the Koran and Hindu and Buddhist writings, were composed by true believers and allegorical storytellers as a means of sharing their convictions with the illiterate people of their time. As a result, I tried to find my own truth. Serendipitously, at this time I was meeting regularly with a friend of my father's. Although there was a difference in our ages, I felt at ease with Emil and able to talk of my interest in the nature and essence of "the good." He gave me the name of a Dr. Kober, a resident of Basel and a publisher by profession. On my return to Switzerland I followed up on his introduction. After listening to me, Dr. Kober showed me several books by an author named Bô Yin Râ, a name adopted by J.A. Schneiderfranken (1876–1943). Dr. Kober explained that the name Bô Yin Râ was created for its tonal quality and had no literal meaning, nor any connection with any eastern religion or philosophy.

The strangeness of Bô Yin Râ's name did not bother me. I accepted that we are all given names without regard to how we might later feel about them. Also, since I had been raised in a rather formal manner, it seemed to me that creating one's own name to express one's own personality was a liberating action. I quickly perused the contents of the books from Dr. Kober and saw at once how they

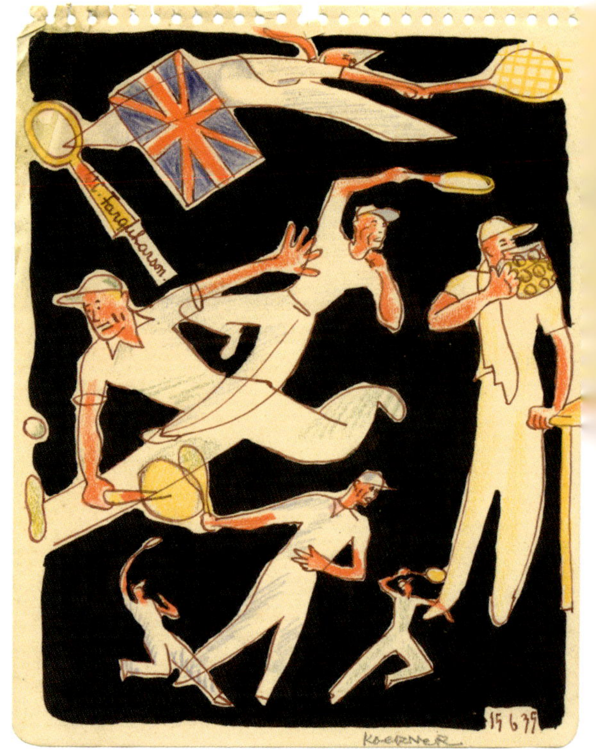

My Passion was Tennis, ink and crayon on paper, 7 x 5.25 inches, dated 1935, collection of the artist

illuminated the human condition, connecting it with the spiritual sphere. On impulse I bought each of the 30 books by Bô Yin Râ.

My initial feeling that these books would provide the answers I was seeking turned out to be right. That night, settling into my lodgings in Geneva, I became absorbed in studying Bô Yin Râ's writings. I found they were in full accord with the teachings of Jesus of Nazareth, they dealt with all important issues, and they used contemporary language instead of arcane parables. The more I read, the more insight I gained into an objective structure of spiritual reality, the all-pervading presence manifest within man's soul on earth. (Seventy years later I am still reading and learning from Bô Yin Râ.) What I did learn was to ask appropriate questions. Instead of questioning the meaning of life, I came to ask what meaning I could give to life. Instead of wondering if a soul exists, I tried to find out how I could become conscious of it. Rather than doubting that there is life after death, it became important to discover what I could do in this earthly life to be prepared for life beyond.

While I was following my passion for art and philosophy (intermingled with some obligatory law studies), my family's forestry business continued a steady and prosperous growth. My father Theodore was a partner in the family firm and was known as a very solid and cautious businessman. Business deals were closed with a handshake, with never any doubt of their validity. As time went on, his three younger brothers joined the firm as partners and their energy and initiative took the enterprise to an international level.

Uncle Otto lived in Amsterdam and looked after the family business interests in Western Europe. From this vantage point he could clearly foresee Hitler's ambitions and was certain they would lead to war. Otto kept warning us that, although our family was known as free-thinkers, our roots were Jewish. Despite his admonitions, we could not perceive the danger and continued our lives as before. The time came, however, when Otto insisted we leave Prague.

One day in early September 1937, I came home from the university library to find no one at home. My parents had fled to Paris, leaving behind instructions for me to follow them. I telephoned Jiřina (Irene), a woman with whom I'd had a close relationship for approximately three years, and threw some clothes into a suitcase. Jiřina drove me to the Prague airport and there we said goodbye, aware that we might never again see one another. In fact, she visited me in Paris a few months later, but by then political events had made our situation impossible. We exchanged letters, but following the outbreak of war our correspondence was stopped. Much later I learned she had died.

At the Prague airport, my uncles Walter and Leon were waiting for me and we all boarded the same DC-3 that uncle Otto had chartered to evacuate their wives and families a day earlier. We flew to Amsterdam and the next day travelled to Paris by train. The only family member left behind was my brother Fred, who was doing compulsory military service near Prague and could not get away at that time. After his discharge, he joined the family firm's office in London.

What an upheaval! I was saddened that I had to leave my home without even a goodbye to my friends, but Paris was dear to me. Relocation was much harder for my parents. Neither of them spoke French. Their lives had been solidly rooted in their homeland. Eventually I was able to find a place for them at Cannes in the south of France where the pace of life was slower and easier.

The move from Prague put an end to my law studies. I enrolled again at the Sorbonne, and found work with Otto Lindner, a designer who later moved to New York and was very successful. He and I worked very well together and enjoyed several excellent design commissions.

Paris in those pre-war days was a marvellous place to live and work. I moved into a mini-studio apartment in the Latin Quarter and ate in bistros frequented by truck drivers where the food was always the cheapest and the best. Through fellow art students at the Sorbonne I met several Comédie-Française actors and became good friends with one of them, René de la Plante. We often went to performances together and I learned a great deal about the Paris theatre scene from him.

My Paris friends also included Madelaine and Maurice de Bestigui who entertained in the grand manner at their elegant residence in Passy. I had originally met them on Ibiza in 1936, when I had painted Madelaine's portrait while Maurice was off spear fishing. Maurice was fond of using phrases connected with hunting and fishing and one of them remains in my memory: "*Vendre le peau d'ours avant de l'avoir tué*" — "to sell the bear's skin before you've killed it."

This then was my social life: the occasional elegant dinner party, conversations with friends over innumerable cups of coffee in sidewalk cafés, and hiking with them all over the surrounding countryside. I thought the cabarets were extremely seedy and that part

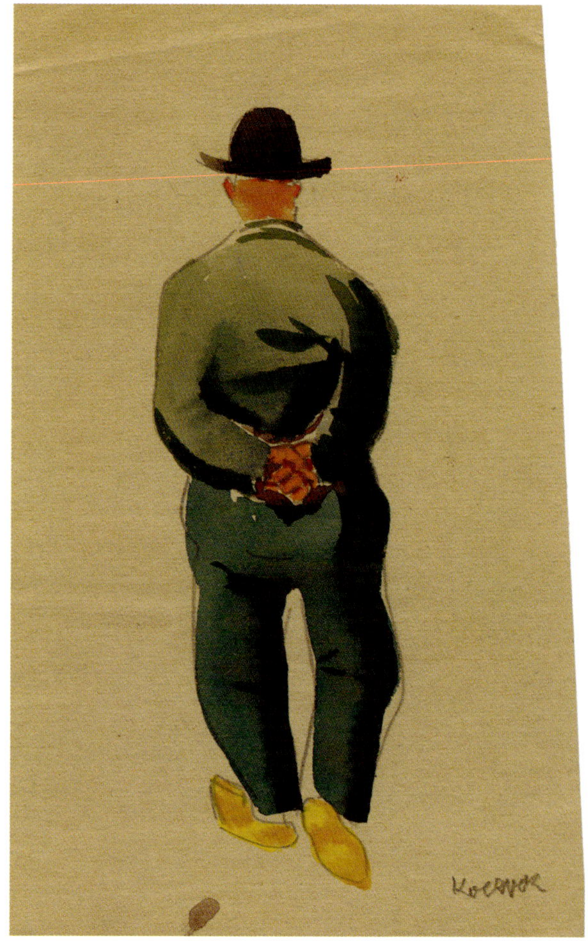

Dutch Farmer, pencil and watercolour on paper, 8 x 5 inches, 1936, collection of the artist

of the nightlife of Paris did not attract me. One evening as I was walking along a street in Montparnasse, a bouncer approached me, praising his establishment. When I showed no intention of stopping, he admonished me with "Monsieur, it will educate you." I did, however, spend some time inside a brothel. A friend I had met in an art history course at the Sorbonne invited me to study with him at "a nice, quiet place that was better than the university library." It was quiet, all right, and very comfortable, with opulent red velvet furniture and no one around to disturb us.

The Viennese painter Victor Tischler was one of my teachers in Paris. He was not much interested in art theory and, instead, told me to observe thoroughly, to "sharpen your vision daily," and to "paint it out." We became good friends, going together to many galleries and exhibition openings, including Salvador Dali's first show in Paris. The Dali exhibition had been highly publicized and the crowd at the gallery near boulevard Montparnasse was huge. Dali appeared wearing a black sombrero and a long black cape lined with red silk. With his extended waxed moustache he looked like a nineteenth-century engraving of Ludwig II, the Mad King of Bavaria.

Dali's paintings were admirably executed, but I found his images too artificial. They seemed to me to be the product of a troubled mind, a mind attempting to escape reality by going into the realm of terrifying dreams. My opinion aside, the show was an instant sensation and Dali's outrageous assertions started him on the road to celebrity. Whatever I thought of his paintings, seeing the show fired up my enthusiasm. I realized how much hard work preceded a successful exhibition. I went back to work with a heightened awareness of the necessity for observation and a desire to be more experimental with colour. More than anything, I started to search for a focussed way in which to express my own viewpoint.

I was now thoroughly settled into Paris with no intention of ever returning to Prague. My affinity was confirmed one day when I was passing the Café des deux Magots. I saw a woman I'd known in Prague and stopped by her table to say hello. She asked when I planned to return to Prague. By this time the Nazis had occupied the city and confiscated my family's property and business. I replied that I now had my *carte d'identité*, needed for foreigners to remain in France as legal visitors, and that I intended to remain in France at least for the time being. She berated me for being fearful and silly, for not wanting to return to my home city as she planned to do in a few days' time. I heard later that she and her family were arrested, taken away, and never heard from again.

While I felt settled in Paris, other members of my family were scattered across two continents. My uncle Walter and his wife Marianne were in London where the family business was now located. My uncle Leon and his wife Thea had left London to look for new business opportunities in North America. The coast of Washington and British Columbia was well known for its forest industry and as they reached Vancouver, Thea came down with a case of mumps. Her illness gave Leon ample time to meet people in the timber business and look at some local sawmills. He saw one in New Westminster that looked promising. It was owned by Kraft Cheese and had not been in operation for some time. With the backing of the London bankers who had previously done business with the family, Leon acquired the mill and invited my brother Fred, two cousins, and me to work for him in the new business on Canada's West Coast.

By that time it was clear to us that Hitler's rantings and threats were real, and that our Czechoslovakia homeland and our homes would be lost. To have the opportunity of a new start in a free country like Canada was a wonderful stroke of luck, even though it meant I would have to temporarily help the family firm and shelve my painterly ambitions. (That it took twelve years before I could devote all my time to my chosen profession was something I didn't anticipate!)

When I told my friends in Paris that I would be leaving for Vancouver, they all asked, "Vancouver? Where is that?" When I showed them its location on the map, they invariably remarked, "*Mon Dieu*, it's at the end of the earth!"

Similarly, I found that many people in Vancouver were so focussed on their own affairs that they were quite unaware of the approaching war clouds in Europe. Some could not understand why anyone would leave his native land and make the trying transition to different customs and standards. In some cases I could sense resentment toward intruding "aliens," which was how we were officially categorized. In other instances, it was a heartwarming experience to be accepted and even welcomed. Later, when war broke out, I volunteered to serve with the Canadian military, but was rejected on medical grounds.

My brother Fred, who had gone to work in the family's London office after the Czech army was disbanded, joined our parents and me at Cherbourg. In May 1939 the four of us departed Europe on the *Empress of Australia*

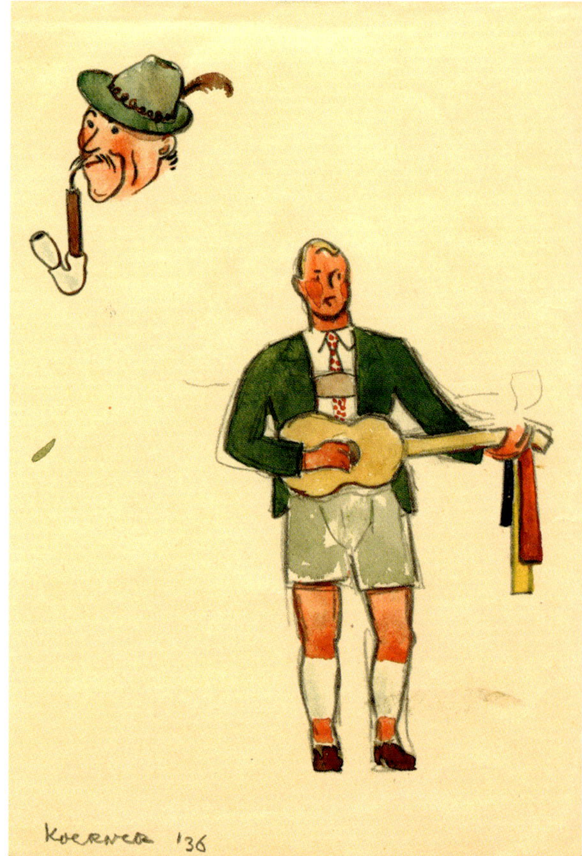

Austrian Guitarist, pencil and watercolour on paper, 8.5 x 5 inches, dated 1936, collection of the artist

(which was later sunk by a German submarine). We landed at Québec City, stayed overnight, then travelled on to Vancouver by train.

What a revelation Canada was! The vastness of the land and the diversity of its geography was overwhelming. As a child raised in a land-locked country I had always hoped I would have the good fortune to some day live by the sea. When I saw Vancouver my first comment was that it was located in the most beautiful setting of any city on the planet. The air was pure, the water clean, the mountains were towering, and the sea was ever changing. Three years earlier the Lions Gate Bridge had been built to link the Guinness family British Properties residential development to the city's downtown core, but at the time there were only a few summer cottages on the north side of Burrard Inlet and many people doubted the bridge's usefulness.

The day after our cross-country train ride ended, I started work in the New Westminster mill, familiarizing myself with the production methods and getting to know the employees and their needs. Later I worked in the personnel department at the company's head office in the Marine Building at the foot of Burrard Street in downtown Vancouver. I worked for the family firm for twelve years.

Soon after war had been declared in 1939, a rumour was started that the family business was broke. A one-week shutdown at the mill fuelled the talk. What actually happened was uncle Leon had flown to England (in a two-engine bomber). He returned with confirmed purchase orders for lumber and the mill started up again. Initially the New Westminster mill concentrated on producing precision-cut kiln-dried western hemlock. The company eventually branched out into pulp and paper production and logging operations.

The name of the new company, Alaska Pine and Cellulose Ltd., resulted from a telephone call between my uncle and the chief forester in Victoria. Western hemlock lumber did not have a good reputation in Europe, where the trees were not a native species. My uncle asked if they could market it as Alaska pine, the other name by which the tree was known. Mr. Orchard replied, "Call it whatever you like, just sell it."

Did I miss Paris? Of course. My thoughts often returned to all that I had left behind in Europe. Being with other emigrés helped ease my regrets. One of them was Otto Lowy, who became a CBC broadcaster and a great supporter of my work when I was unknown. Another supporter was Poldi

(Leopold) Bentley. He had come to Vancouver from Vienna with his family and founded Canadian Forest Products. Oddly enough, I had met Poldi when he and my father were playing in a golf tournament in Prague. I'd been my father's caddy. In Vancouver I met Poldi's son, Peter, who eventually took over his father's lumber business and became one of Vancouver's most prominent benefactors of hospital charities.

Out of this nostalgia for times past, I painted a series entitled *Lost City*. As an artist in Vancouver, I was often lonely. Not only was I a newcomer, I worked quite independently and in my own direction. As well, Vancouver's population at that time was predominantly English and Scottish. My formal demeanour and European manners too frequently made my Canadian contemporaries uneasy. With the exception of Doris and Jack Shadbolt and later Bert and Jessie Binning and Lawren Harris, my overtures of hospitality to fellow artists were not returned.

Privately, although I kept such opinions to myself, I felt that as far as art and culture were concerned, I had landed in the backwash of the Empire. The Vancouver Art Gallery on Georgia Street was a small, sad edifice with a small, sad art collection. The Group of Seven was represented by a motley group of sketches and minor canvases, works that an amateur collector might have gathered at auction, and there were no Emily Carr paintings. Vancouver's one commercial gallery, run by a very nice older man named Mr. Wood on Robson Street, provided framing services.

In 1983 the Vancouver Art Gallery moved to its present location in the neoclassical palace that was formerly the Vancouver court house. Its permanent collection (which includes eight of my works) has increased enormously since the 1950s. Unfortunately, considerable money and storage space has been squandered on self-indulgent garbage masquerading as art, such as Andres Serrano's *Piss Pope*, a plaster portrait submerged in a glass container of urine. It seems that whenever the New York or London critics embrace petulant or provocative products, gallery directors uncritically accept the works as examples of freedom of artistic expression. If the liquid in the glass container evaporates over time, will it be replenished by a staff member, or would ethnic origin or gender be a consideration? A more serious comment concerns the *Massive Change* exhibition. It was a popular success, but emphasized Vancouver's desperate need for another venue which could focus on design, technology, and the crafts. Instead, *Massive*

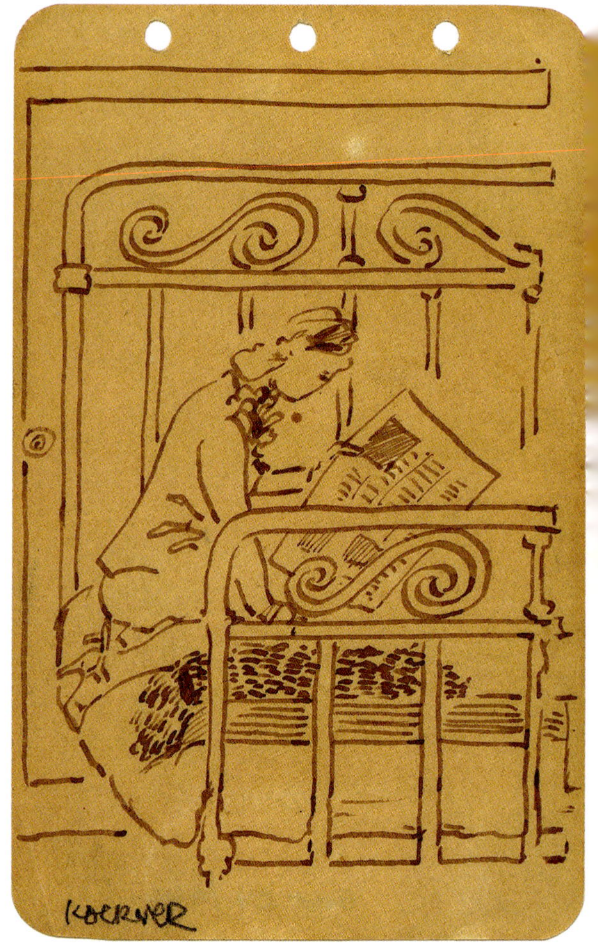

Eileen Reading, brown ink on paper, 5 x 3 inches, dated September 1944, collection of the artist

Change continued the prolonged tradition of diminishing the stature of the Vancouver Art Gallery as an art gallery in the true sense of the word.

I had been in Vancouver about two years when I had the good fortune to meet and become friends with Bill Trapp, a heart surgeon and avid sailor. I enjoyed our day trips in his boat and especially our longer voyages sailing around the Gulf Islands. On these trips I got to know the British Columbia landscape from the water level, and out of this came a series of paintings called *Coast Glitter*. I also became increasingly aware of the aesthetic value of West Coast native art which, at that time, was of little interest and not considered to have any artistic value. The general opinion was that the Northwest Coast peoples' traditions and culture would soon disappear completely.

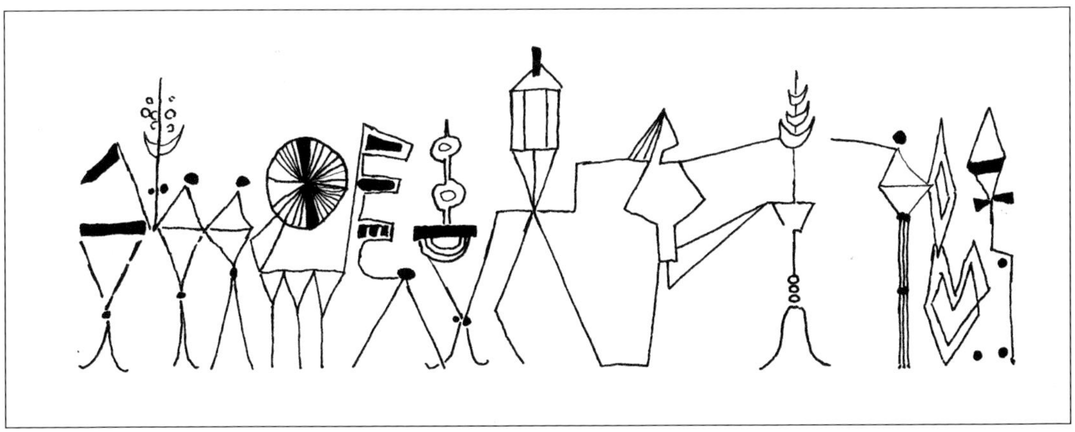

Rhythmic Progression, ink on paper, 4.25 x 7.5 inches, dated January 27, 1953, collection of the artist

In 1943 I met a young woman on a blind date. Eileen Newby had been working at the Vernon Hospital after getting a degree in bacteriology at the University of British Columbia. Initially she had wanted to study medicine, but was discouraged by the dean who favoured men for that profession. At the time we met, Eileen had returned to Vancouver because of her mother's poor health. One of Eileen's girlfriends, Eleanor Boyd, was dating my cousin Peter Sloan. She arranged the blind date between Eileen and myself, and the four of us went to a small Saturday night house party. It was war time and there was a chronic shortage of men, so phone calls were made to redress the social balance. Some fellows from a naval crew brought along two of their shipmates, shifting the equation to two girls short, and the phone calls resumed. Eventually, we all gathered around a large table at the Commodore ballroom. No one at the table seemed to get along except Eileen and I.

Our next date was again with Eleanor and Peter. We went horseback riding and Eileen wore an elegant riding outfit. I had no idea it was borrowed from a friend or that she had never been on a horse before. My suspicions were stirred, however, when she repeatedly let her horse stray into the bushes. Each time this happened I followed her and led the horse out by the bridle. It was clear that this was an omen of things to come. Later, she would become indispensable to me in her understanding, warmth, and intelligence, and I would follow her anywhere.

That same afternoon the four of us called at the home of my aunt Marianne and uncle Walter. Always hospitable, they welcomed visits from family and friends. Little did any of us know this was my future bride's introduction to my family. My parents came to know Eileen only much later when they invited her to lunch. This turned out to be a very formal and tense occasion because my father (as I later found out) believed I should marry a European woman who would properly attend to his precious son. Nevertheless, after our marriage, my father became extremely fond of Eileen and often came over to our home with a little present for her.

Our wedding took place at St. Augustine's Church in Marpole, with a joyous wedding reception at the Georgia Hotel in downtown Vancouver. Afterwards, because of gas rationing, we took the train to the Okanagan. Our destination was a small hotel above Kalamalka Lake, but because there was no direct rail connection to Kelowna we first had to travel to Sicamous. We arrived there to find that on Sundays the station restaurant was open only for dinner so we spent the first day of our honeymoon fasting by the lakeside. The hotel, about two miles from Kelowna, was surrounded by orchards. We rented bicycles and explored the countryside. We didn't want to appear to be newlyweds and were perplexed when the hotel's other guests seemed to avoid us. Later we found out that an announcement about our wedding had appeared in the newpaper.

Eileen and I settled in a small house in Vancouver with a nice little garden, realizing too late that the rackety interurban tram ran right below it. But these were very happy days. In 1947 we became parents of Sidney and, two years later, of Diane.

During these years I remained employed at the family business and continued to paint and immerse myself in the study of art. With Eileen's support, I left the family company in 1951 and six years later joined the teaching staff at the Vancouver School of Art (now Emily Carr Institute of Art and Design). Jack Shadbolt, who had been a friend since I first arrived in Vancouver, was the school's principal teacher at the time. I liked him enormously and was very fond of his wife Doris, a prominent art writer and historian.

My friendship with Jack began to weaken one day in late 1980. He and I were sitting

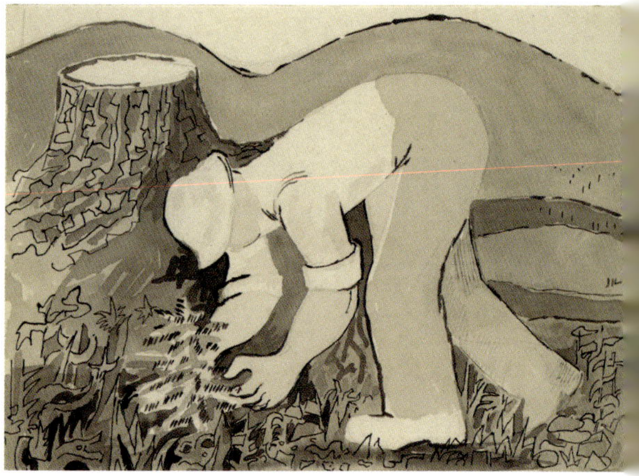

Tree Planter, ink wash on paper board, 6.25 x 8 inches, 1943 (possibly 1946), collection of the artist, an industrial poster design

opposite each other at the kitchen table. We were both quite clear by this time about our individual artistic objectives. The more we talked, the more obvious it became that our directions and motivations ran along different paths. Jack had a very intellectual outlook, very critical expectations, and quite materialistic values. He also had a flamboyant temperament and was the strongest atheist I had ever met. He vehemently denied the possibility of any other view. Sharp, dramatic contrasts suited his energetic style: the "push and pull" of colour in space that he had learned while studying in New York with Hans Hoffman.

I, too, felt strongly about colour, but held to more value-oriented treatments that featured far less dramatic and far more peaceful solutions. What Jack and I shared was the excitement we felt when a painting "came to life." We also agreed that the colour of light within a painting can be the main theme of the work, as it did, for instance, in the first of my *Lighthouse* paintings — although I don't think Jack understood what they were about.

Other colleagues at the Vancouver School of Art included Molly and Bruno Bobak, Don Jarvis, and Orville Fisher, all accomplished artists and more experienced teachers than I was at that time. My relationships with each of them was friendly enough, but I always had an uncomfortable feeling I was not a very welcome newcomer. When Abe Rogatnik and Alvin Balkin opened the New Design Gallery in the mid-1950s, we all exhibited our work there, but our individual styles and attitudes toward painting were so dissimilar that a closer association never developed.

At about the same time as the New Design Gallery opened, Alan Jarvis was hired as the director of the National Gallery in Ottawa. Alan was a knowledgeable art historian and a very urbane, witty man. Soon after his appointment he made a tour of artists' studios from coast to coast, something that no subsequent director has done. He came to my studio and acquired seven works for the National Gallery. That gave me a tremendous boost.

I did make friends with other colleagues at school, particularly Bert Binning, Joe Plaskett, Lawren Harris, Tak Tanabe, and Gordon Smith and his wife Marion. Joe Plaskett moved to Paris in the early 1950s and bought a seventeenth-century house in the Marais. I visited him there and later saw him when he came to my show in Cambridge. He even bought one of my paintings — the only artist ever to do so! Joe now lives in Suffolk in a charming cottage with a Monet-type garden. We meet whenever he comes to Vancouver. He has established a reputation as an important Canadian artist, an achievement that, remarkably, remains unrecognized by the Vancouver Art Gallery.

I enjoyed many evenings with Bert and Jessie Binning and Lawren and Bess Harris, looking at what we had produced and discussing in great detail the directions our work was taking. Bert was a man of ideas and had an enchanting sense of humour. He left the Vancouver School of Art in the early 1950s to start the art department at the University of British Columbia. A decade earlier he had designed the first truly contemporary post-and-beam house on the West Coast. Constructed at the end of Mather Street in West Vancouver, it was completed in time for Bert and Jessie to move in after their marriage. Below, through the heavily wooded ravine on which the house had been built, was a stunning view of the sea. We would sit near the fireplace wall built of local stones, Bertie sprawled in an easy chair, with their Scotch terrier Lucy lolling at his stockinged feet.

Jessie Binning is an interesting woman, always groomed and dressed to perfection. She was very knowledgeable, particularly about Japanese art. Her father was an importer and she had accompanied him on many trips to Nippon. Through her, Bertie developed an interest in Japanese art and, since it was something we all shared, much of our talk was on that topic. I had seen and admired *ukiyo-e* woodcut prints by Katsushika Hokusai, Utagawa Hiroshige, Kitamara Utamaro, and other eighteenth-century masters in the Louvre when I was in my teens, and it was wonderful to be able to discuss them with friends.

A Japanese influence was not evident in Bertie's artwork; rather, he produced distinctly personal statements. The simple, nervous lines in his drawings and paintings showed the personality of their maker. Later in life, Bertie focussed on more formal aspects, transforming signals, ships, and sails into composed units of great beauty. Regrettably, his contribution to West Coast art has also been undervalued. In the recent book, *Masterworks from British Columbia* by Ian M. Thom, Bert Binning is barely mentioned. It was a savage blow to me when Bertie died suddenly in 1978.

Lawren Harris and I became close friends in the late 1940s, and when he later asked me to join the Vancouver Art Gallery's exhibition committee we spent even more time together. We would go on long walks and discuss everything from art making to walking shoes. I found his cosmopolitan attitude and sensi-

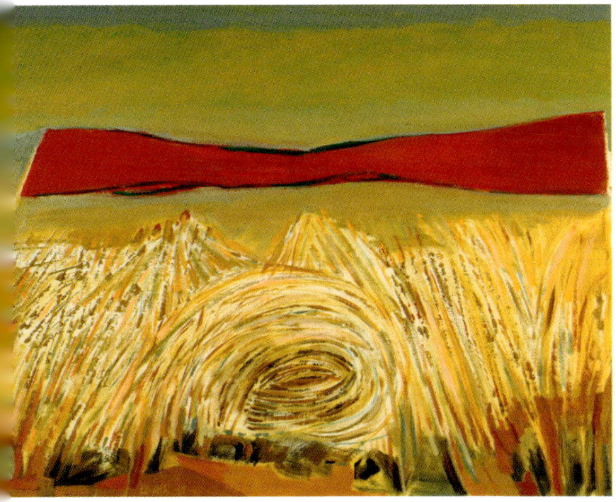

Mrs. Satvedi's Sari, acrylic on canvas, 18 x 24 inches, 1977, collection of Jane Rule

tive manner most appealing. Whenever an indifferent painting was being considered by the committee, he would lean back laughing and remark, "Now there's a painting." I never heard him use a more critical expression.

It was widely reported at the time and has since been repeated as gospel that Lawren was deeply involved in Theosophy. This was simply not the case. His interest had been satisfied while he was in New Mexico in the 1940s, and by the time he moved to Vancouver he had long since relinquished any ties with Theosophy. In New Mexico he and his wife Bess has been associated with Raymond Jonson, Emil Bistram, and Agnes Pelton. Kandinsky (an advocate of transcendentalism) was a strong influence on them and Lawren's work changed from the representational style of his Toronto years when he was a principal member of the Group of Seven. However, after he left Theosophy behind, his abstract style of painting showed he maintained a strong belief in the spiritual sphere of life.

Lawren and Bess made many friends in Vancouver and soon their Saturday musical evenings became popular gatherings of interesting people. These evenings helped widen my musical range just as our discussions broadened my visual knowledge. It was Lawren who first drew my attention to Emily Carr and, quite apart from the intrinsic value of her work, the significance of her depictions of coastal villages in sensitizing the "white" population to native life.

Keeping up my friendship with Tak Tanabe was somewhat haphazard. Tak was very concentrated on his work and I only saw him occasionally when he came to Vancouver from his studio residence in Parksville on Vancouver Island. He would phone and ask, "Can you give me a cup of coffee?" I'd assure Tak he was welcome and inquire when he planned to visit us. "In fifteen minutes," he'd say. He would arrive promptly, regale us with his exploits for an hour, then abruptly take his leave.

Tak was born in Seal Cove, near Prince Rupert. When he was fifteen, his family was forcibly moved to the interior of the province at the start of World War II in 1939. Relocation to an internment camp was a stressful experience that he could not forget. He went back to Japan to decide if he really belonged there, but returned to British Columbia and re-established his roots here. Without much help he became an outstanding painter.

Tak tells the story of searching for a street address in Tokyo. When he could not find it, he asked a passerby for assistance. The fellow assumed that Tak was Japanese from Japan and simply pointed to a sign. Tak could speak Japanese, but reading calligraphic signs was beyond him.

I first met Gordon and Marion Smith so long ago that I can't recall when I didn't know them. Gordon and I taught together at the Vancouver School of Art and later at the University of British Columbia. We both were friends of Arthur Erickson, who I should mention was a wonderful dancer. Gordon was the only artist in western Canada to commission Arthur to design not one, but two houses. They were both masterpieces, especially the second one which spans a small ravine near Lighthouse Park on the North Shore. Like Bert and Jessie Binning's home, it also features a tree-framed view of the sea.

By this time my circle of friends had extended beyond those solely engaged in visual arts. One of my earliest supporters was Max Wyman, then the editor of the magazine section of the *Vancouver Sun* newspaper. He was very knowledgeable and perceptive in all that he wrote about the arts. The *Vancouver Sun*'s art critic at that time was the novelist David Watmough who reviewed some of my shows with great enthusiasm and became a collector of my paintings. Another close friend since the early 1970s has been Dr. David McLean, whom I met while I was a patient at the Vancouver General Hospital skin clinic.

Friends are the lifeblood of an artist. In my case, because my art was and remains totally different from anything that could remotely be described as "cutting edge," the support of my friends has been invaluable.

My major focusses from the late 1950s onward evolved from questions concerning beauty in art, colour, and form. What is beauty in art? The term "beautiful" seemed useless to me in the discussion and criticism of art, or even in the description of what some found pleasing in nature. Different people used the word for disparate reasons, and it was often impossible to reconcile the differences because they were based on subjective outlooks and perspectives. Yet it was obvious that the word "beautiful," as well as the experiencing of it, is exceedingly important to every human being. Even early man rejected the purely utilitarian, choosing instead to create fine, voluminous curves in the earthen pots required for gathering and storing food.

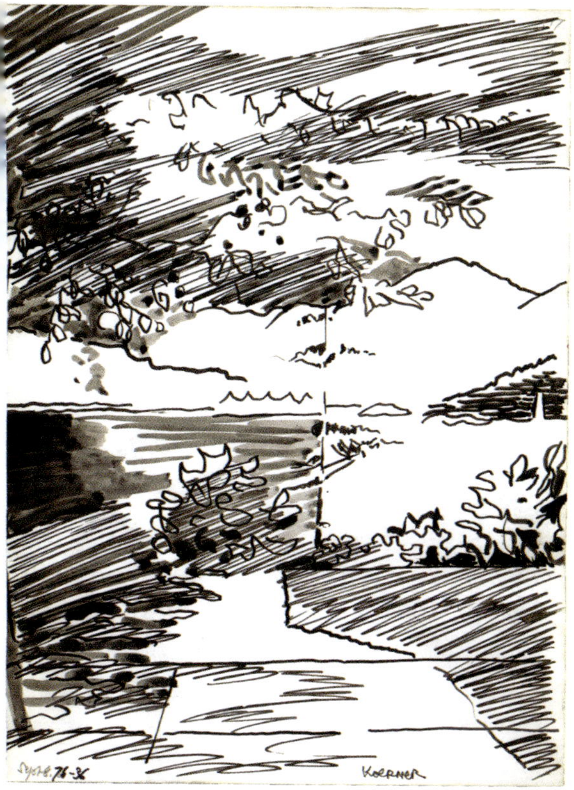

Provence, ink sketch on paper, 11.25 x 8 inches, dated Sept. 8, 1976, collection of the artist

Another conundrum was the question of colour, which had started tantalizing me in my early teens. The colours in a tube or jar of paint, or on the surface of a canvas, are inert materials. How best to bring colours to life? We perceive colour when the retina is stimulated by energy coming from light. The input is then converted according to the eye's pre-programming. So colour resides inside our brain, yet our entire body and emotional system respond to the colour input the brain receives. How we respond is very individual. Our perception of colour can be partly acquired by study, but its main source is an enigmatic predetermined disposition we cannot change or escape from. Our colour sense is part of our make-up, perhaps rooted in our individual genetic code.

The notion of what is beautiful and how to make colour sing absorbed a lot of my thinking. Finally, I decided to do what Victor Tischler had told me in Paris. "Sharpen your vision daily and paint it out." This is the route I am still following.

By nature I have never been doubtful that man has a spiritual life, an invisible life beyond the material one. I've never stopped studying the teachings of Bô Yin Râ which I began in Switzerland when I was nineteen. Those readings have helped develop my awareness that all human beings are rooted in a field of spiritual energy. We cannot perceive this energy with our physical senses; we can, however, partake of it and put it to use by awareness of and respect for the latent spiritual sphere. It is possible, if we pay enough attention, to become fully awake to this field of spiritual energy while we are still on this earth. Either way, we enter this sphere once our physical existence comes to an end. This basic belief was what I wanted "to paint out."

Three models were most meaningful to me. One was the distinctive painting style of the Japanese *emaki* scrolls, dating from the twelfth century, and the monumental screens of the Taiga style which evolved later. They fascinated me because they were so consistent and so powerful, despite — or rather because of — their restrained use of colour.

A second model was provided by Hans Hoffman. I had not attended his famous school in New York, but I was aware of the influence of his teachings. He stated that the perception of colour lies in its relation to adjacent colour, an idea that corresponded with Einstein's hypothesis and his perception of relative speed.

The third model was Giorgione, whose paintings had so impressed me during my student days. To me, sharp contrasts of colour have always seemed like marks of aggression. Giorgione did not try for maximum contrast; instead, he chose close colour relationships, so that the juxtaposition of one colour next to another resulted in a vibrant surface. Aside from the warmth of the colours' glow — which, in itself, has a welcoming, comforting effect on the beholder — such a painting offers in its tonality the explicit impression of luminosity, a metaphor for serenity, calm, and peace.

My investigations of beauty, colour, and form continued while I was teaching at the University of British Columbia. I enjoyed teaching and remember two students in particular whose work I hold in special regard. One was Ann Kipling. From the beginning she showed an original vision and great dedication. The other was Barry Wainwright, an outstanding printmaker, who went on to New York, then taught at Concordia University in Montreal, and finally settled on the Sunshine Coast where he maintains a very functional printshop.

In 1962, I resigned from my teaching position so I could paint full time. Eileen and I had bought a home on the University Endowment Lands that had a garage which I converted into a studio, a garden in which I loved to work, and a beautiful view of the sea with the Point Atkinson lighthouse and the Coast Range mountains in the background.

I had now completed three series: *Lost City*, a nostalgic remembrance of things past; *Coast Glitter*, a series of 34 paintings which focussed on the British Columbia landscape from water level; and *Compass Rose*, a series based on the navigation device used on ships. The latter related directly to my belief that the course our lives take is often dependent on decisions we take as individuals.

After a trip to Italy with Eileen, I wanted to express some of the spirit of that country. When we returned home I started *The Italian Series*, which alluded to fourteenth-century Italian art and the Italian landscape. Two other unrelated themes that developed into series were the *West County Set* and the *Numbers* motif. The *Numbers* motif came about in an unexpected way. I was walking down a back lane and, on top of an overflowing garbage can, was a piece of metal. As I moved closer I saw it was a template of the numeral five. I took it home and placed it on my work table. It lay there for weeks. Looking at it every day, I began to see its significance as an abstract thought, as well as an abstract form. I realized that there is no substitute for any number; that numbers, such as the five petals

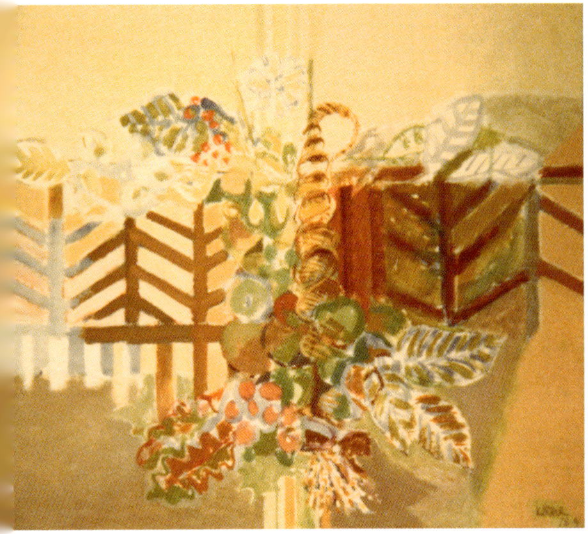

Still Life with Corn Dolly, acrylic on canvas, 24 x 26 inches, 1978, collection of the artist

on a flower or the three parts of a maple leaf, are part of nature. For the first time I understood that numbers are an integral part of life, and out of this realization I started the series.

I did not work on any theme consistently, but switched from one to the other as it suited me. I don't know if this is how other painters work, but this is how it was and continues to be for me. The *West County Set* was a tribute to the English sculptor Grinling Gibbons (1648–1721), as well as the English countryside. Gibbons designed *The Wood Room* at Midhurst Castle outside of London. Perhaps I was drawn to his large Baroque-style carved panels because there is so much Baroque art and architecture in Prague.

Despite this venture back into the Baroque, I had over the years developed a strong, if contrasting, interest in West Coast Indian art. When I first arrived in Vancouver in 1939 neither Northwest Coast people nor their culture was valued. First Nations people, or "natives" as they were then called, lived on reserves as wards of the government. Most men worked in fishing or logging and the women were employed in fish canneries.

British Columbia's first chief forester, H.R. MacMillan was one man who thought otherwise. So did my uncle Walter. He was born with a special talent for recognizing good and, more often, outstanding works of art. When he was eight years old he began collecting ceramics created by Czech and Moravian peasants sold in the town square of our birthplace, Nový Jičín. Next came an enthusiasm for Bohemian glass and rare books. He brought his collections with him when he moved to Vancouver.

On business trips to timber sites on Vancouver Island and in the BC Interior, Walter encountered First Nations artwork and immediately started collecting. Marianne, his wife, took longer to appreciate the artefacts, so Walter kept his collection in a basement storage area. Knowing of my interest, he would often take me there to show off his new acquisitions.

Walter was particularly concerned about the preservation of Haida carvings. He had seen numerous house poles and commemorative "totem" poles deteriorating in the forests and in the late 1940s organized an expedition to bring them to Vancouver where they could be cared for, preserved, and available to the public. The expedition participants were Bill Reid, anthropologists Wilson Duff and Audrey and Harry Hawthorn, and a Canadian Navy ship. Replicas of the poles were made by Mungo Martin and members of the Hunt family, then given to First Nations villages to be installed in their place of origin.

In 1950 Walter organized another expedition, this time to Gitxsan village sites along the Skeena River that had been uninhabited since their populations were decimated by smallpox in 1884. Some of the poles had fallen, others were covered with moss and threatened by undergrowth. Knowing these treasures should be properly housed and preserved, he began negotiating with the provincial government about saving the carvings and was instrumental in getting the Arthur Erickson-designed Museum of Anthropology built on the University of British Columbia campus in 1976. He gave all of his First Nations carvings, jewellery, and baskets, as well as his ceramics collection to the museum. Walter's long-term commitment and patronage, which included commissioning the gigantic *Bear* (1962) and the famous *Raven and the First Men* (1980) by Bill Reid, contributed substantially to the renaissance of West Coast native art.

I first met Bill Reid in the early 1950s, when he was working as a goldsmith replicating traditional Haida motifs on jewellery. We got on easily, were friends, but never close friends. During one of our conversations he mentioned that he had never made any jewellery of contemporary design. If I would design something, he said he would make it. I came up with an abacus theme for a bracelet, broach, and earrings, and he executed them in silver and ebony. The set is now in the collection of the Bill Reid Foundation.

Bill's life changed when he met Martine de Widerspoch-Thor, a French anthropologist who had studied under the renowned Claude Levi-Strauss. Martine had spent a year and a half among the Kwakwaka'wakw at Fort Rupert, Alert Bay, and Campbell River. In the 1970s, Eileen and I sailed with Bill and Martine to Haida Gwai (Queen Charlotte Islands) where Bill's mother had been born. There I gained some understanding of these mysterious, heavily wooded islands. Standing in knee-deep moss amongst ancient trees, feeling the isolation and great silence, is a unique contemplative experience.

As the years passed, Bill developed a powerful and distinctive style far beyond the traditional native art themes he used in the 1950s and 1960s. Perhaps his greatest works are *The Spirit of Haida Gwai* (1991) bronze sculpture installed at the Canadian Embassy in Washington D.C. and its sister *The Jade Canoe* (1994) at the Vancouver International Airport. On the other hand, I believe Martine

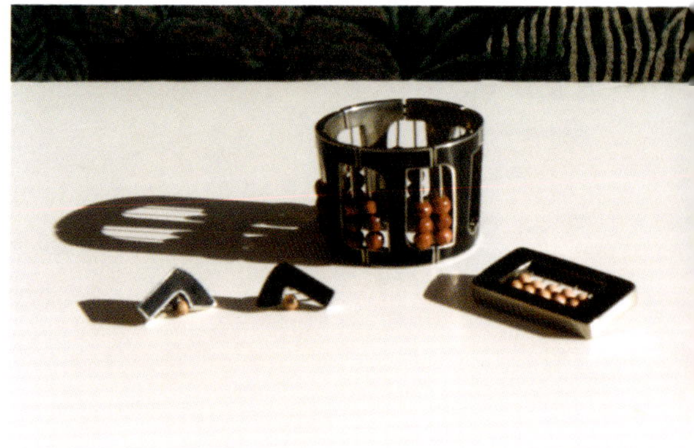

Silver jewellery by Bill Reid, designed by John Koerner

knew more about West Coast native art than Bill. She studied art and anthropology for years, has a doctorate in the subject, and speaks two First Nations languages.

During the 1970s and 1980s I started on several new painting series, including *The Garden of Eden* and *The Pacific Gateway*. If there is a subject that interests me, I can usually find many different ways of dealing with it. One variation suggests another. *The Garden of Eden* series, for instance, focusses on the spiritual realm, which is the true home of all humans. In these paintings I referenced the West Coast landscape as I have found it to be a worthy analogy. *The Pacific Gateway* series — which now numbers 312 works — suggests the peaceful arch from here-and-now to another world. It also juxtaposes the British Columbia shoreline with Japanese temple gardens on the other side of the Pacific Ocean.

I had not yet travelled to Japan when I started *The Pacific Gateway* series, although I had long been interested in the East and its art. After my first visit to Japan in 1986 I discovered the similarities between the Japanese coastline and the coast of British Columbia. Since then I have visited Japan several times, and exhibited my paintings there in 1995.

I began *The Lighthouse* series when I was living in our home on the University Endowment Lands and had a view of the Point Atkinson lighthouse across Burrard Inlet. I telephoned the lighthouse keeper one day to see if it would be possible to have a look at the interior of the structure. He promptly invited me over for tea. Taking a drawing as a small gift, I went to visit him. Once inside the building I was astonished to see he was an art collector. The lighthouse walls were covered with drawings he had collected over many years. *The Lighthouse* series now numbers 115 works and uses the marine beacons as a metaphor for "the fiery pillar that can guide onto dry land through the midst of a stormy sea," described in the Gospels.

These years brought other changes. Our daughter Sidney was about to graduate in art history from the University of British Columbia when some friends came to Vancouver for a visit. Mari and Stewart Williams lived in Palm Springs, California, where Stewart practised architecture. Their son, Erik, was an intern in medicine at the University of California at Los Angeles. Through all our years of friendship with the Williams, our children had never met. On this trip Erik accompanied his parents, met Sidney, and their marriage soon followed.

Our other daughter, Diane, was in her last year of high school when she met Stephen Owen, the son of Eileen's good friend Marion Owen. Their home was near ours and we'd often see Steve racing by on his bicycle. Six years later, he had graduated in law, Diane had her BA, and they were married and living in London. There, Diane attended the Cordon Bleu cooking school, Steve got his Masters of Law at the University of London and then an MBA at the University of Geneva.

In 1975 Diane and Steve went to Nigeria as teachers under the auspices of CUSO (Canadian University Services Overseas). They invited us to join them for a visit and at the end of 1976 the four of us spent two months travelling around Africa. I sat with Steve in the front of their Volkswagen and had the task of holding on to the car door which unlatched every time we hit a bump in the road.

What an experience to see the great expanses of grass, the vultures, the villages, the brilliant sunsets, the men in their caftan-like *rigas* sitting in the shade of enormous baobab trees, drinking coffee and smoking, while the women worked the fields or pounded corn. At one point in our journey a grass fire, a yearly occurrence that sometimes destroyed the straw huts in its path, came uncomfortably close to where we were staying.

On Christmas Day we attended a church service in Biu, Nigeria. Built of stone in the neo-Gothic style common in England, the church was filled with parishioners dressed in their most festive attire. "Sunday best" meant a lot in those parts where even everyday clothing was very colourful. Women wore elaborate headscarves wound into turbans, and men were garbed in pastel-hued robes. An animated nativity scene began with a procession of Mary enacted by a woman carrying a very pink, very nude plastic doll in her arms, accompanied by her (actual) husband and some live sheep. A big star made of coloured cardboard suspended on a rope was pulled closer and closer to the altar at the same time as three wise men approached. As a finale, a group of men dressed in military uniforms representing Roman soldiers came running down the aisle. With guns drawn, they started firing blank bullets. The children were terrified and everyone raced toward the exit. When calm was restored, the service resumed with everyone laughing and hugging their neighbours.

Those months in Africa were a powerful experience and, on my return to Vancouver, I painted an *African* series. Interestingly, until I became involved in writing these memoirs, I could not remember doing more than eight

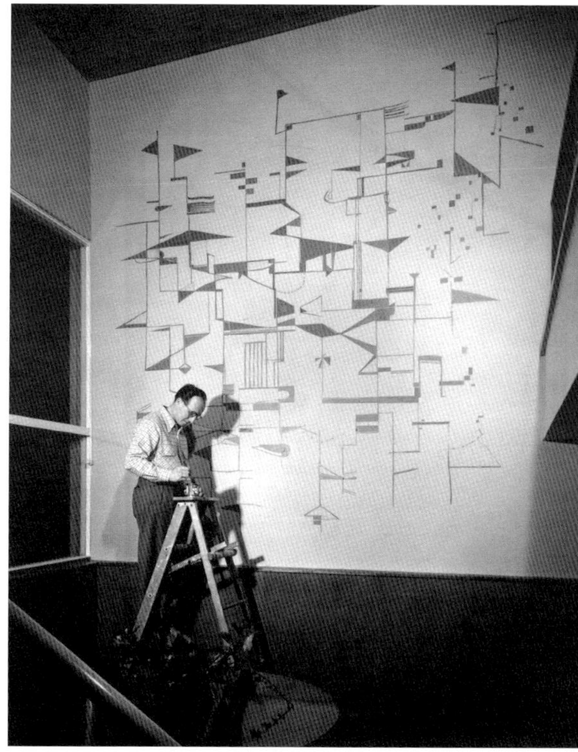

Mural, R.J. Young residence, West Vancouver, BC
Photo: Graham Warrington, architectural photographer, Vancouver, BC

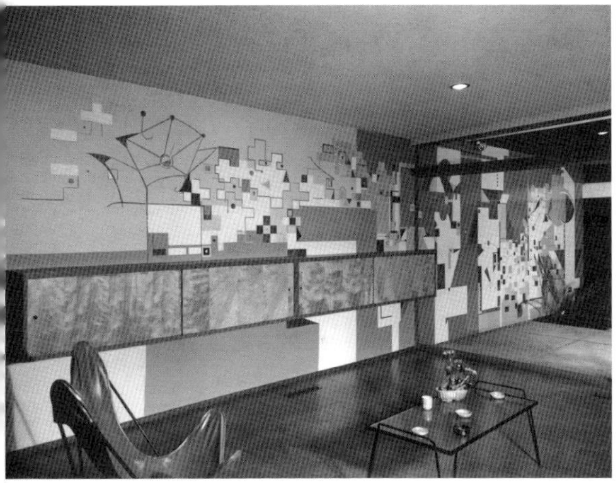

Mural, Douglas Simpson residence, West Vancouver, BC
Photo: Graham Warrington, architectural photographer, Vancouver, BC

paintings. Checking my records, I discovered that I had done 63. It was the only figurative series I've ever done, and all but four of the paintings went into private collections.

In 1986 I was commissioned to do a painting for the Queen Elizabeth Theatre in honour of Vancouver's centennial year. It turned out to be the largest painting I ever did and, appropriately, was the one-hundredth work in *The Pacific Gateway* series. It comprises four panels, each four by six feet in size, and hangs in the northwest corner of the theatre lobby.

The creation of an art work, especially a large canvas or sculpture, can be totally exhausting. Yet the number of people who regard the artist's work as a pleasant hobby is quite extraordinary. If I had a dime for every person who has asked me, "Are you still painting?" — as if I really should be doing something less self-indulgent and more responsible — I'd be doing well.

During these years I also completed a number of murals which allowed full play of my interest in abstract art. Most of the murals were commissioned for residences and many of these houses have since been renovated or torn down. As far as I know, none of them is still in existence. One mural, however, had a lasting effect. In the late 1960s, architect Douglas Simpson commissioned me to do a very large mural for his modern West Vancouver home. Completely abstract, the mural extended right across the living room wall, past a glass wall, and across the wall of the patio. Doug's son, Greg, who was about twelve years old at the time, has since told me that the mural interested him so much that he decided he, too, would become a painter, an ambition he has successfully achieved.

My best known mural was commissioned by David Lemon in 1993 and installed on the rear wall of The Magic Flute, his classical music store in Vancouver. Recently, ownership of the store changed hands and the mural is now in the collection of the Vancouver General Hospital.

In 1990, shortly after the "Velvet Revolution" — the non-violent uprising of the Czech people which led to the end of Communist rule in 1989 — Eileen and I travelled to Prague. The visit was of tremendous importance to me. Unlike many European capitals, Prague had been physically undamaged by World War II and the Soviet occupation. The city's cultural life was humming. There were over fifty small theatres, all well attended. Bookstores were busy. At concerts or the opera, it was not unusual to see teenagers following the score.

I had always been an admirer of Václav Havel, the dramatist who became president of the new Czech Republic. He had twice been imprisoned as a dissident by the Soviets and all his plays, books, and essays had been banned. His meditations on freedom and art in *Letters to Olga*, written to his wife during his imprisonment, were in harmony with my own beliefs. Several years after our trip to Prague, I was invited to show at an international art exhibition there. The three paintings I offered all sold and I was pleased to learn that one of them, an improvisation of my memories of Prague as a young man, had been bought by President Havel.

In these ruminations on work and friendships, I have overlooked mentioning four friends whose interest and support was — and in two instances remains — very important to me. One is Jean Paul Lemieux, whom I met in 1958 at the Galerie Agnès Lefort in Montreal. At the time, he was a well recognized Montreal artist. The occasion was my first exhibition in that city. We had a very amiable chat which developed into a warm friendship. He lived on the Isle de Coudres, an isolated location not far from Québec City, and at his invitation I visited him there. Although he was a very friendly person, he was also very private and liked to be left alone to get on with his work. I recall the long afternoon we spent together, seated on the lawn outside his house overlooking the St. Lawrence river, talking about everything from painting to poutine, Québec's unique contribution to Canadian cuisine. American abstractionism was *de rigueur* in the 1950s, and Jean Paul loved the *isolation indépendente* the Isle de Coudres provided to him, supporting the deviant course of his art work away from the mainstream. Our friendship continued until his premature death in 1981.

Another friend is Herbert Sax, a Swiss artist who lived in Japan for twenty years. I met him in a curious way, through a friend in Berkeley, California, who suggested I get in touch with Herbert as he thought we had a lot of common interests. We started corresponding and when I went to Japan in 1995 we met at the airport. Even though Herbert and I had only exchanged letters, we felt we had known each other for years. We travelled together in Japan, where his fluent Japanese was of great help. We also exhibited together in Tokyo, Kyoto, and Tokushima on the island of Shikoku. Herbert now lives in his native Switzerland and we remain in regular contact.

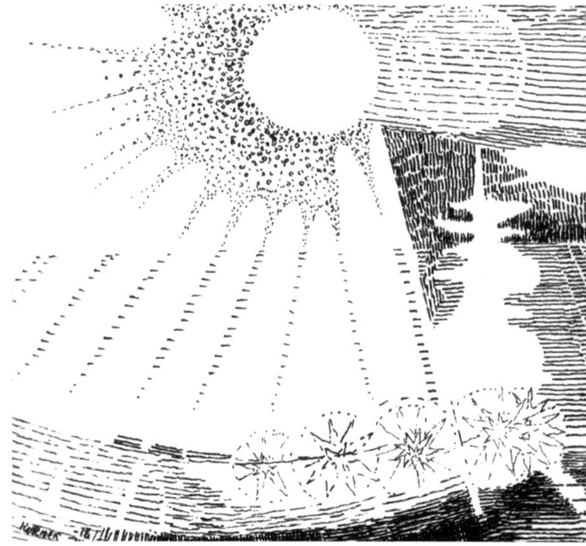

Drawing for a Lighthouse Painting, ink on cardboard, 6 x 15 inches, 1981, collection of the artist

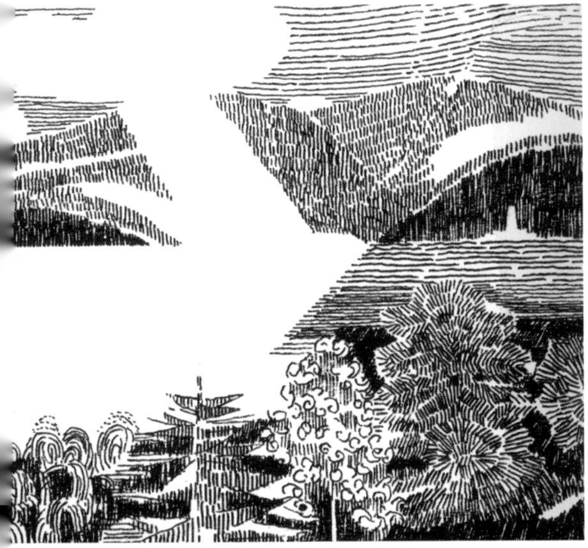

A younger Vancouver friend who has remained close is Jamie Evrard, a woman of originality, wit, and enormous zest. We have met regularly for many years, exchanging experiences and comparing notes connected with our work. Her paintings, like mine, do not attempt to be cutting edge and thus are less valued than they should be.

Outside Vancouver, another colleague was the witty Bill Roberts, whom I met during an exhibition of his work at Vancouver's Equinox Gallery. Bill lived in Nova Scotia in a house on a cliff overlooking the ocean. His wife was the local postmistress. We corresponded frequently and, once, in reply to my query about what he was working on, instead of a letter he sent a large sheet of paper covered with pen and ink drawings that I framed and hung in my hallway. "These are some of the paintings I am working on," he wrote on the sketch. "Some are almost finished, nearly finished, getting close to finished — some might just not make it." Bill died about three years ago. This is the great curse of aging — the loss of friends.

In the spring of 2000, my life took a terrible turn. During intermission at a chamber music concert we were attending, Eileen turned to me saying she wasn't feeling well and would I please take her home. Then followed a series of medical tests, emergency admittances, hospitalizations and discharges, more tests, nursing services at home, another hospitalization — where she suffered the pain of having her wedding ring stolen — and a final transfer to palliative care a few days before the end.

The loss of Eileen devastated me. Throughout her illnes I was totally unable to work and after she was gone I fell into a desperate state of grief.

My habit in times of crisis has been to consult Bô Yin Râ's teachings. In his *Book on Solace* he says that the sorrow we feel is, in part, for ourselves, grieving our loss: "All suffering is evil, but it must be surmounted." It took time for me to realize I was wallowing in self-pity, not just sorrow over the loss of Eileen. She would not have wanted me to be in such a depressed, inactive state. A letter I received during this time I particularly cherish. It was from our long-time friend, the author Jane Rule. "It was your last gift to her, to outlive her," Jane wrote.

In my lowest moments I thought that age had finally caught up with me, that my career as a painter had come to an end. On a brighter day, I'd tell myself, no, artists don't retire at sixty-five, they hope to drop at the easel the way Titian did at ninety-one. Gradually I understood that there was still work to be done, that my purpose, the purpose of all human beings, was to keep striving towards a deepened inner consciousness. There is no age limit at which this striving should stop. It was up to me to produce work, in image and word, that would be imbued and in harmony with the spirit and teachings of Bô Yin Râ.

I turned more and more to my work and, in time, felt its beneficial influence. Soon I could concentrate for longer periods and, finally, found myself again fully absorbed in projects that had been put aside. As I worked, I felt Eileen's strong presence. Our connection had not been broken. I knew that by striving to reach my spiritual objective I was helping her reach hers, even though Eileen had not been a believer in Bô Yin Râ or his teachings about life after death.

"If some calamity has struck you," Bô Yin Râ writes, "above all else do not allow it time to gain a foothold in your thoughts, for if it once overwhelms your mind you will not easily escape its possessive grip. You must be master in your mind and soul, allowing nothing to defy your will, not even grief, no matter how profoundly you might feel its power. Resolutely show the door to all who come ostensibly to 'comfort' you but know nothing better than digging up new graves. The grief you have experienced needs peace and quiet in your soul so that it may come to rest within your depth."

And that is what finally happened; grief came to rest within my depth. But my former energy seemed to have diminished, I did not have the same powers of concentration, and living alone was lonely.

I did not know that great happiness lay ahead of me. I met Lisa Birnie, a former journalist and writer who had lost her husband at almost the same time I lost Eileen. Lisa and I were introduced at one of my exhibitions by Eilish McKendy, a mutual friend and art aficionado, who, from that day on, has quite rightly claimed that "I owe her one!" I had accepted that I would spend the rest of my days alone and was dumbfounded when I realized that luck, coincidence, or karma had found me an exquisite alternative, an instantly recognized and quickly verified soul mate.

Lisa changed my life, and invigorated my mind, soul, and body. My creativity surged and I returned to painting, living, and loving life. We were married four months later and travelled to Vietnam and Australia for what I later told our friends was "the mother of all honeymoons."

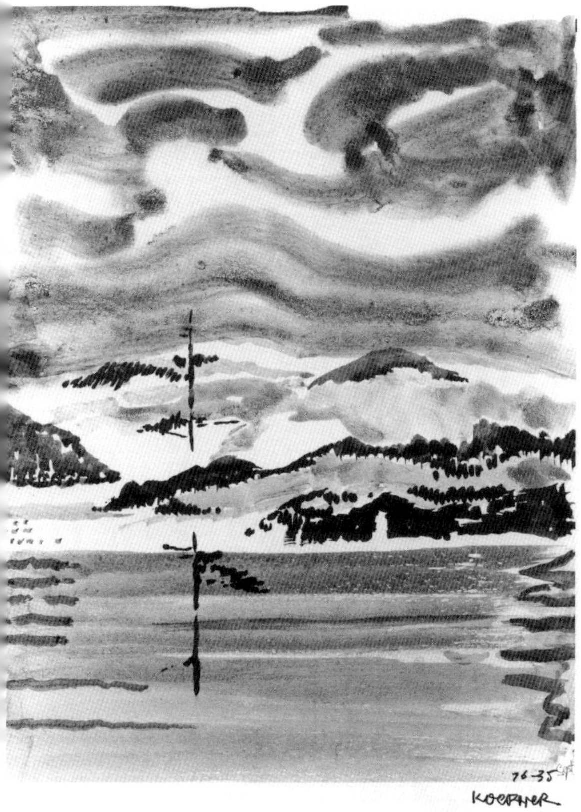

Early study for *Lighthouse* series, 9 x 7 inches, 1976, collection of the artist

We found great beauty in Vietnam, in the industry of the people, the magnificent landscapes and volcanic peaks, the lotus-strewn rivers where water buffalo wallowed in mud. In Australia we swam in the surf along the east coast, hiked through fern-bordered mountain trails, and camped on the red desert sand near Uluru. In Australia's cities I was astonished by the amount of state and federal support given to the arts, by the number of public art galleries, museums, and concert halls, and the widespread involvement of ordinary citizens in cultural activities.

I am now fully immersed in my new life and new work. As Longfellow wrote on the subject of aging:

> Ah, nothing is too late
> Till the tired heart hath ceased to palpitate;
> Cato learned Greek at eighty, Sophocles
> Wrote his grand *Oedipus*, and Simonides
> Bore off the prize of verse from his compeers
> When each had numbered more than four score years.

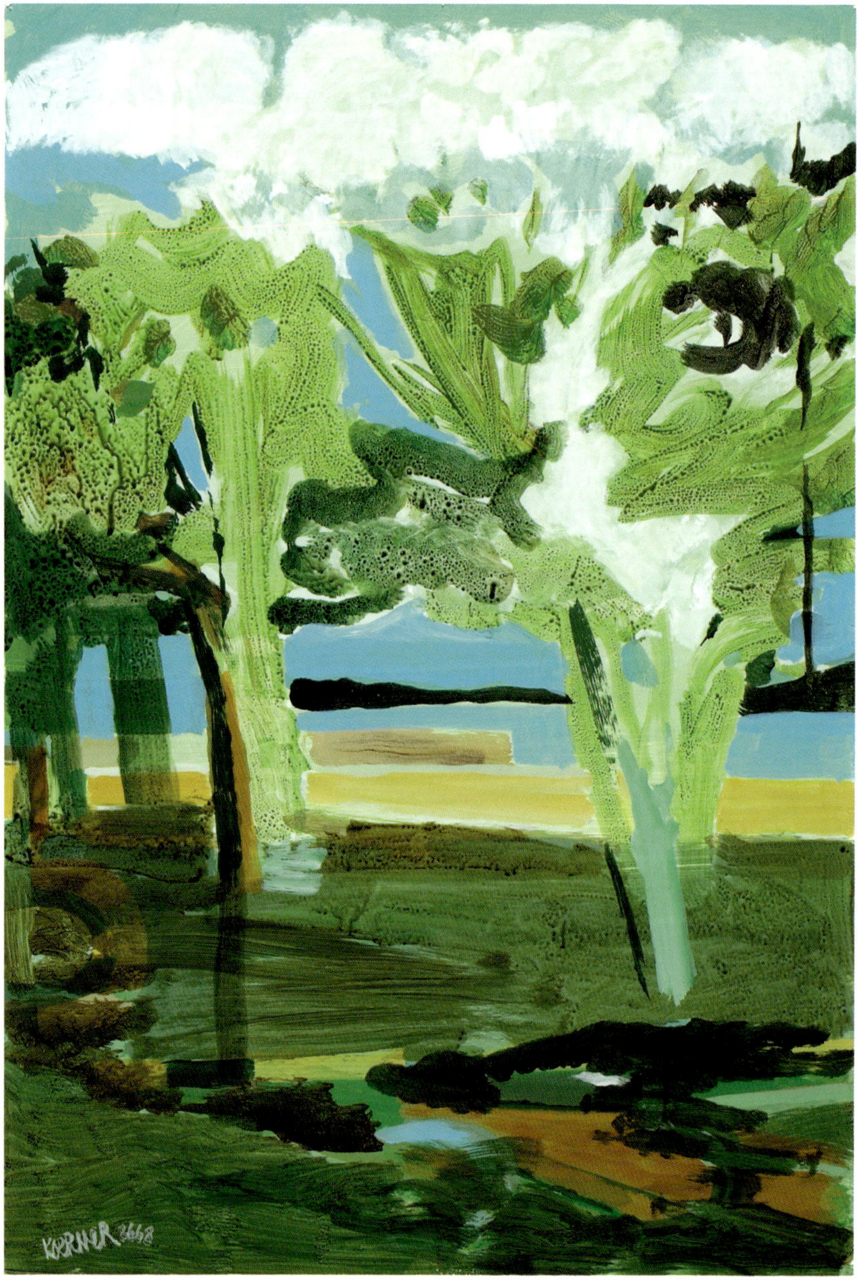

Pacific Gateway (97), acrylic on paper, 33 x 22 inches, 1986, private collection, Vancouver, BC

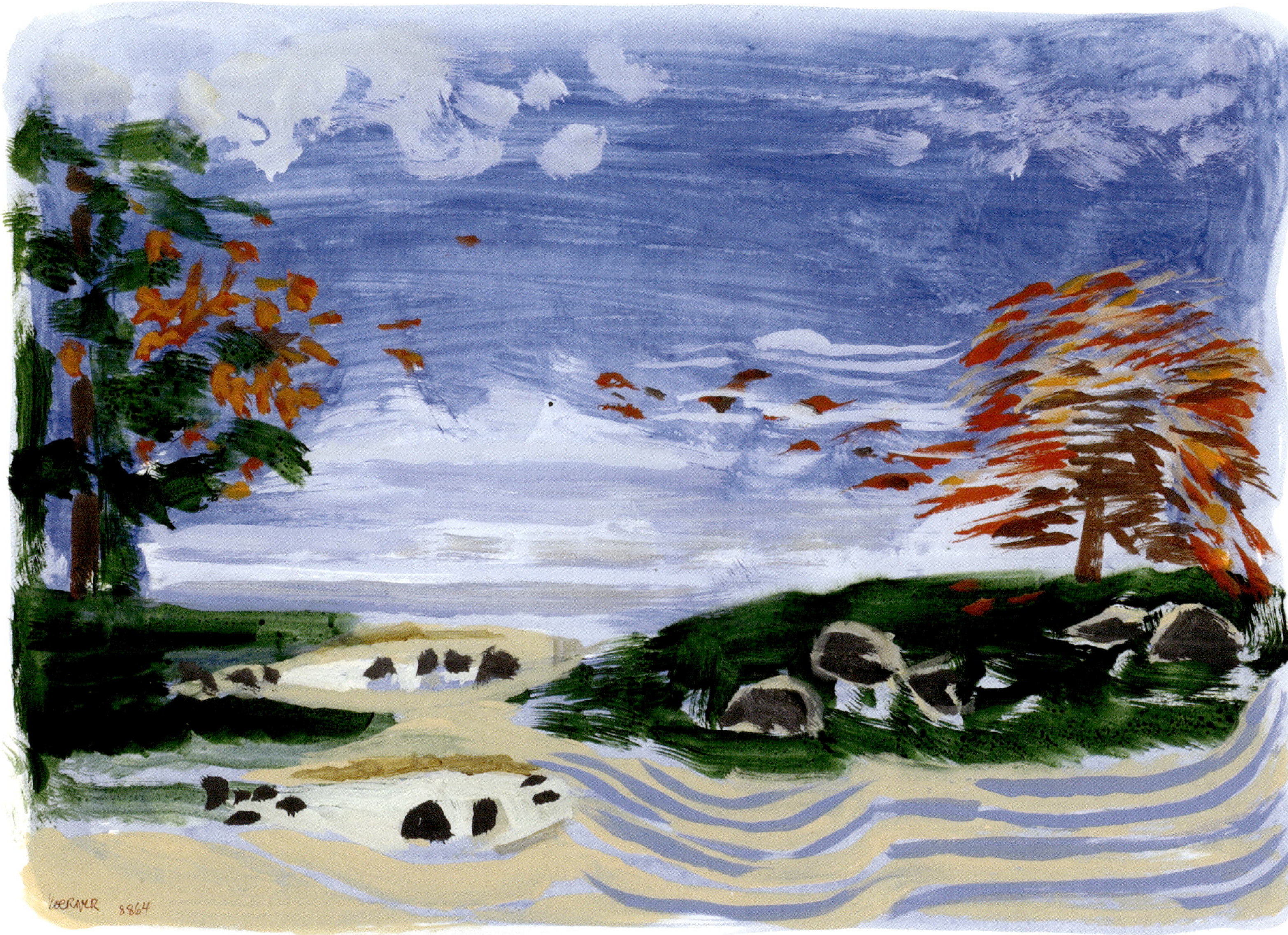

Pacific Gateway (215), acrylic on board, 14 x 19 inches, 1988, private collection, Vancouver, BC

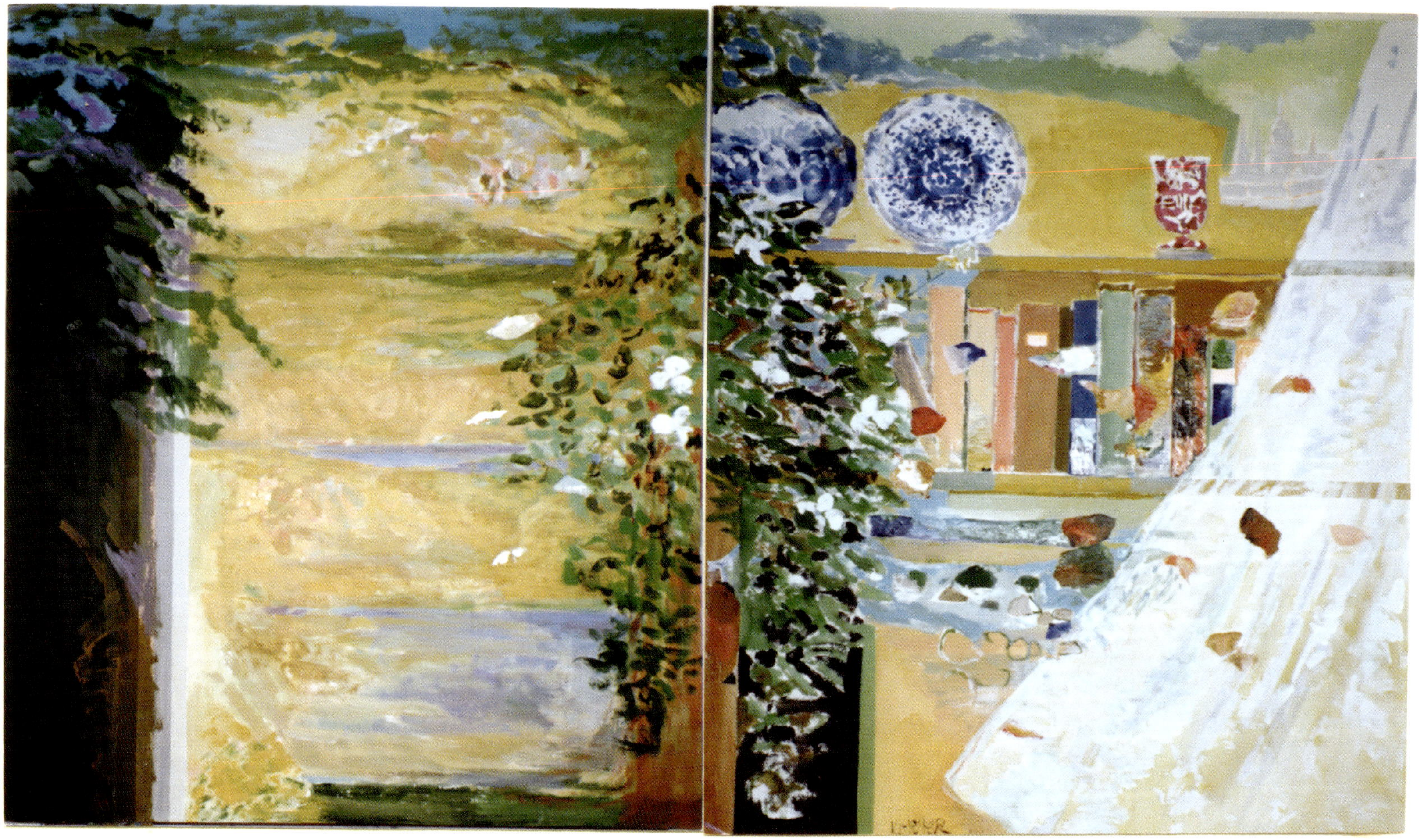

Pacific Gateway (288) The Balcony with Curtain, acrylic on canvas and collage, 50 x 84 inches (diptych), 1990, collection of John Bishop

The subject of the *Balcony* series is inside/outside: inner security looking out on the world.

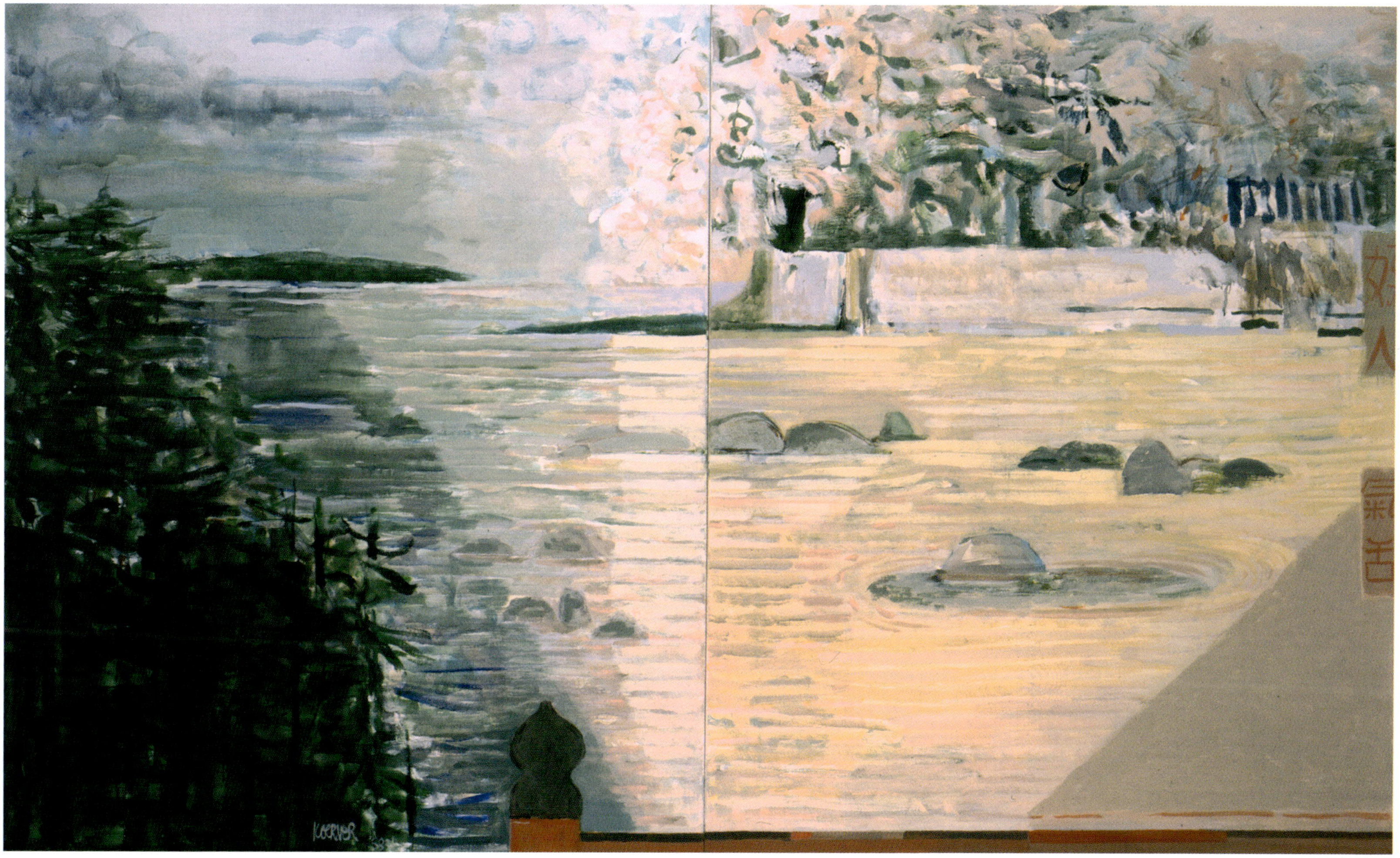

Pacific Gateway (183), acrylic on canvas,
100 x 160 cm, 1988, collection of the artist

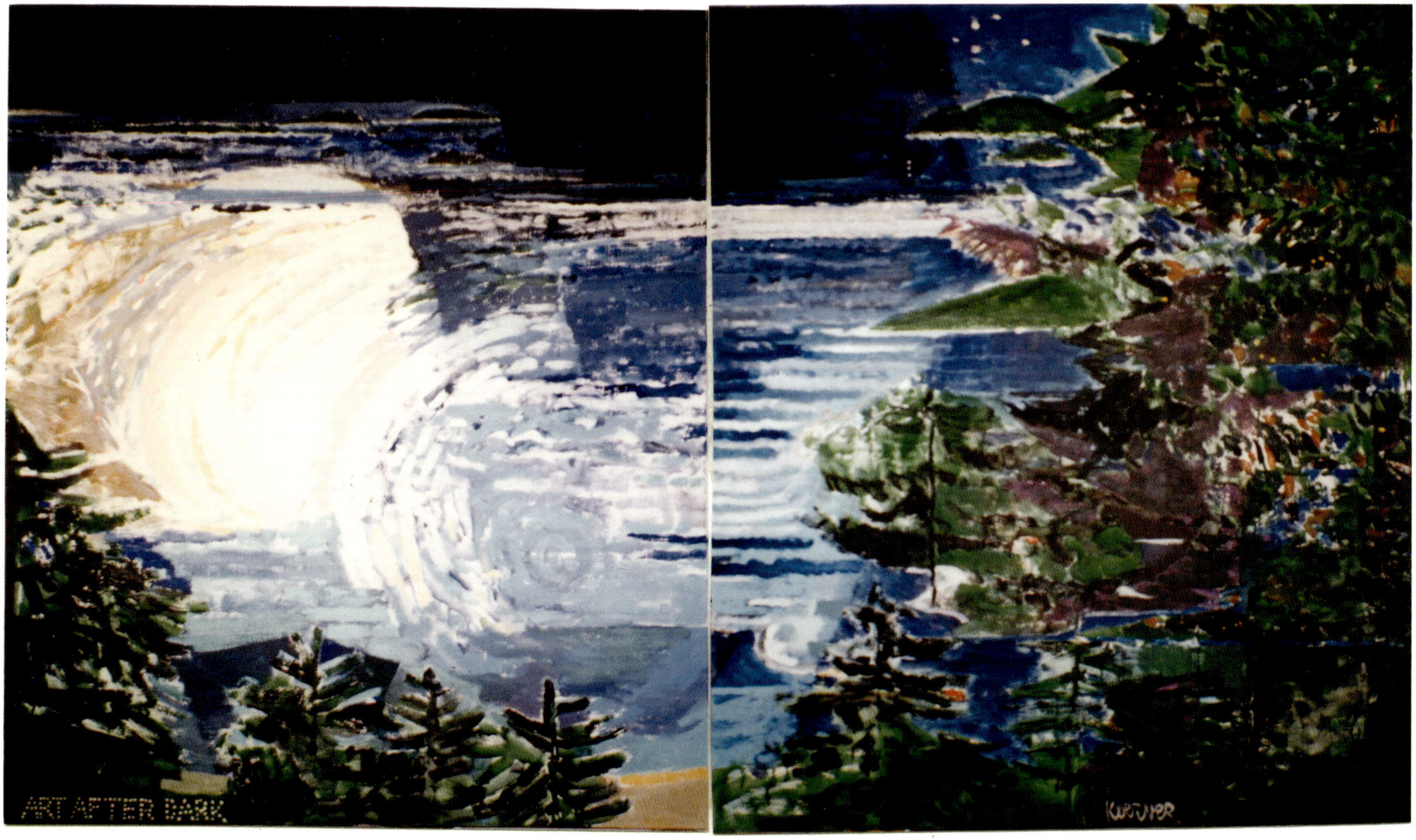

Pacific Gateway (276), acrylic on canvas, 50 x 84 inches, 1990, private collection, Vancouver, BC

In art, as in nature, beauty is in the eye, the mind, and the gut of the beholder. Our perception of beauty cannot be categorized or pinned down in an objective way — but that does not make it less beneficial, for it is soul food.

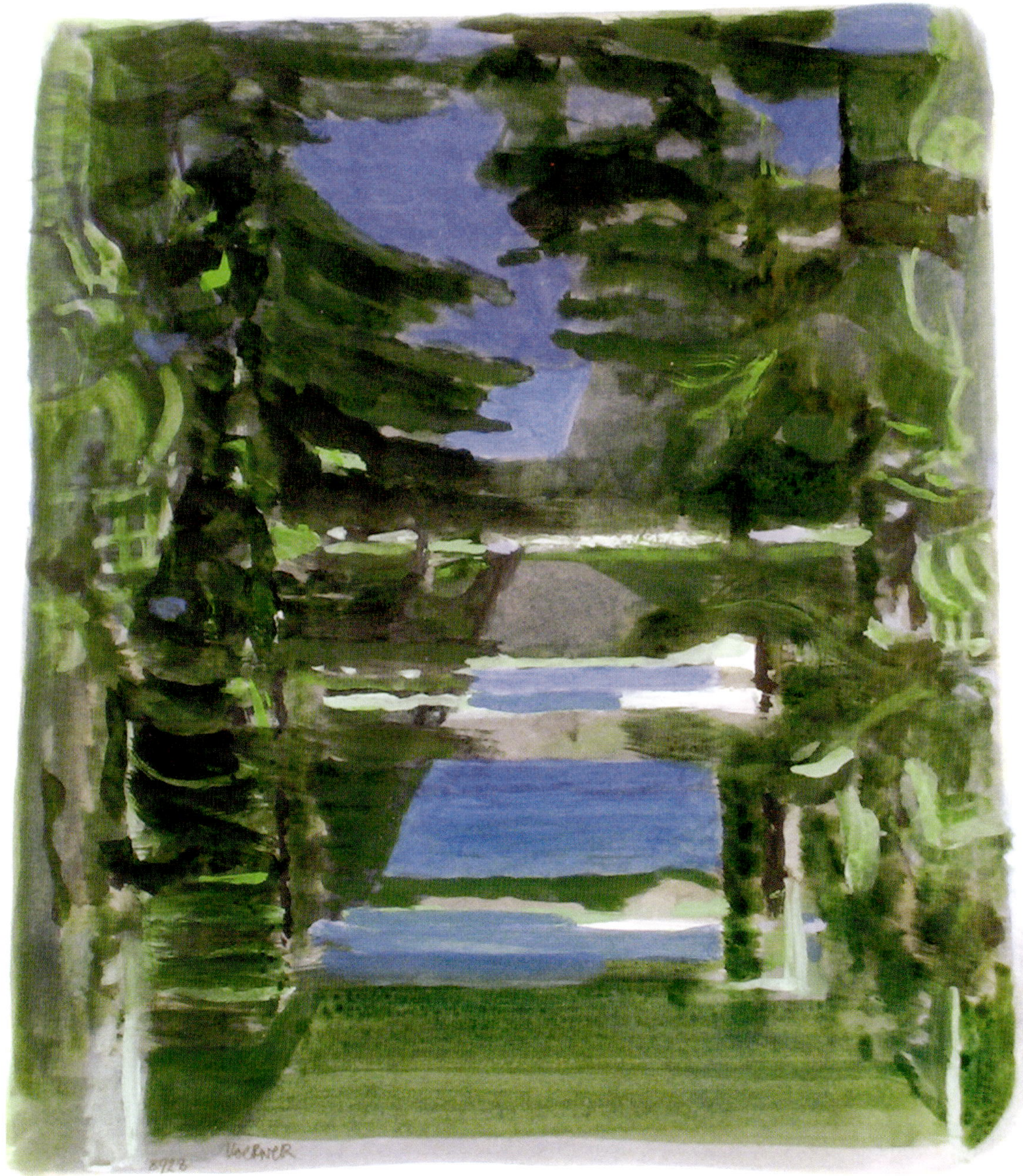

Pacific Gateway (251), acrylic on canvas, 13 x 11.25 inches, 1989, private collection, Vancouver, BC

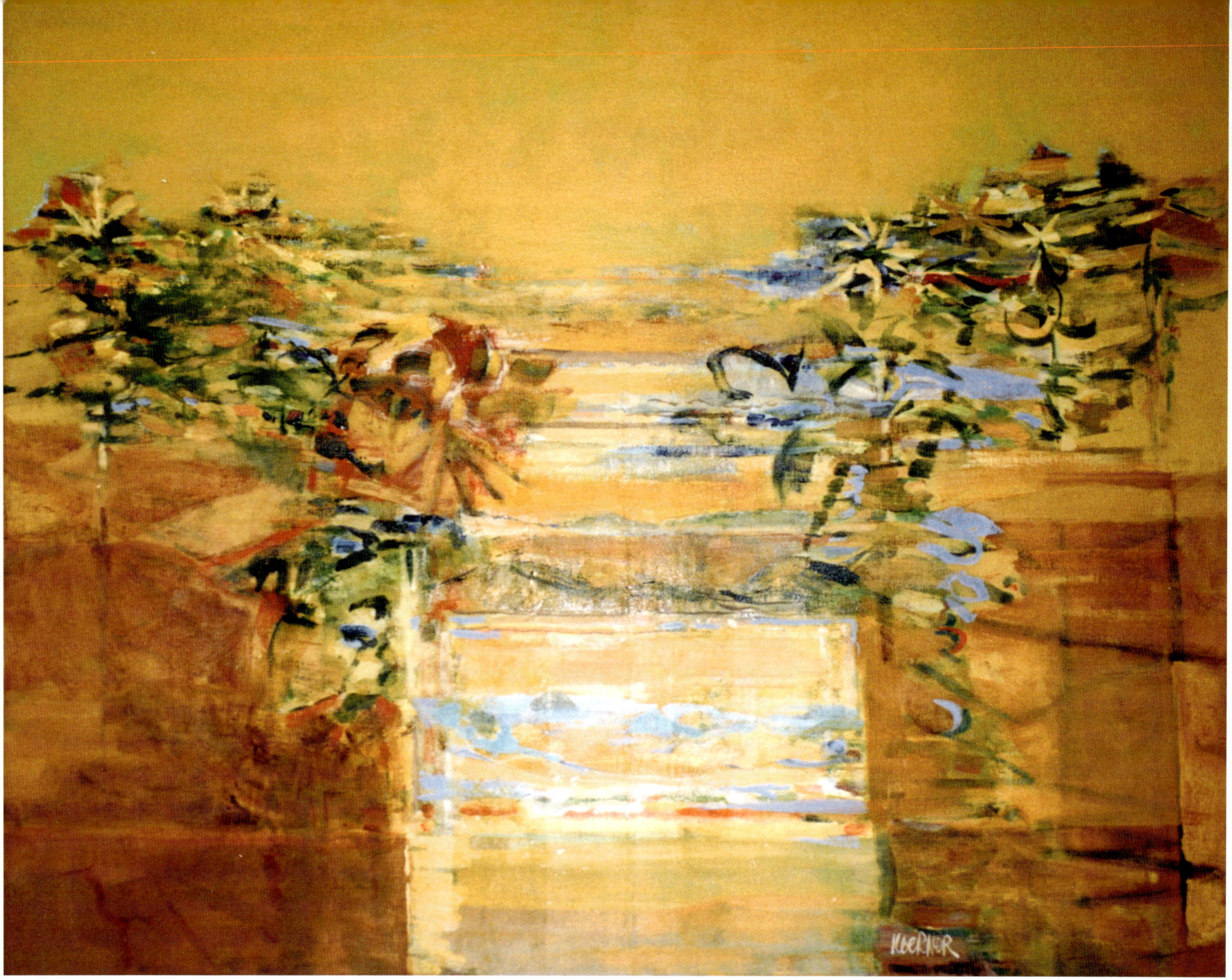

Pacific Gateway (299), acrylic on canvas, 42 x 50 inches, 1999, collection of the artist

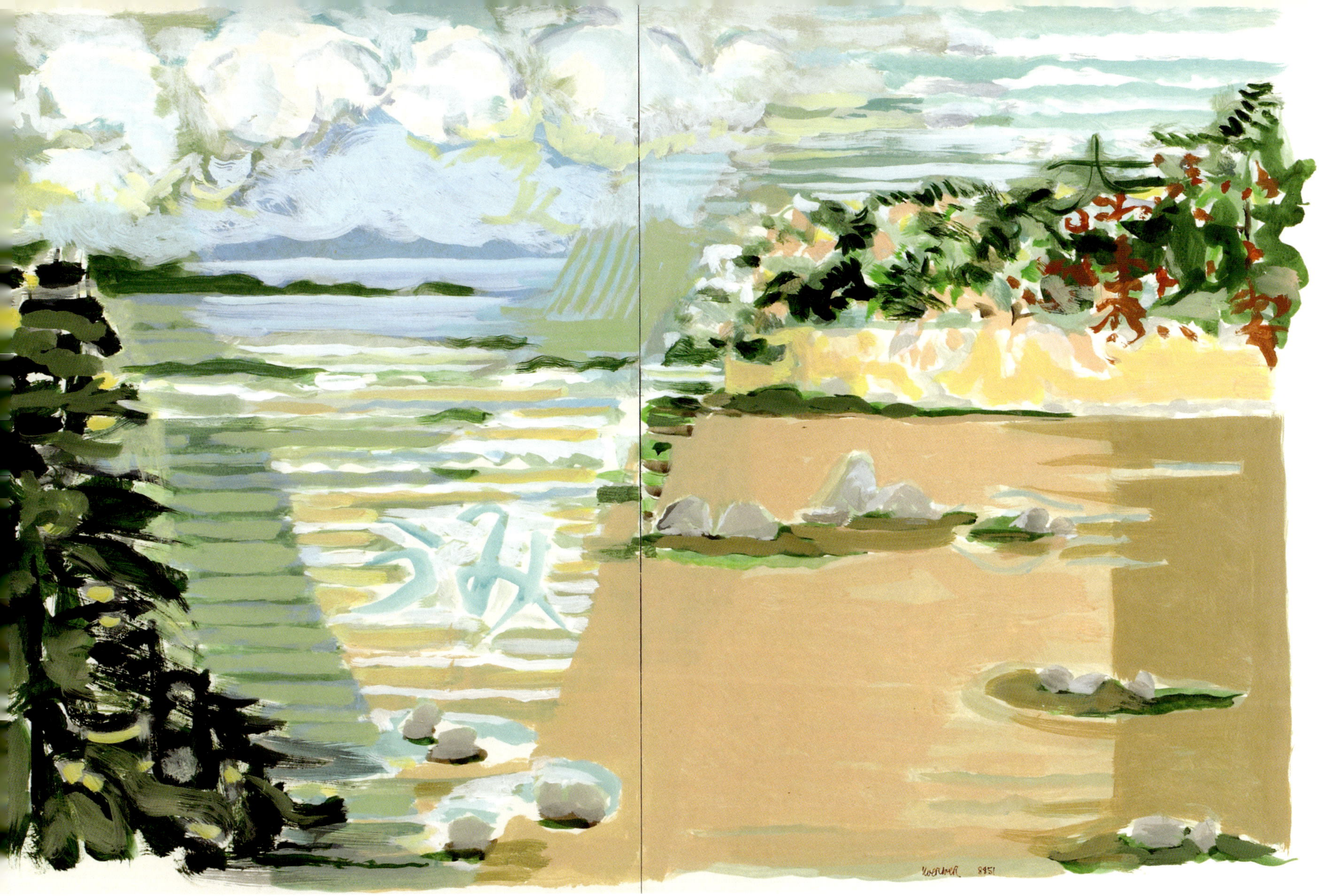

Pacific Gateway (203), acrylic on board, 22 x 30 inches (diptych), 1988, private collection, Vancouver, BC

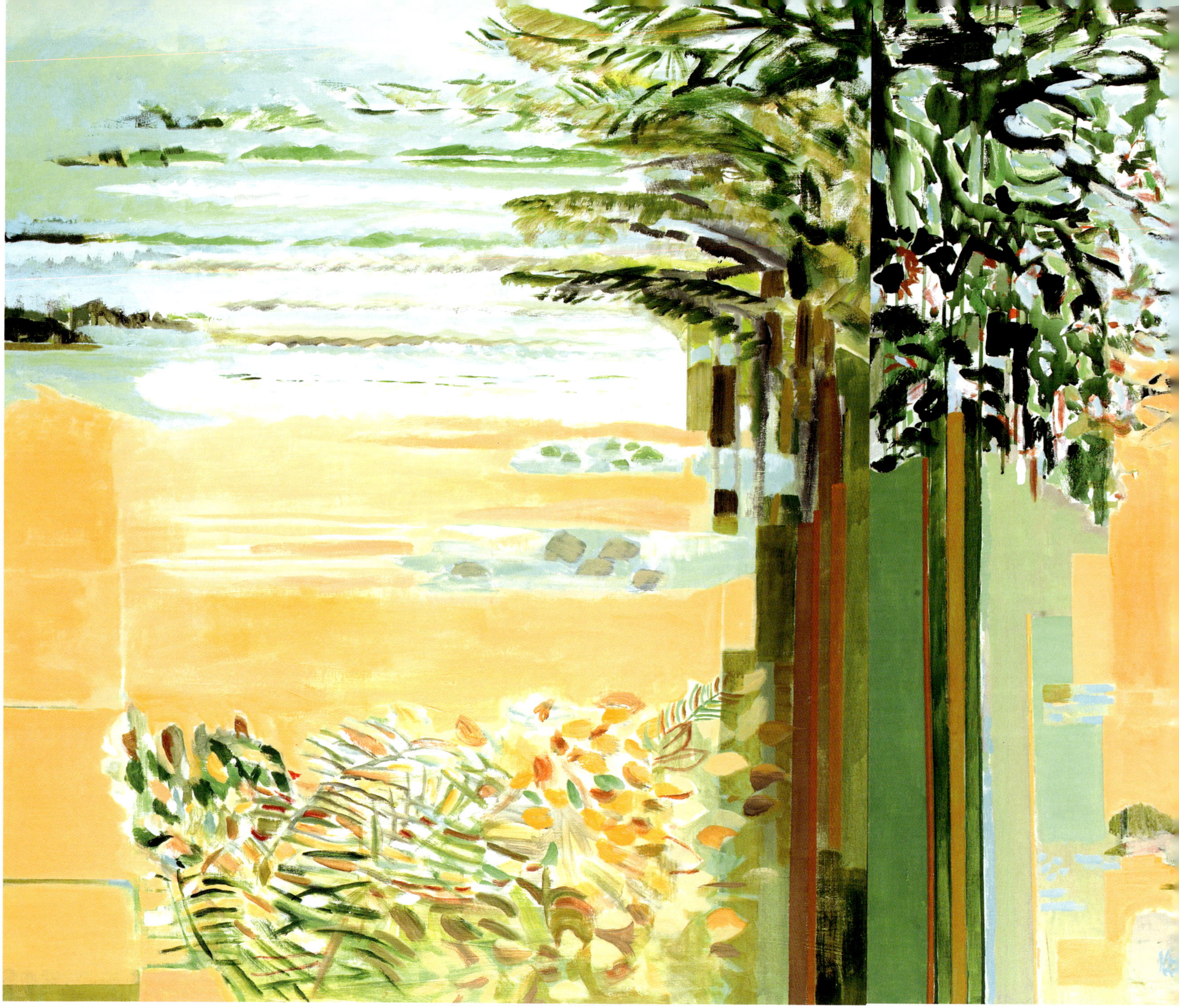

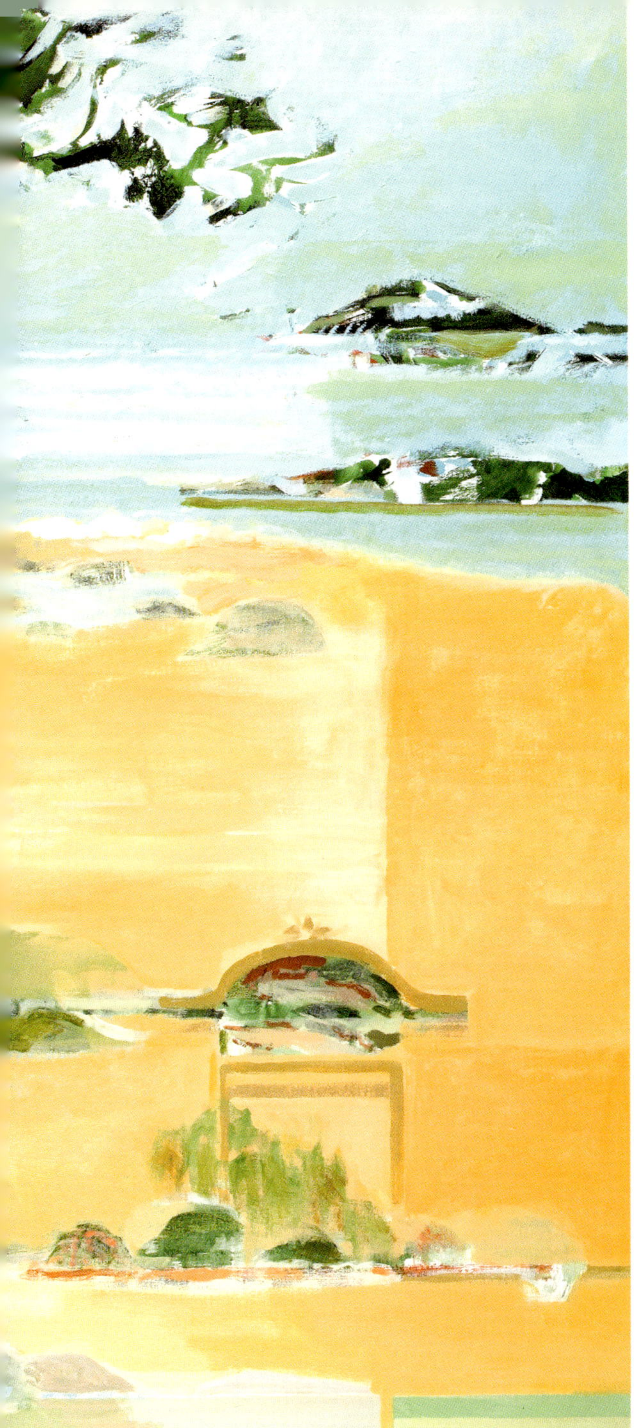

The diptychs and triptychs often begin as single panels that need additional space. Sometimes they are joined together, as in this painting. Sometimes the seams between the panels are emphasized by "hinges," firming the fusion of the two or three parts.

Pacific Gateway (310), acrylic on canvas, 50 x 125 inches (diptych), 1993, collection of Lisa Birnie

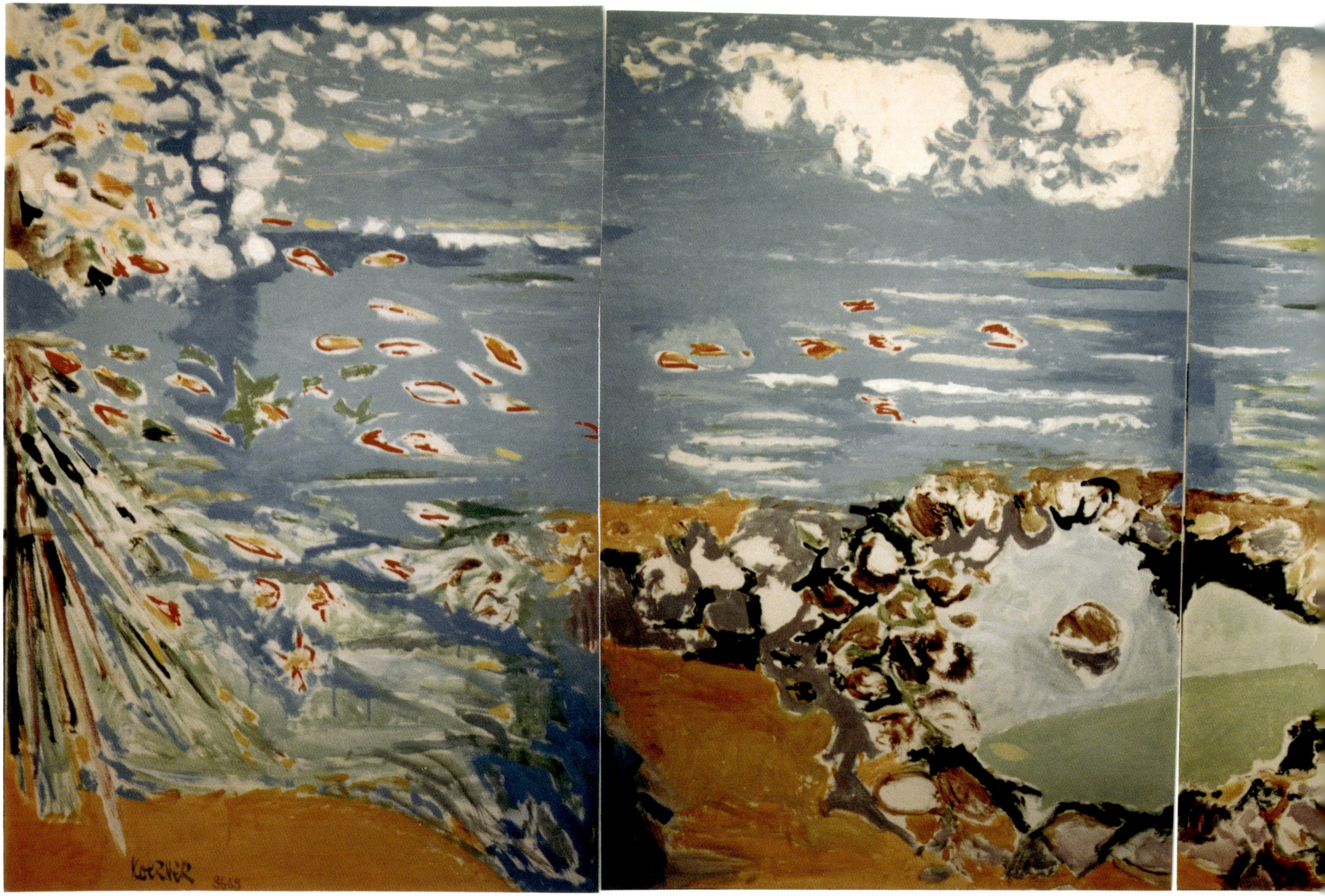

Pacific Gateway (100), acrylic on canvas, 50 x 168 inches, four panels installed in Queen Elizabeth Theatre, Vancouver, BC, 1991

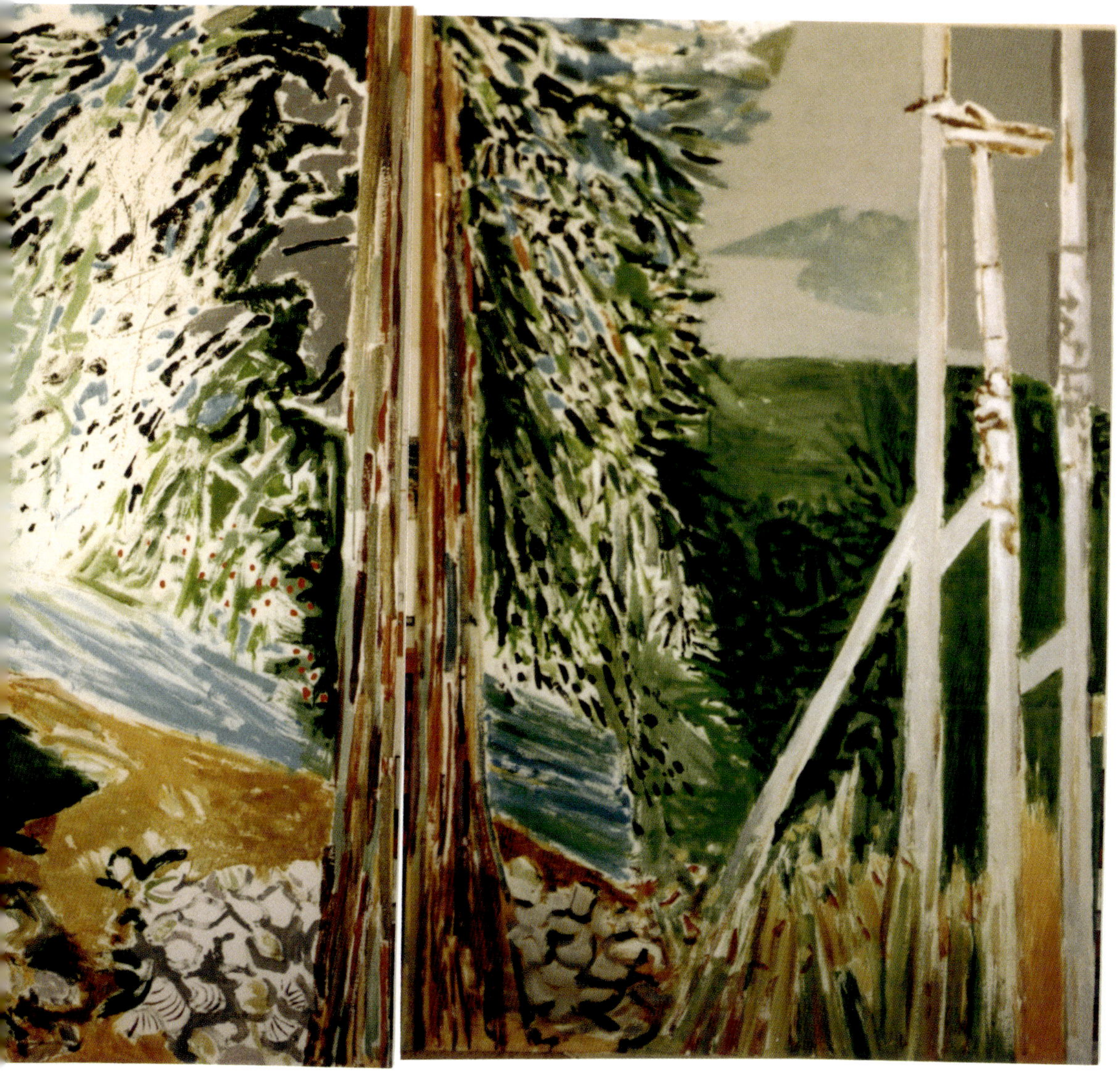

Aside from murals, this is the largest piece I have painted. Anything larger seems to me to be too far from human scale and too pompous; it would have the mistaken sense that bigger is better.

The tidal pool is a recurring theme in my paintings. It could be a symbol for the individual facing the riddle of existence, or a small island in an ocean. Or is this a pond teaming with small marine life such as crabs, spiders, and snails, a remnant of a previous flooding, a temporarily serene world that will soon be engulfed again by the inevitable turn of the tide?

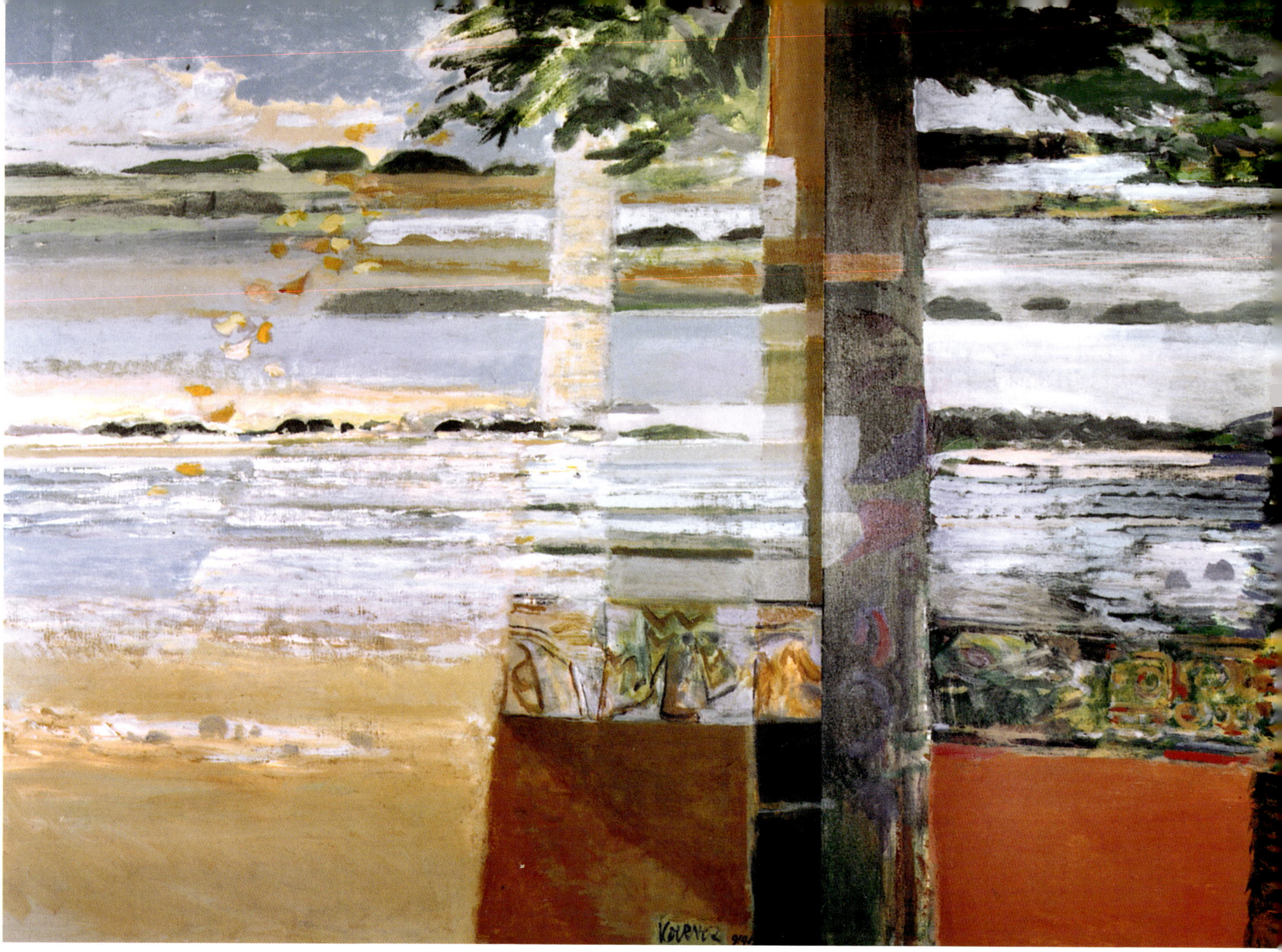

Pacific Gateway (285), acrylic on canvas, 50 x 126 inches (triptych), 1993, collection of the Art Gallery of Greater Victoria, Victoria, BC, 2000.012.006.1-3

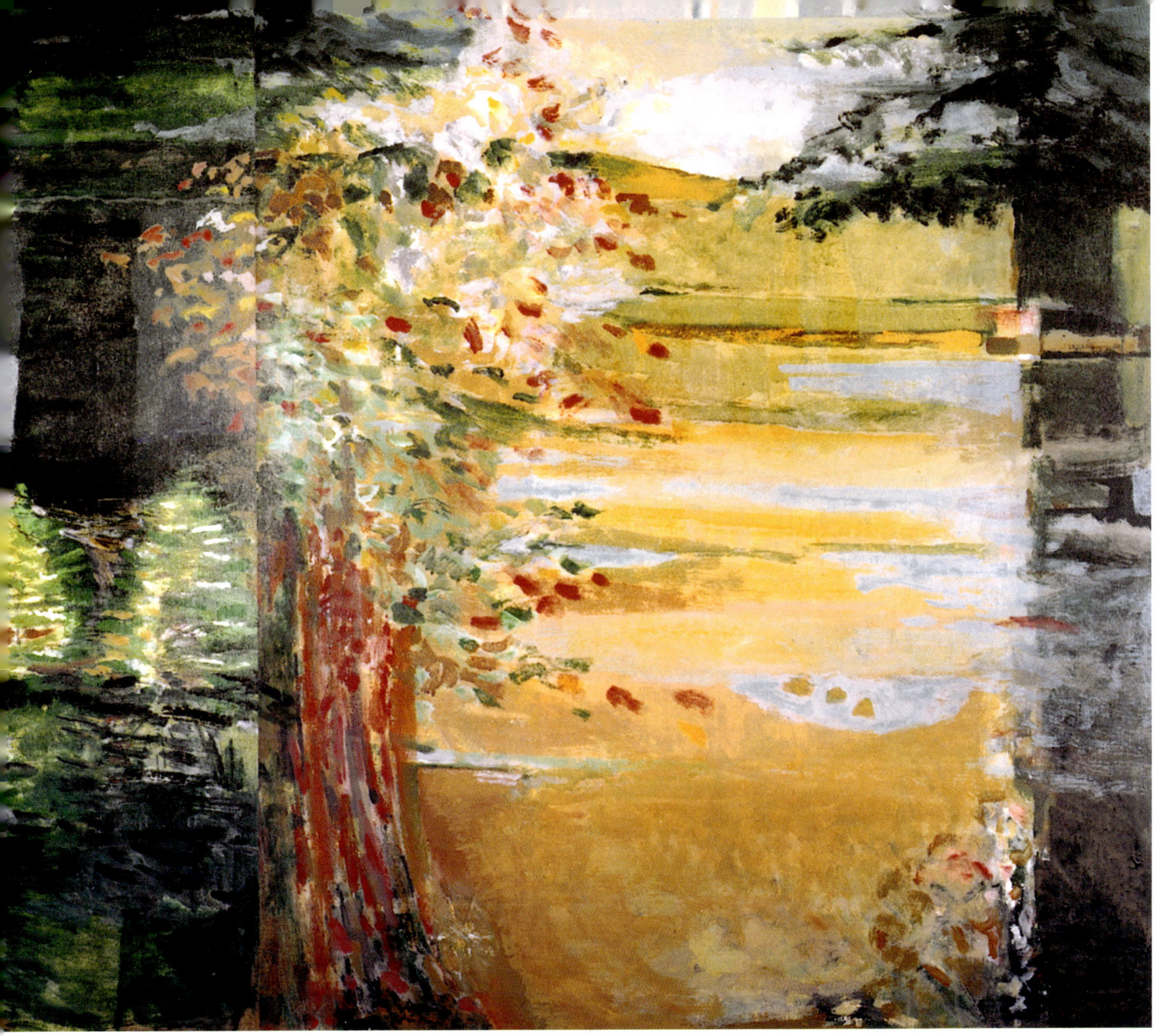

Our vision is often deceived by our imagination. Multiple horizons are a kind of contrapuntal invention alluding to the many aspects of nature and the diversity of human vision. Phenomena are often interchangeable.

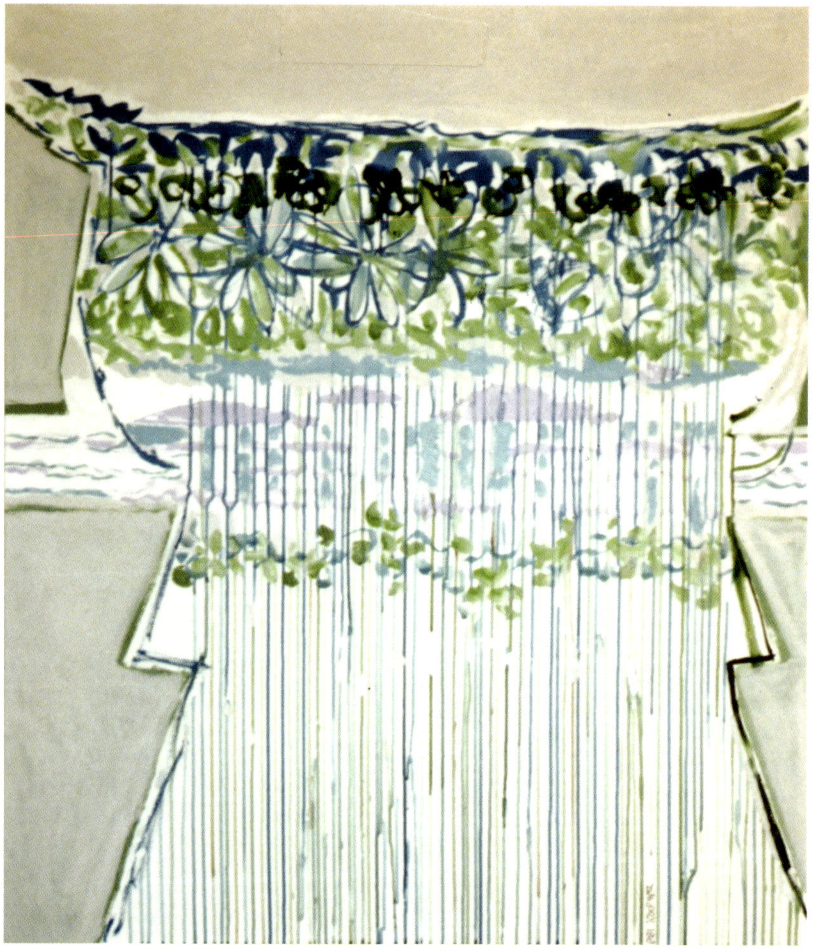

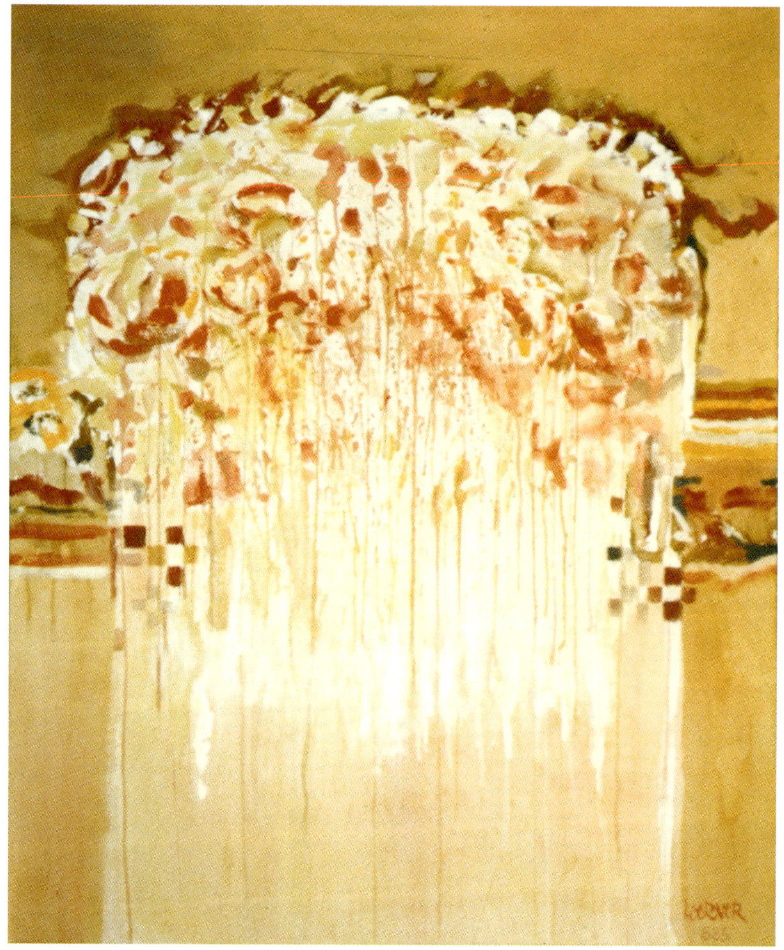

Pacific Gateway (163) Karaori Theme, acrylic on canvas, 50 x 42 inches, 1988, Rideau Hall, Ottawa, ON

Pacific Gateway Kosode Series, acrylic on canvas, 50 x 42 inches, 1988, collection of the artist

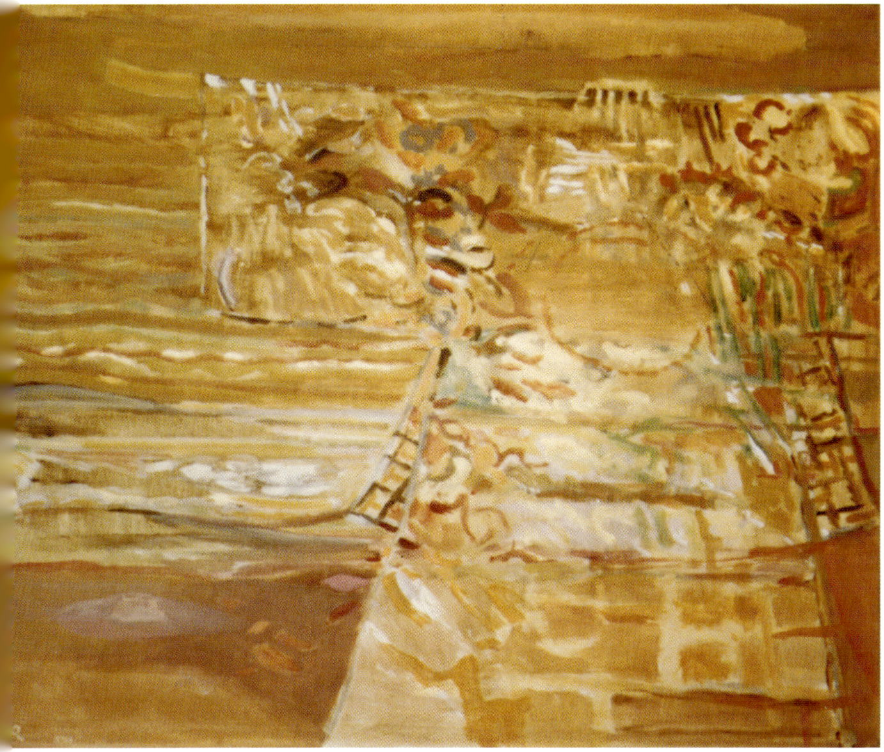

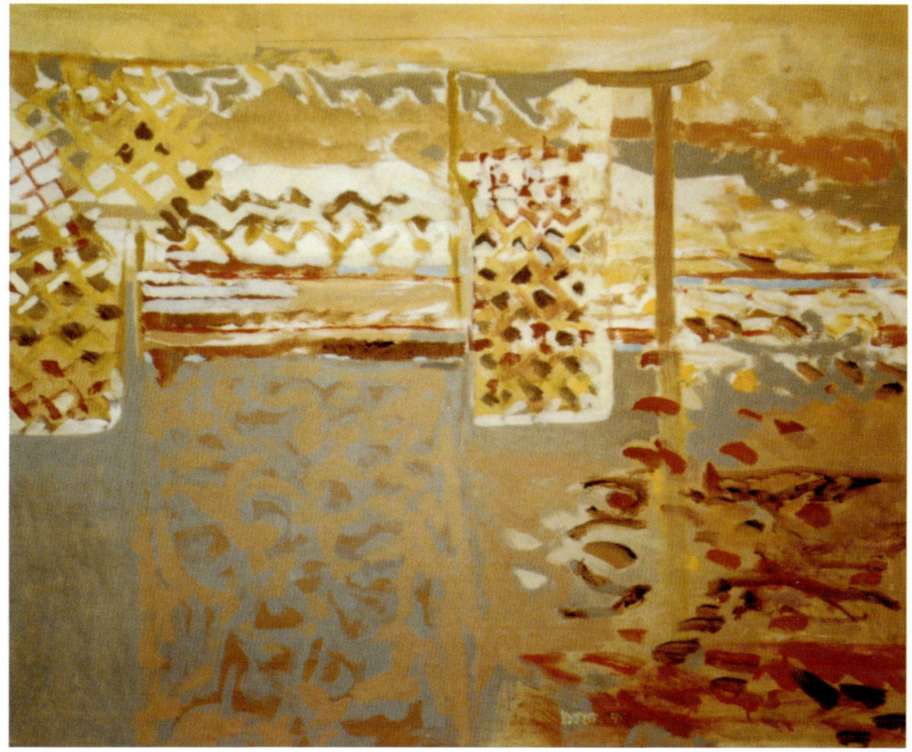

These "gateways" were painted after a stay in Japan. Here the kimono, the *kosode*, becomes transparent, allowing the sea and the land to show through.

Pacific Gateway (146) Kosode Series, acrylic on canvas, 42 x 50 inches, 1988, collection of S. Wood, Toronto, ON

Pacific Gateway (147) Kosode Series, acrylic on canvas, 42 x 50 inches, 1988, collection of Dr. Peter Tryneberg, Palm Springs

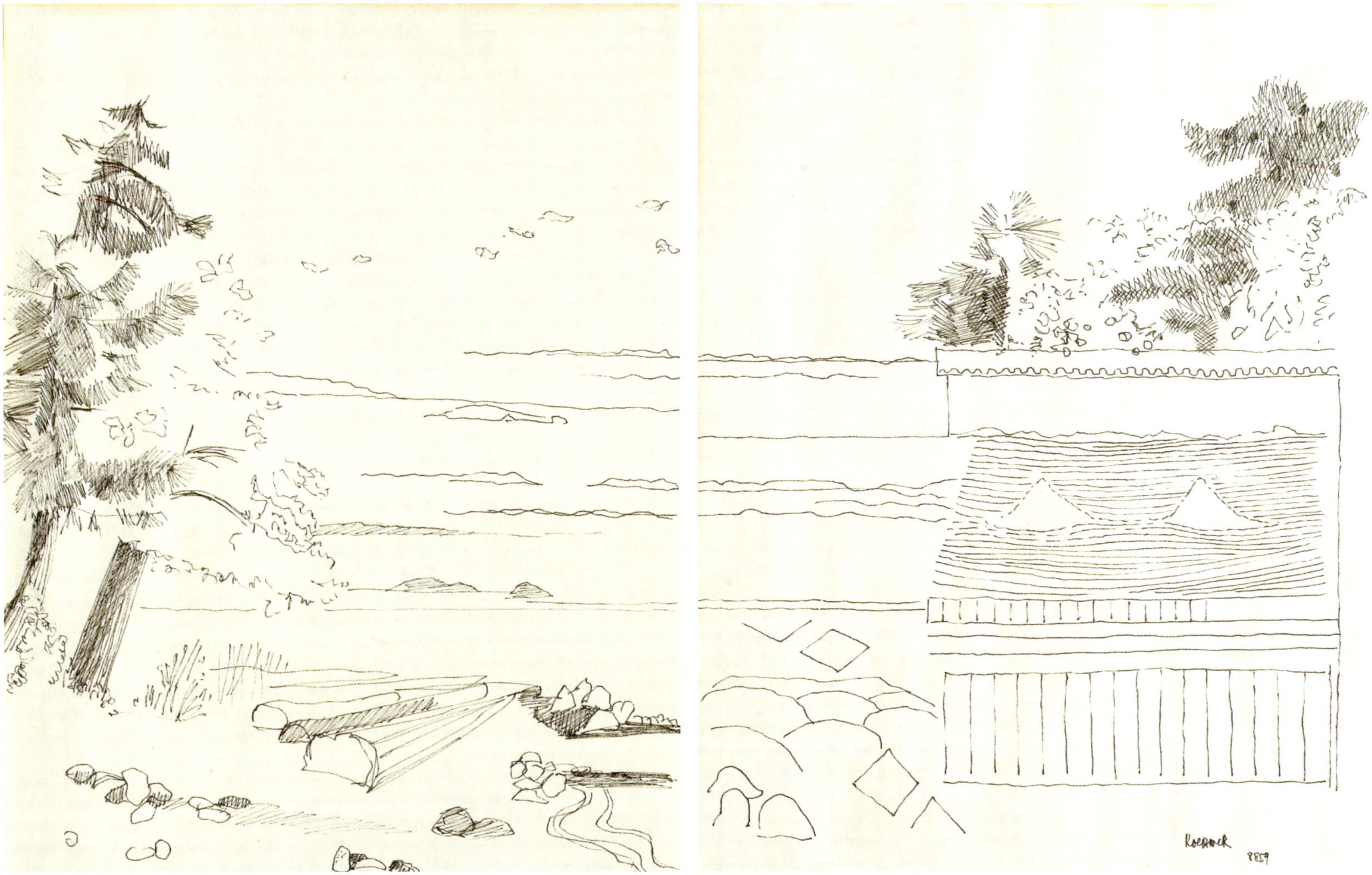

Pacific Gateway (210), pen and ink on paper, 13.5 x 21 inches (diptych), 1988, private collection, Vancouver, BC

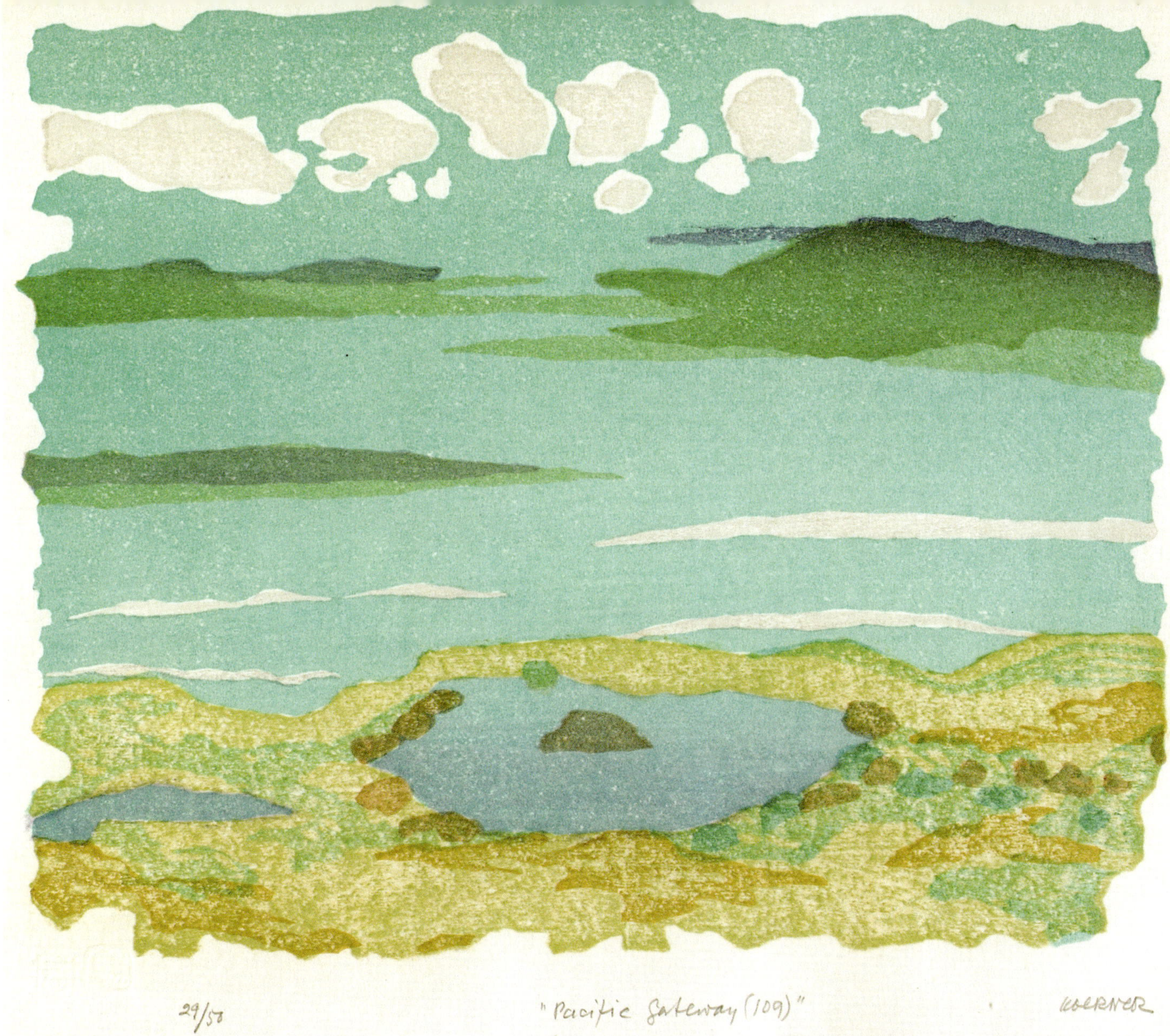

Pacific Gateway (109), woodcut, 11 x 13 inches, 1991, collection of the artist

Drawings and prints are often undervalued. At the age of seventy-four, printmaker Katsushika Hokusai (1760–1849) bemoaned his lack of talent and claimed that "of all I did prior to the age of seventy [there] is truly nothing of great note." It took fifty years before his mastery of the art of *ukiuo-e* was fully recognized.

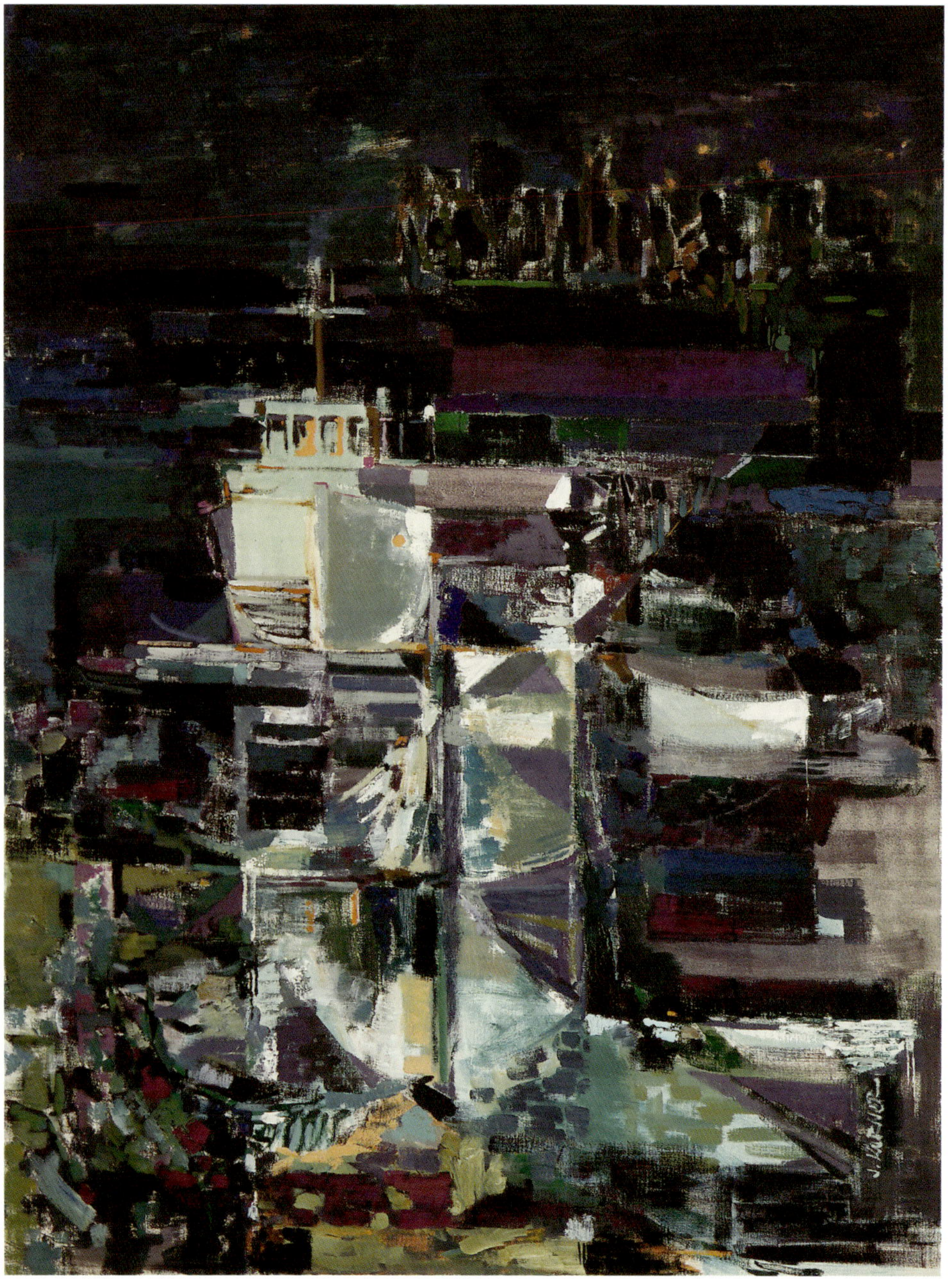

Coast Nocturne, oil on canvas, 46 x 34 inches, 1957, Vancouver Art Gallery Women's Auxillary Picture Purchase Fund, VAG 58.2

Photo: Tim Bonham

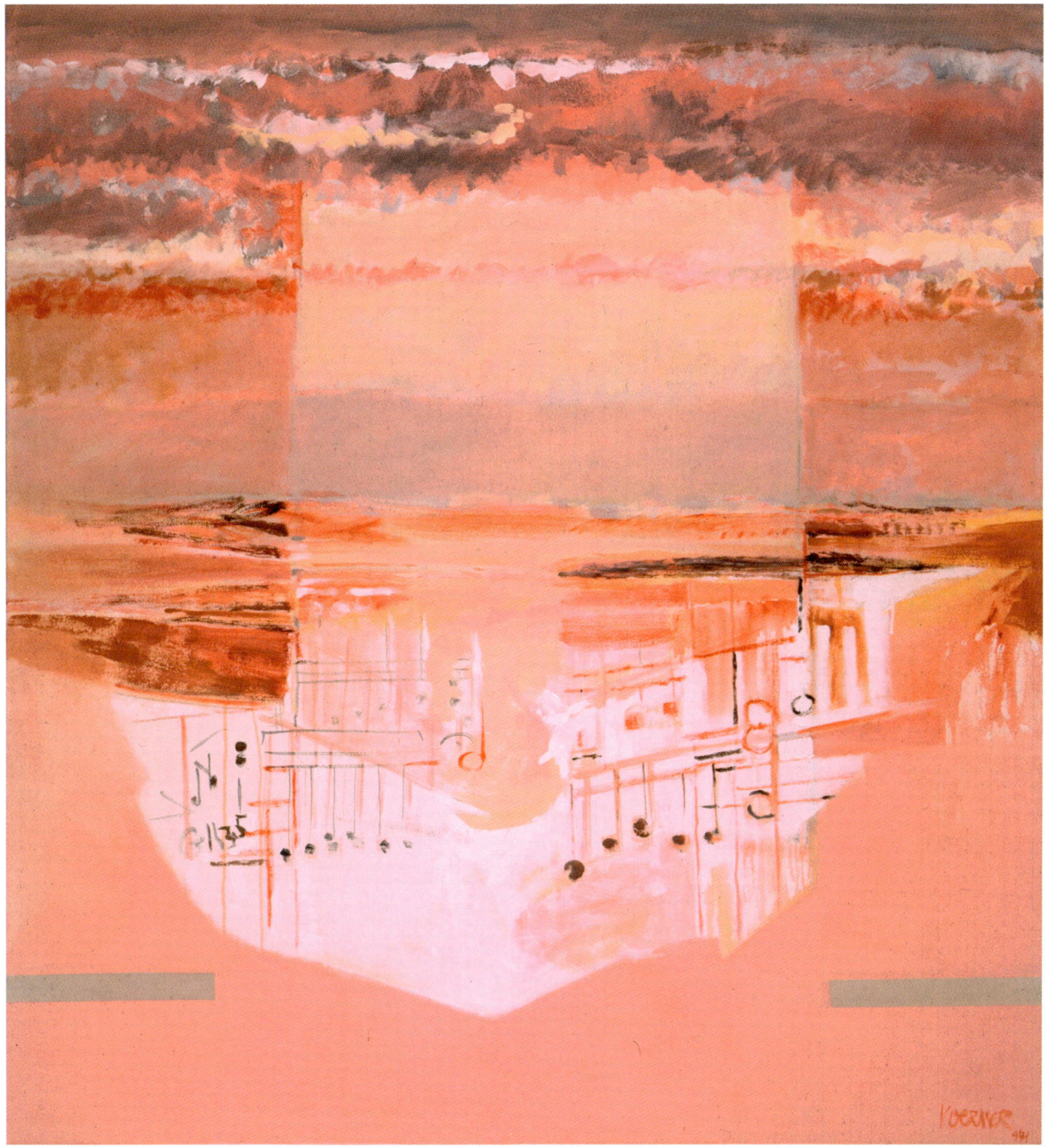

The Balcony (20), acrylic on canvas, 60 x 54 inches, Dec 1993 – Jan 1994, collection of the Vancouver General Hospital, Heather Pavilion

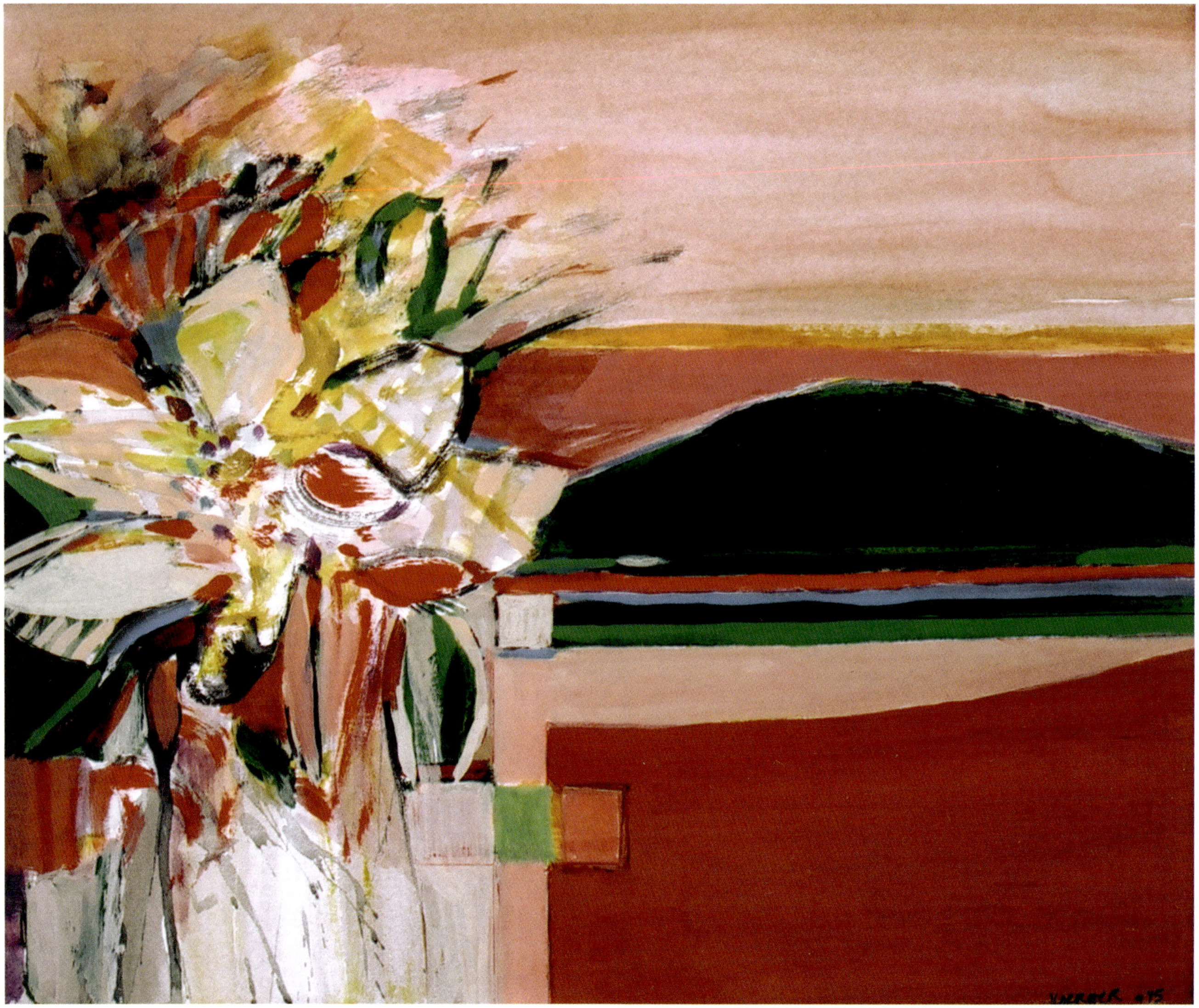

The Balcony (24), acrylic on paper, 13.25 x 16 inches, 1999, collection of Merle McKee. Photo: Merle McKee

The flower still life always turns out to be a symbol for celebration, commemoration, and festive events — perhaps for the gift of life.

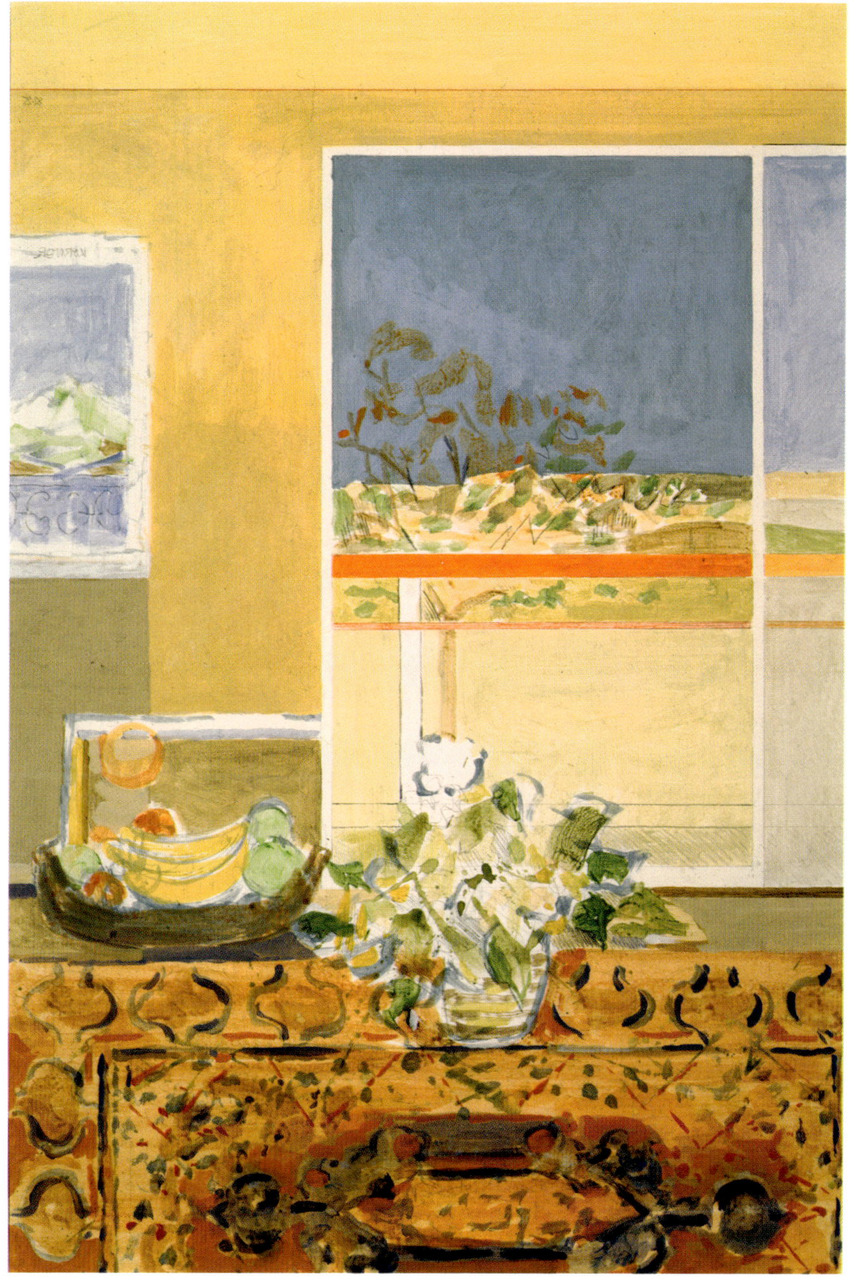

Balcony with Fruit Bowl, acrylic on board, 30 x 20 inches, 1982, private collection

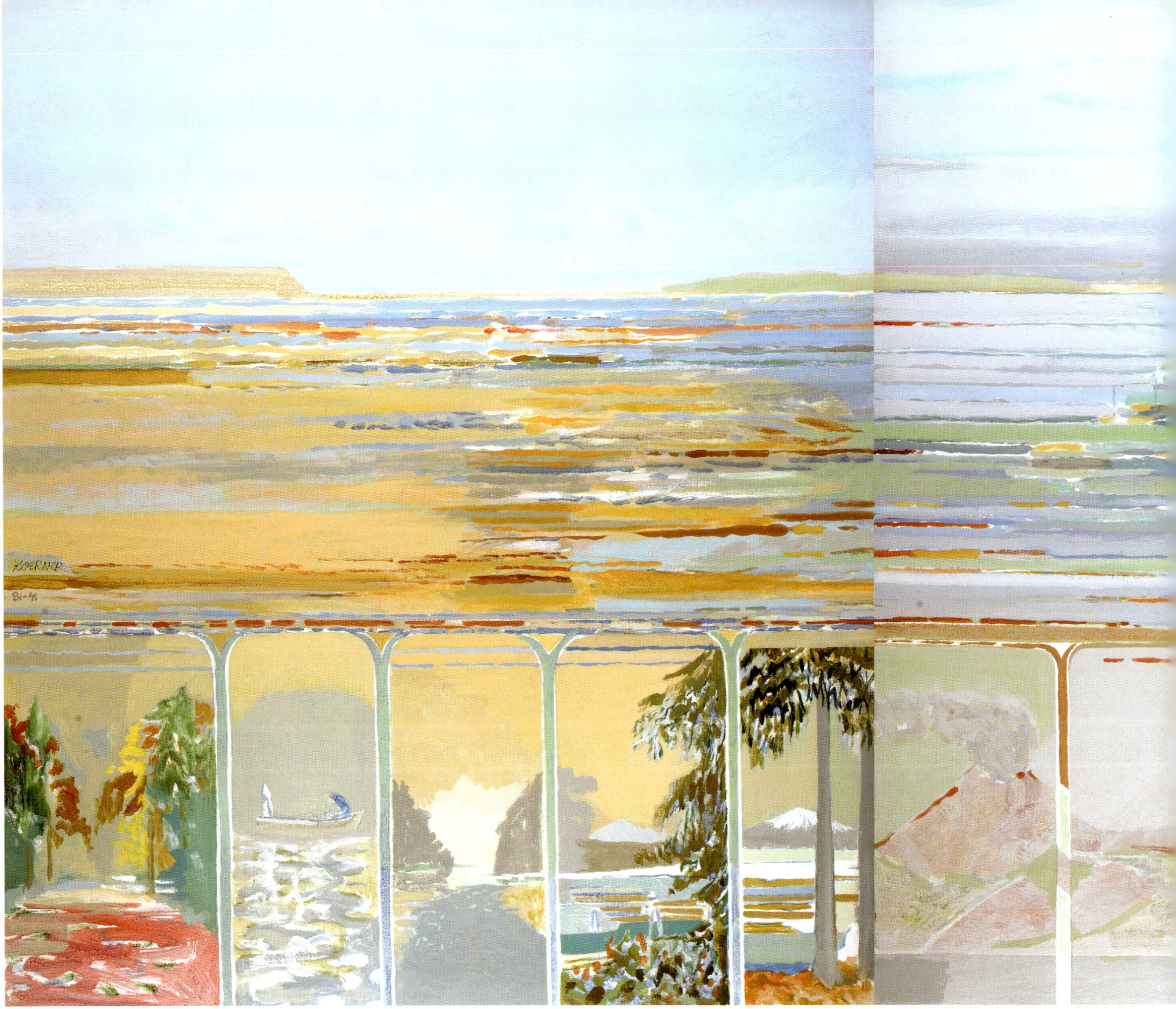

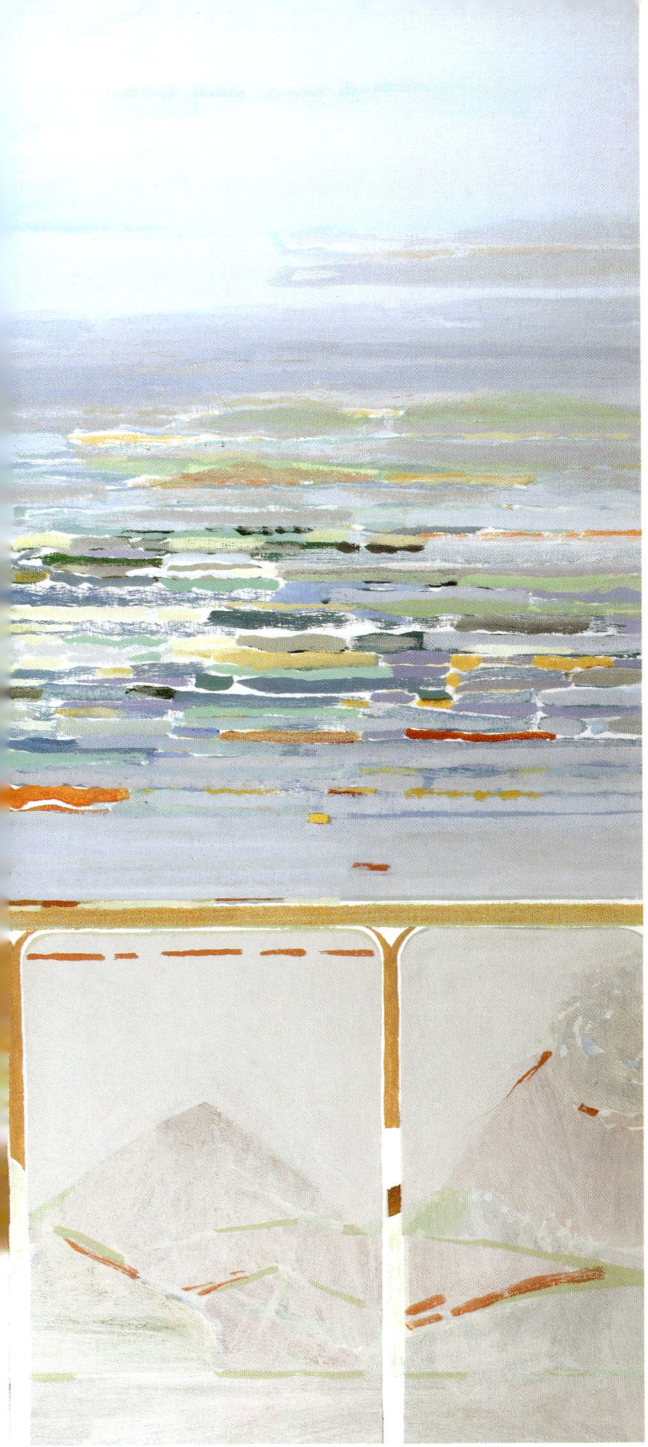

An imaginary balcony overlooking an ocean with friendly waves and various phases of volcanic action. Above, the sky, the light.

Oceanic, Balcony with Volcanos, acrylic on canvas, 50 x 84 inches (diptych), 1981, collection of the artist

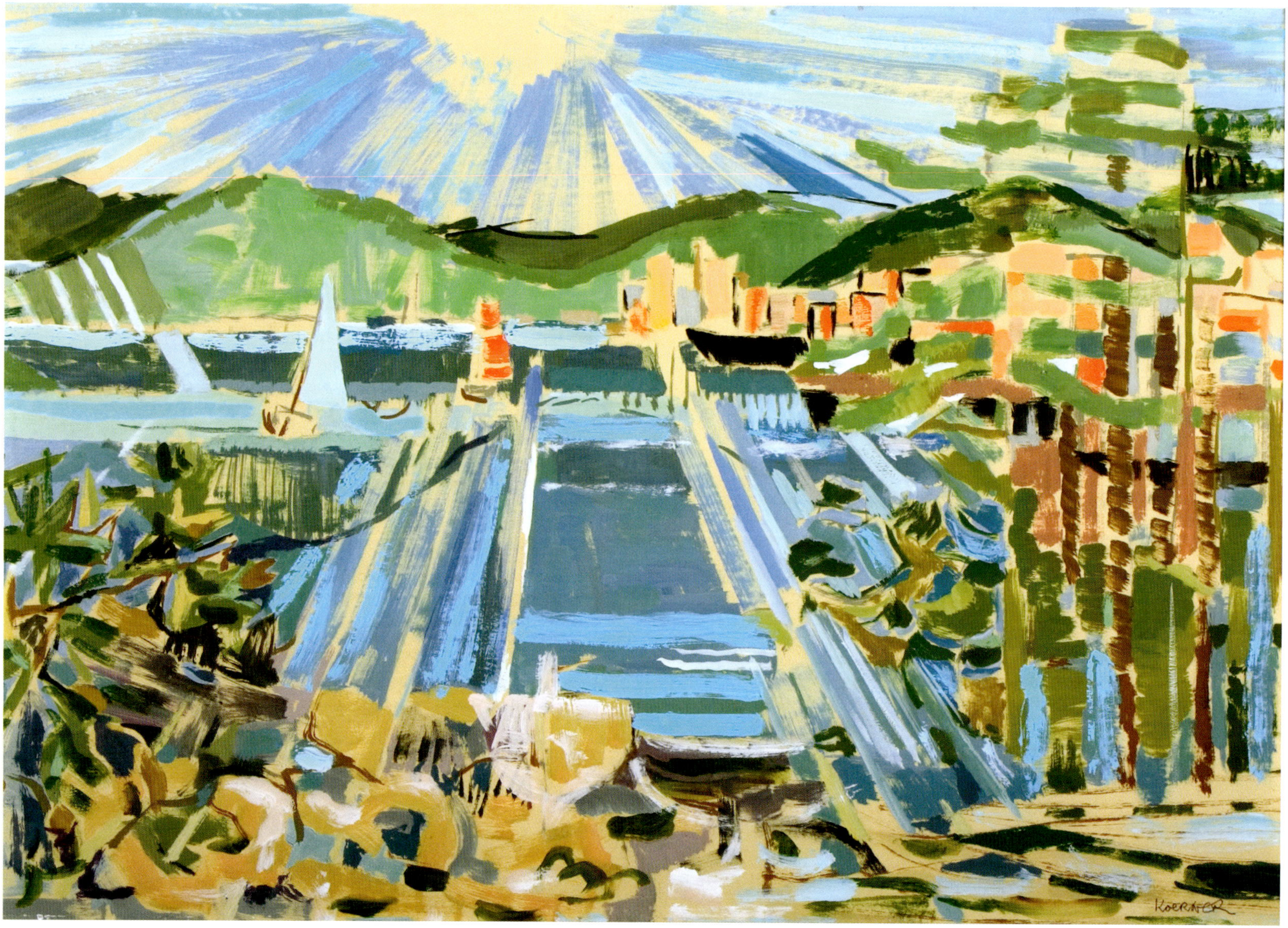

Inner Harbour, acrylic on board, 18 x 25 inches, n.d., private collection

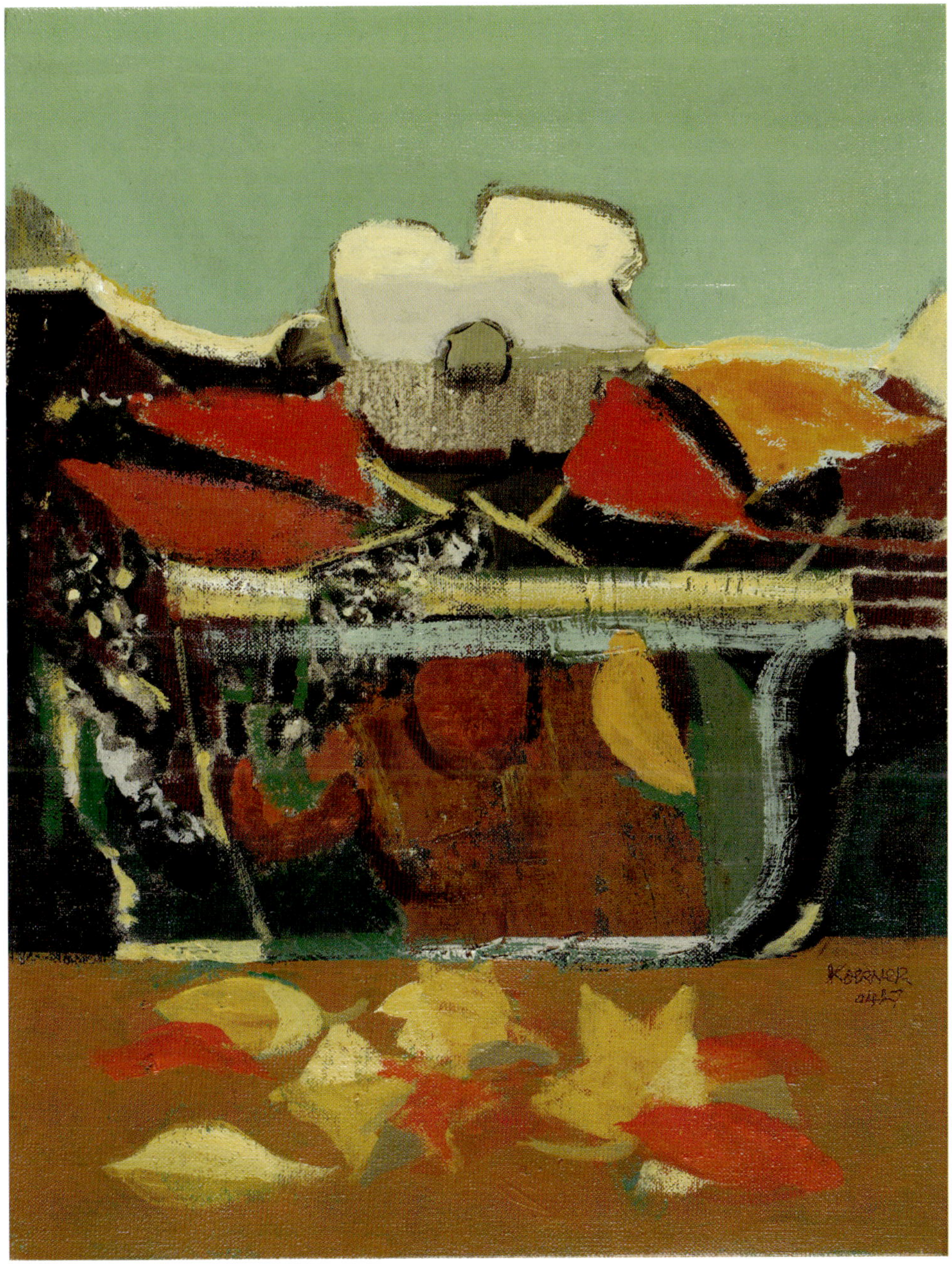

Autumnal, acrylic on canvas, 16 x 12 inches,
n.d. 61-21, collection of the artist

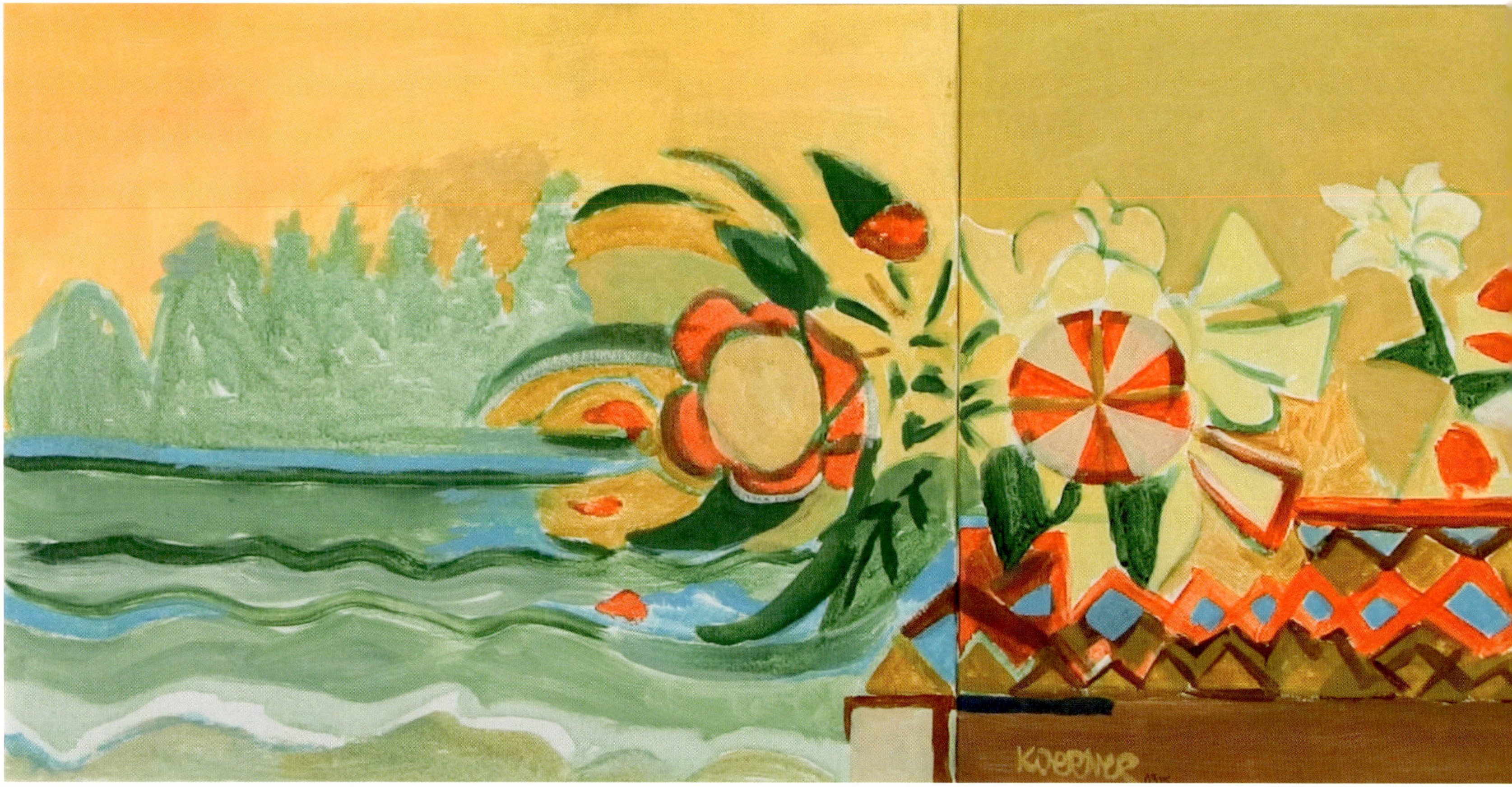

Still Life with Ocean, acrylic on canvas, 18.75 x 68.5 inches (triptych), 2003, collection of Lisa Birnie

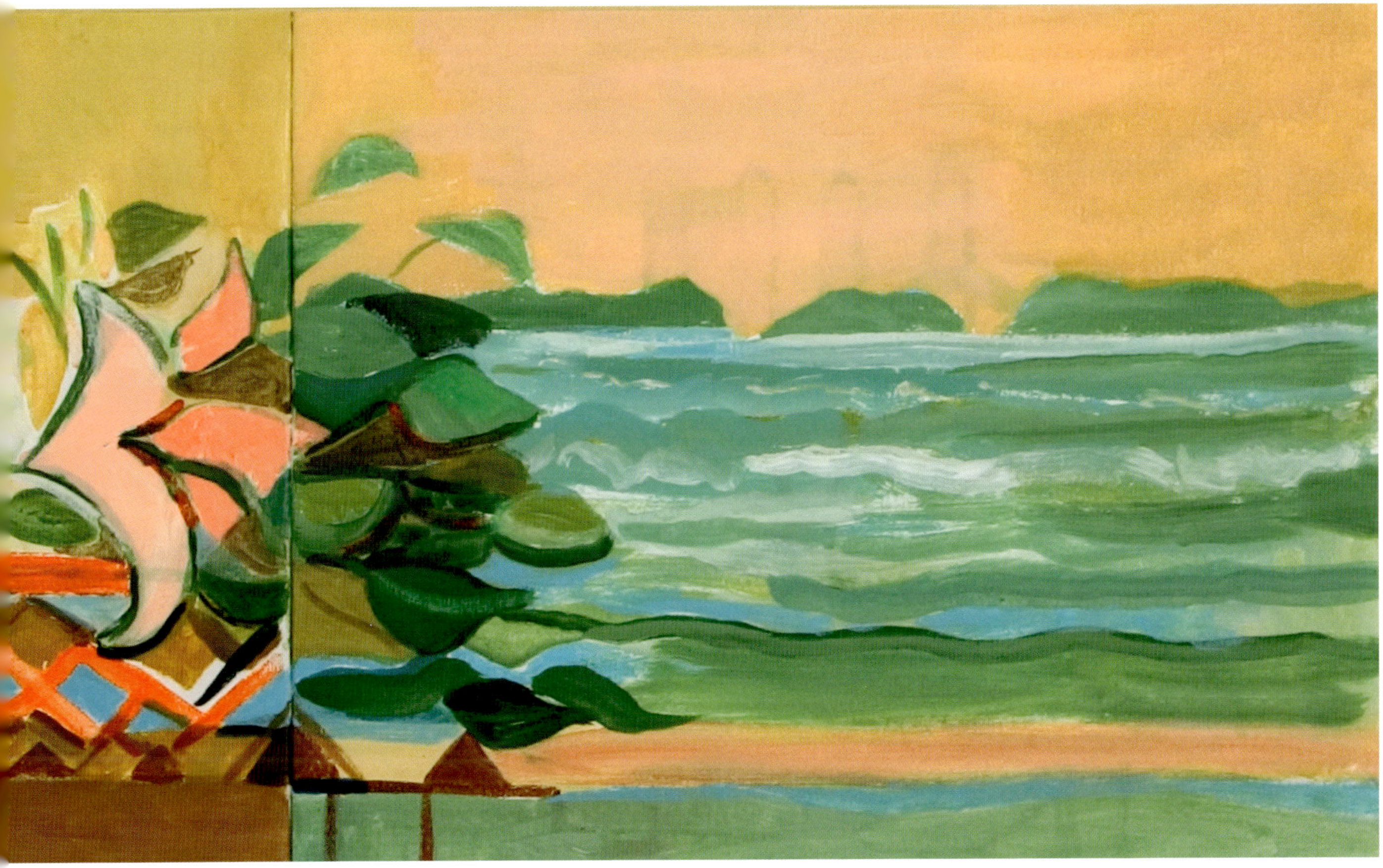

Here the theme is symmetry — the correspondence of size, form, and the arrangement of parts.

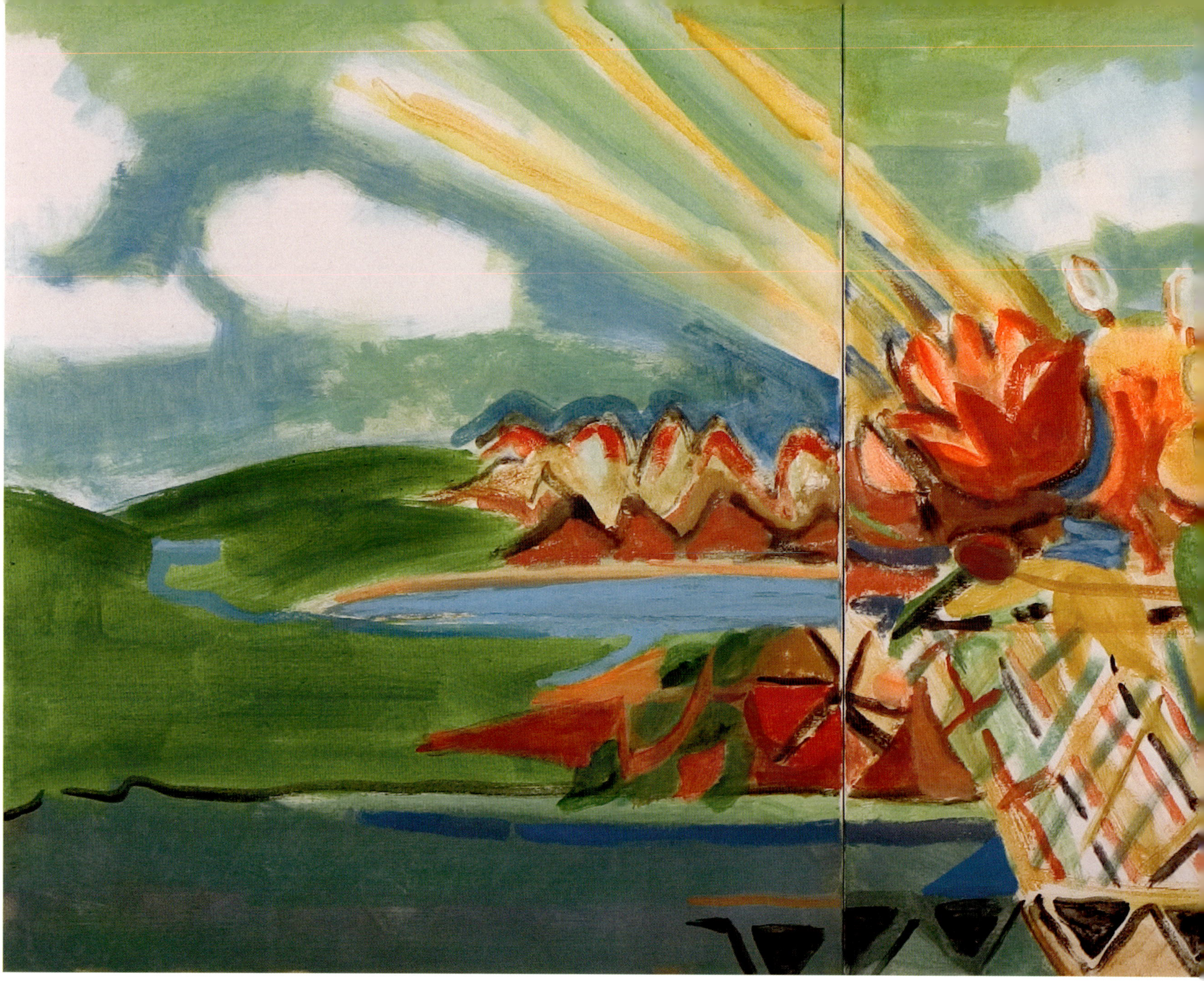

Still Life With Rays, acrylic on canvas, 24 x 60 inches (triptych), 2003, collection of the artist

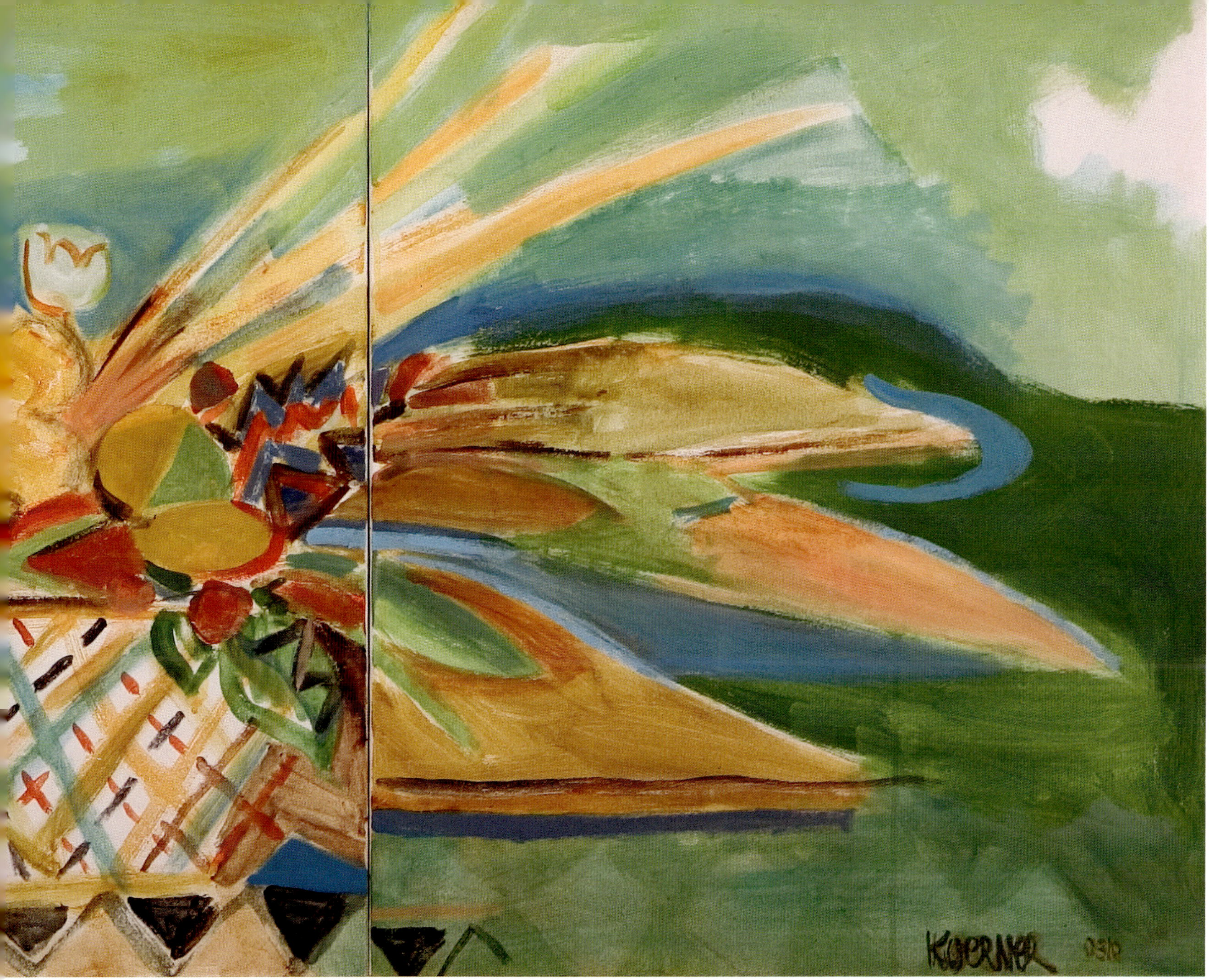

This painting was done as a joyous reaction to a surprising event.

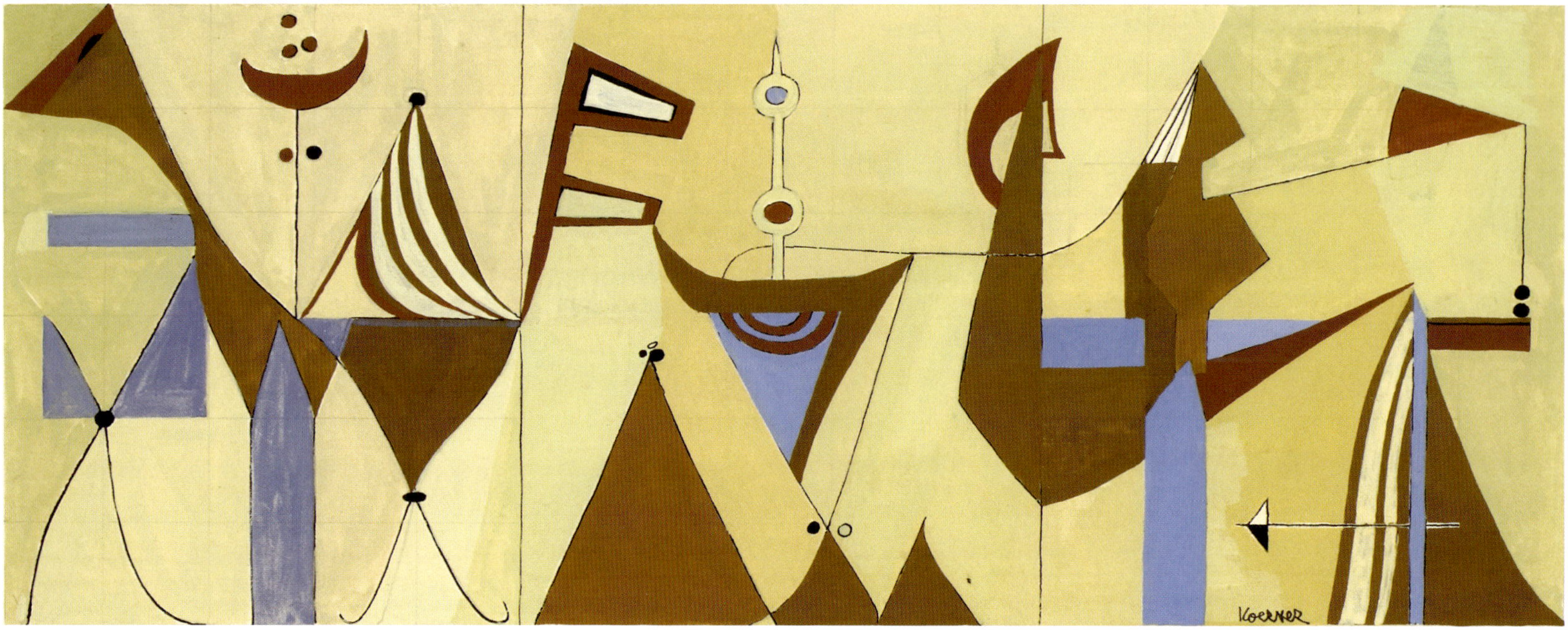

Rhythmic Progression, ink on paper, 4.25 x 7.5 inches, dated January 27, 1953, collection of the artist

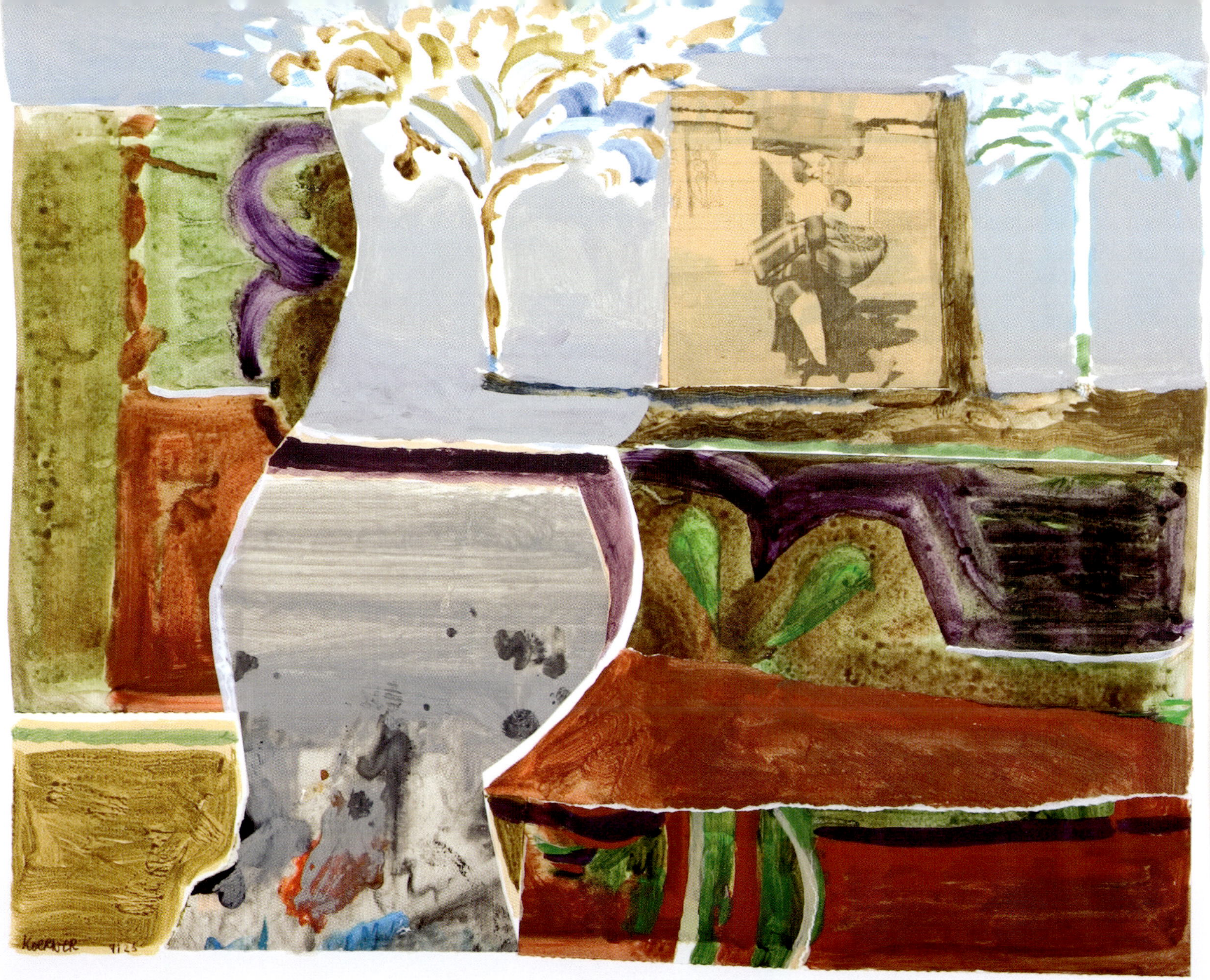

African Study, acrylic and collage on paper, 12.5 x 15 inches, 1997, private collection

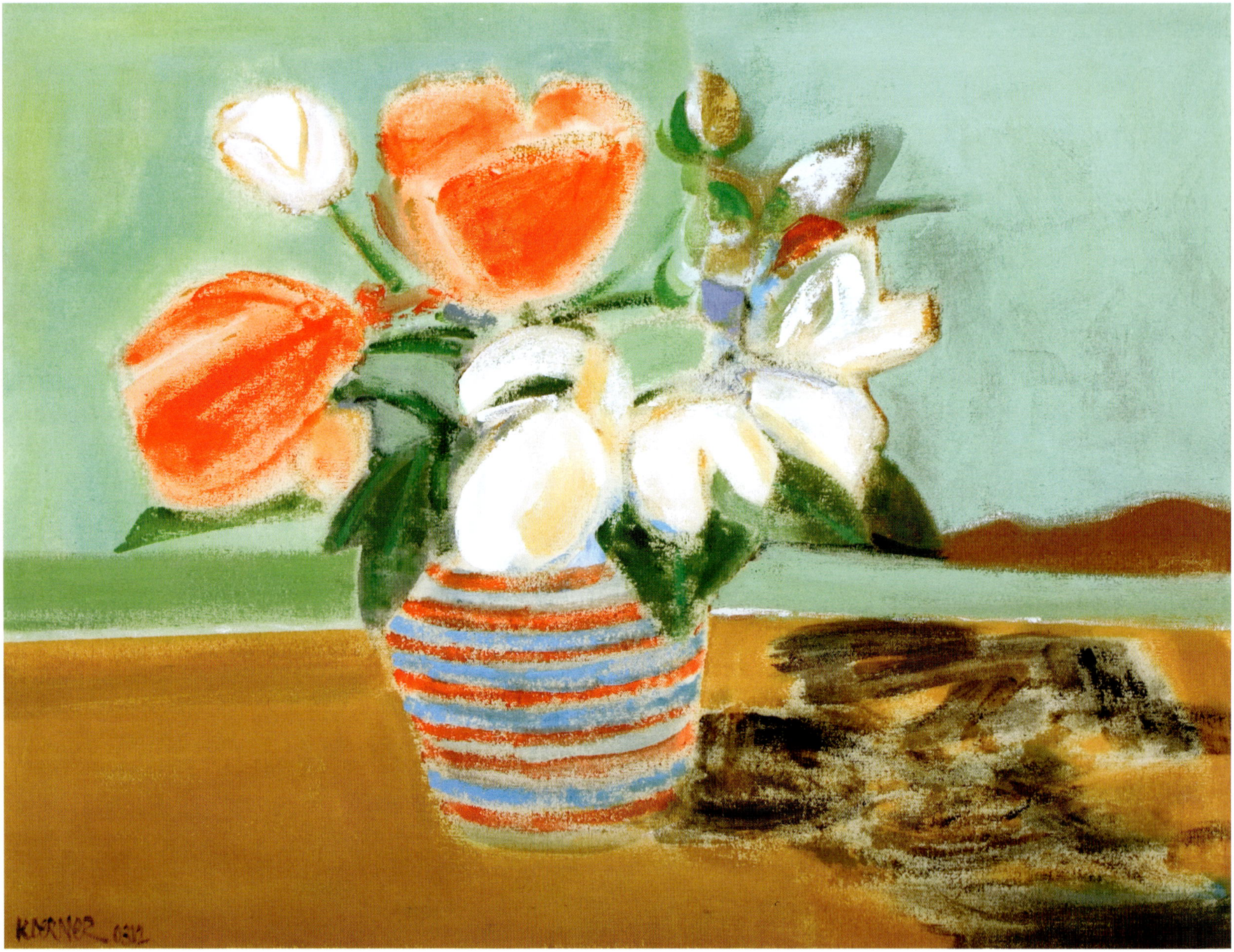

Winter Flowers, acrylic on canvas, 20.75 x 26.75 inches, 2003, collection of the artist

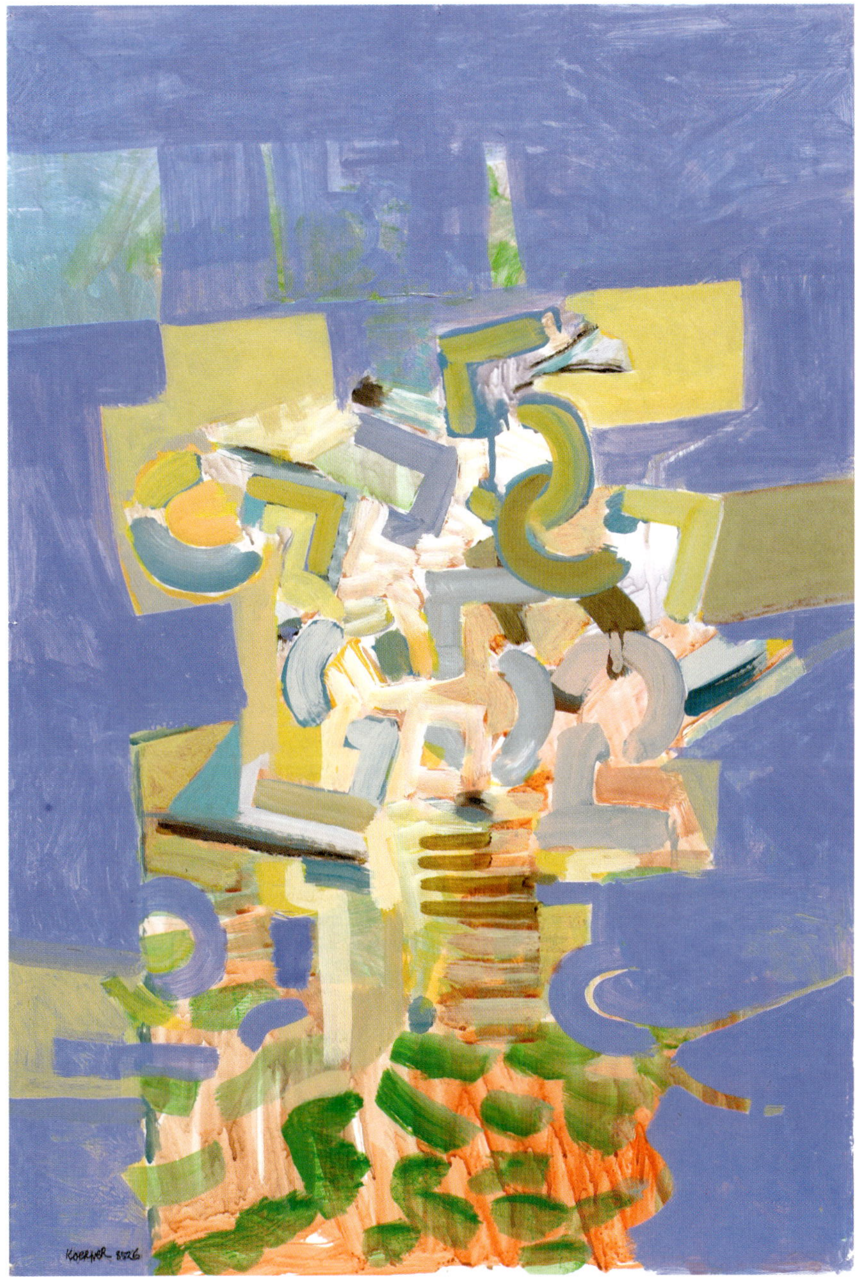

Totemic Number Motif, acrylic on board, 30 x 20 inches, n.d., collection of the artist

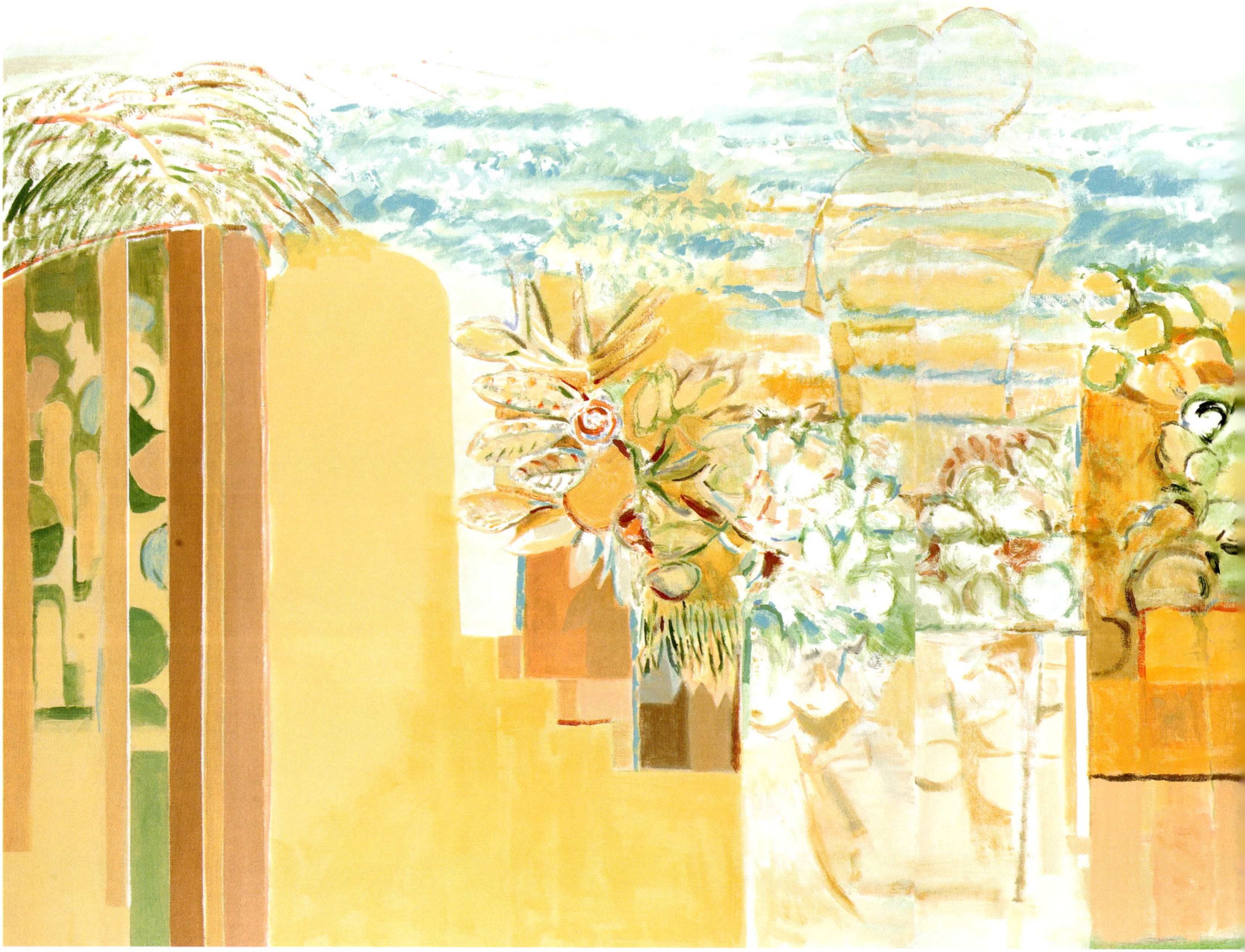

This *Garden* was completed during a very happy stage in my life — a kind of celebration.

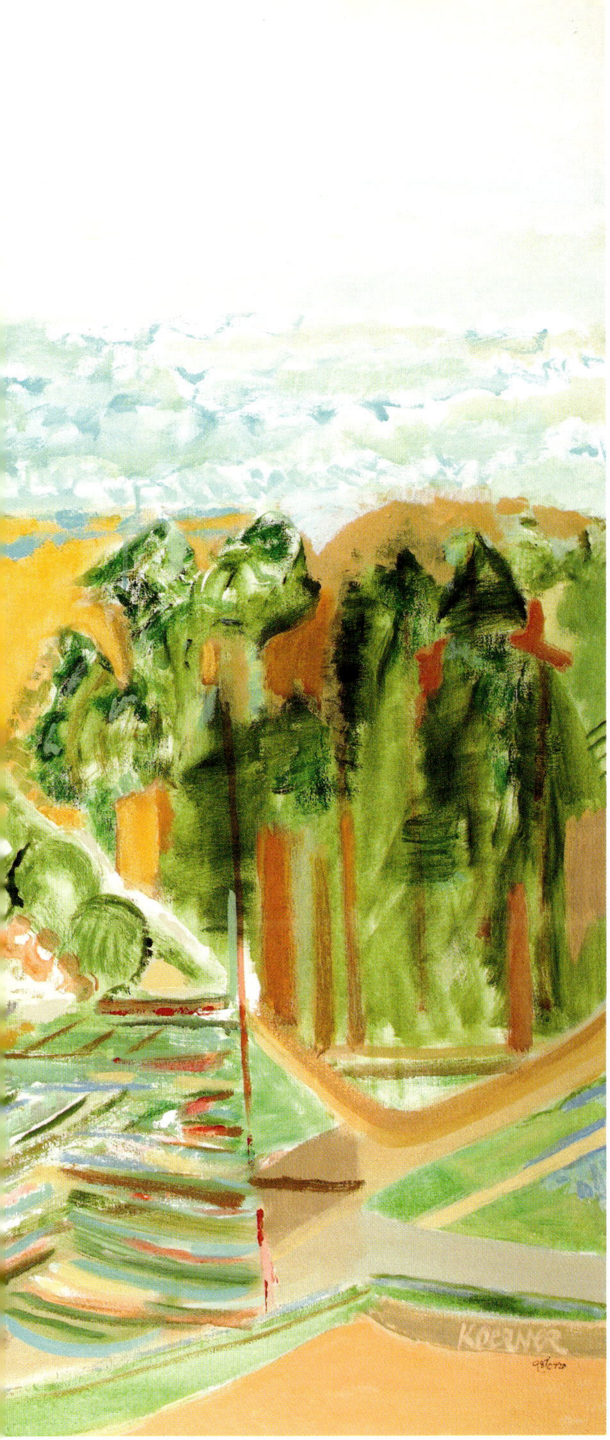

The Garden of Eden (28), 50 x 84 inches (diptych), 2002, collection of Lisa Birnie

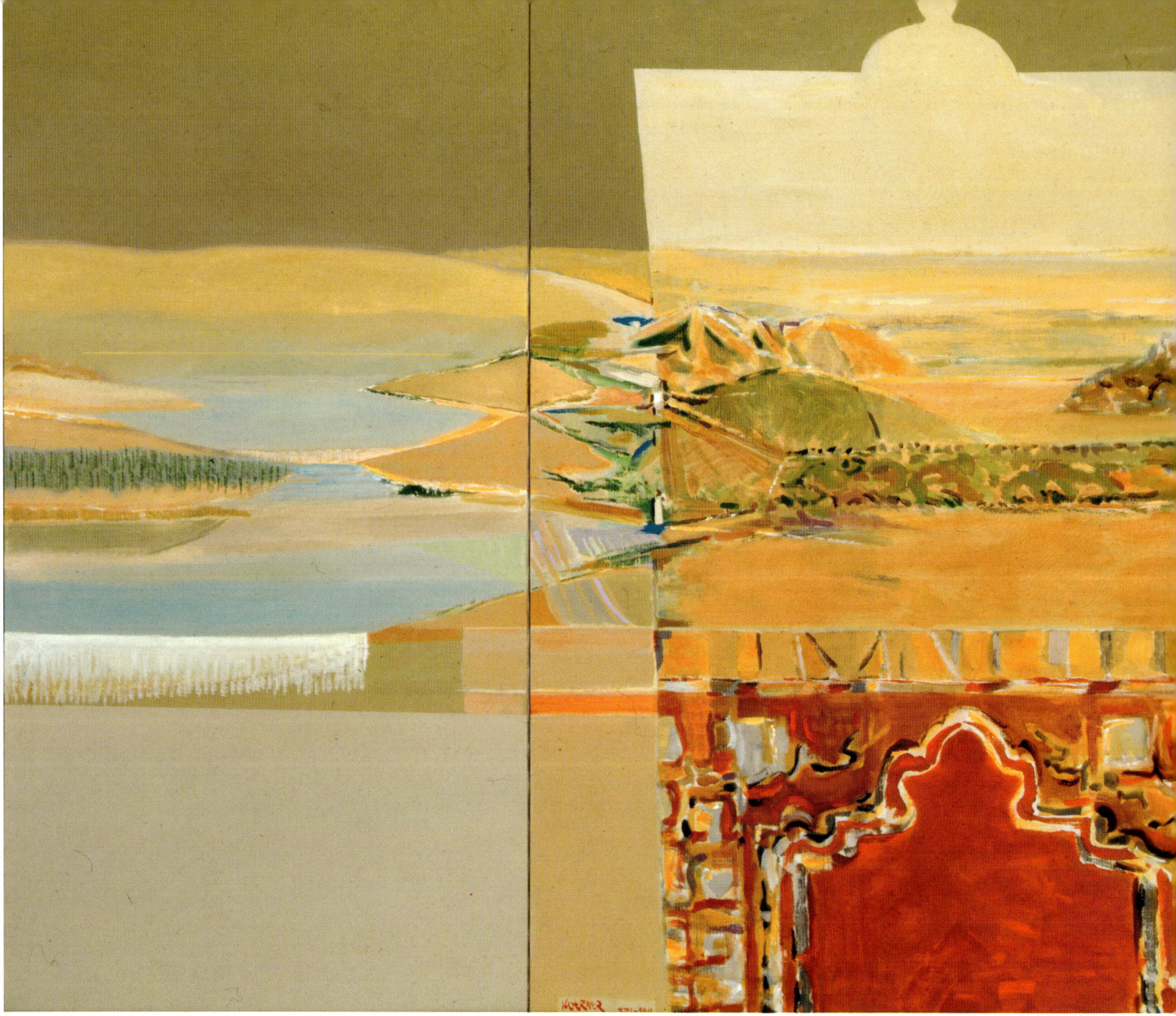

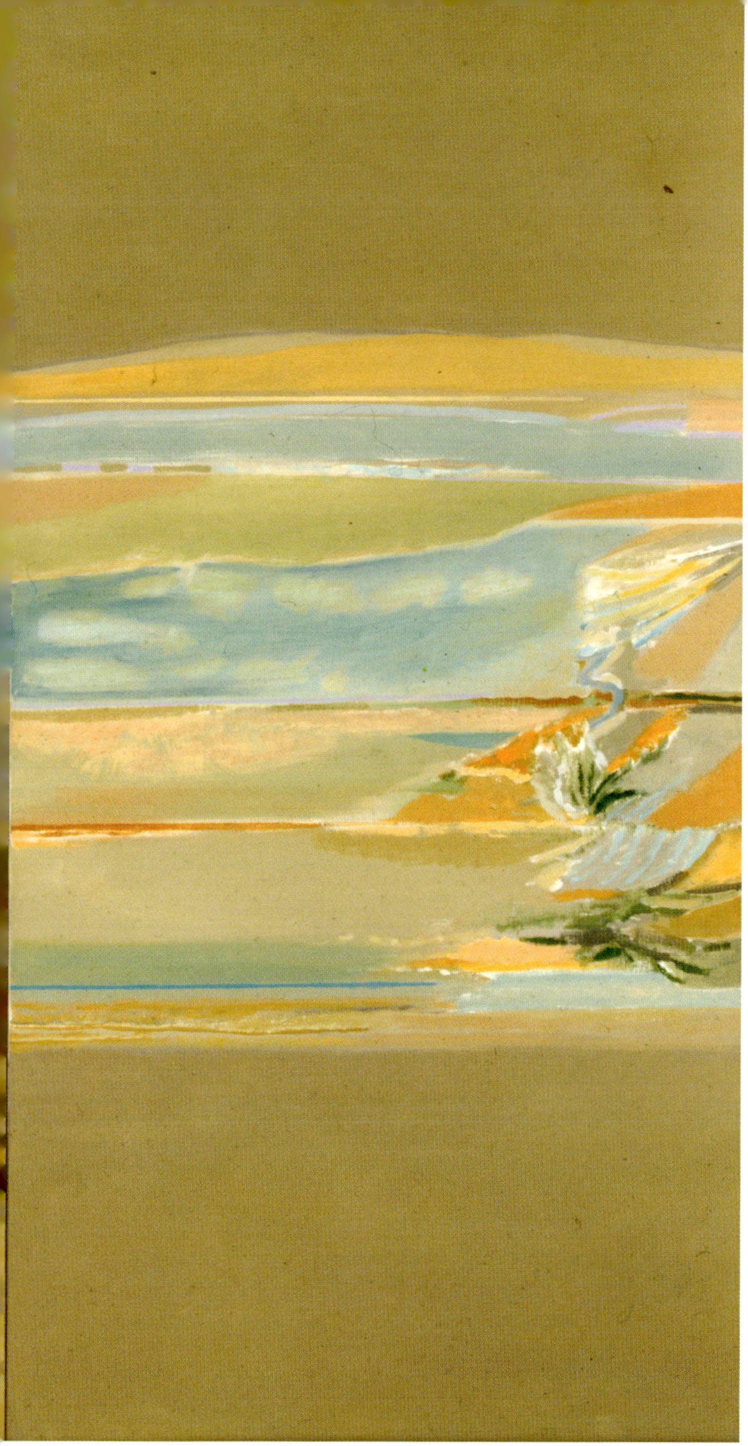

The Garden of Eden with Prayer Rug, acrylic on canvas, 48 x 84 inches (triptych), 1998, collection of the Art Gallery of Victoria, 2000.012.009

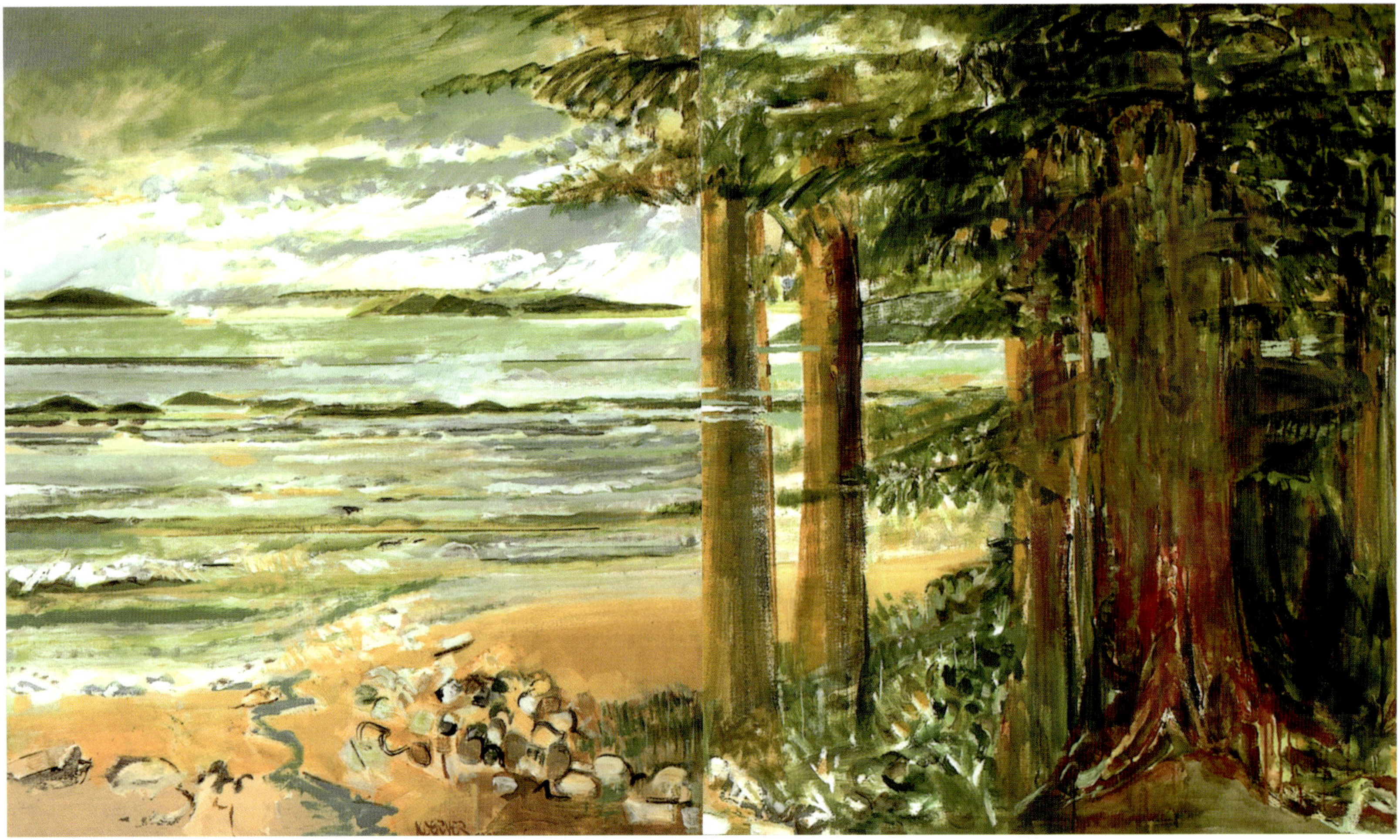

The Garden of Eden (29), acrylic on canvas, 50 x 84 inches (diptych), 1998, collection of Simon Fraser University, Dialogue Centre, Vancouver, BC

The sun never sets
it is we who rise
and think
to shine.
– Earle Birney

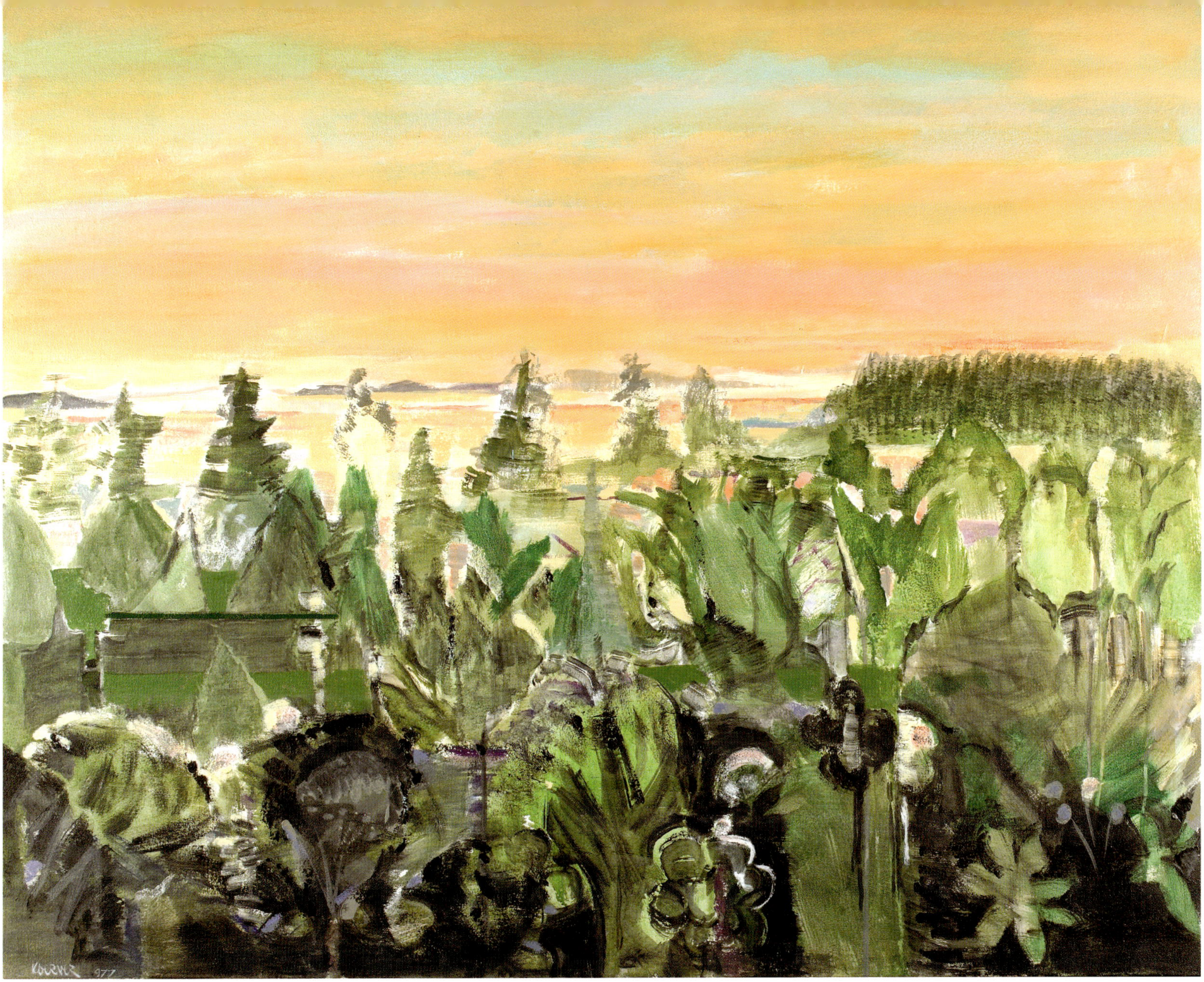

The Garden of Eden (5), acrylic on canvas, 42 x 50 inches, n.d., collection of the artist

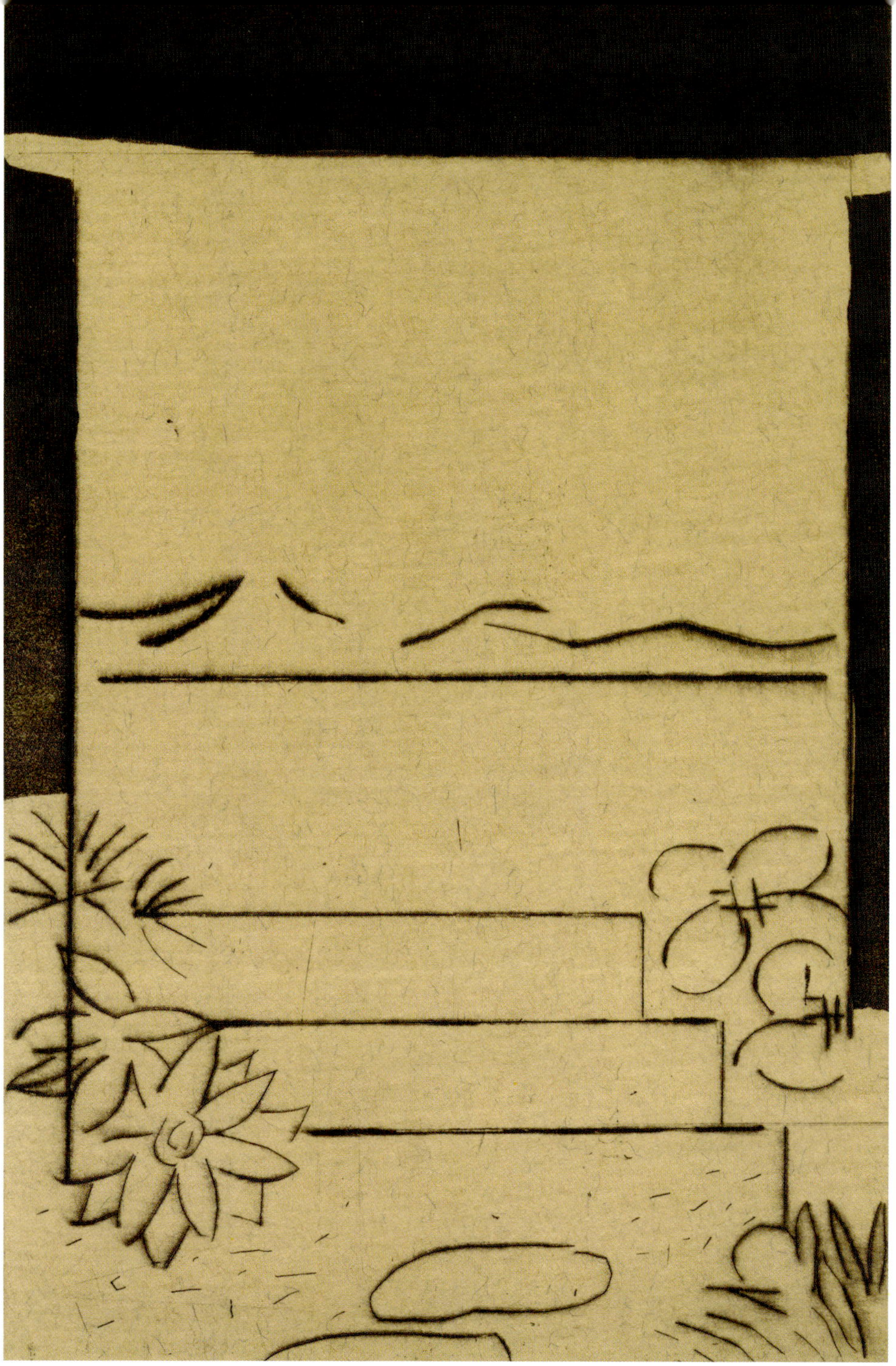

Garden of Eden (15), dry point etching, 10 x 9 inches, edition of 100, artist's proof, collection of the artist

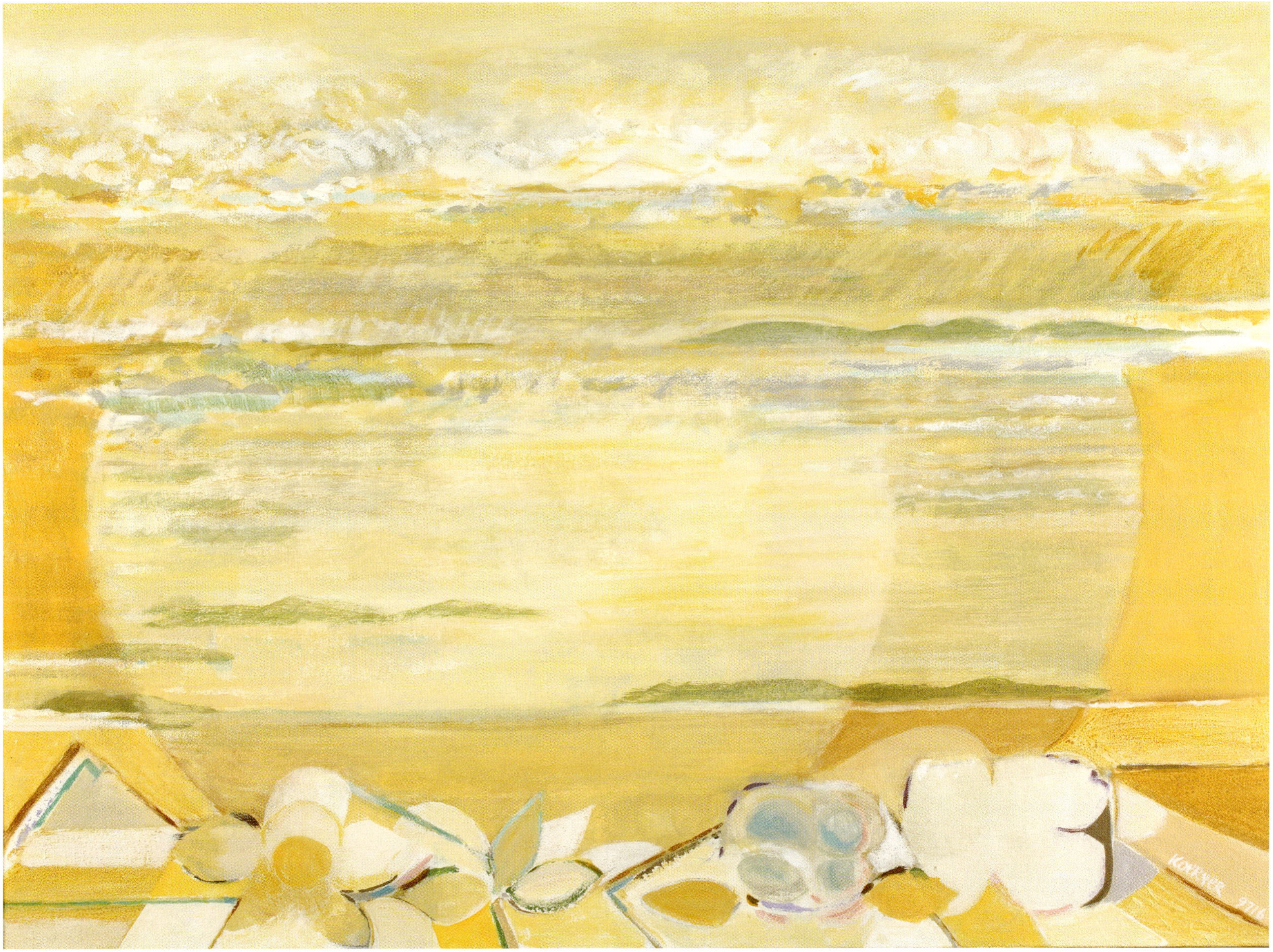

Garden of Eden (14), acrylic on canvas, 30 x 40 inches, 1997, private collection, Vancouver, BC

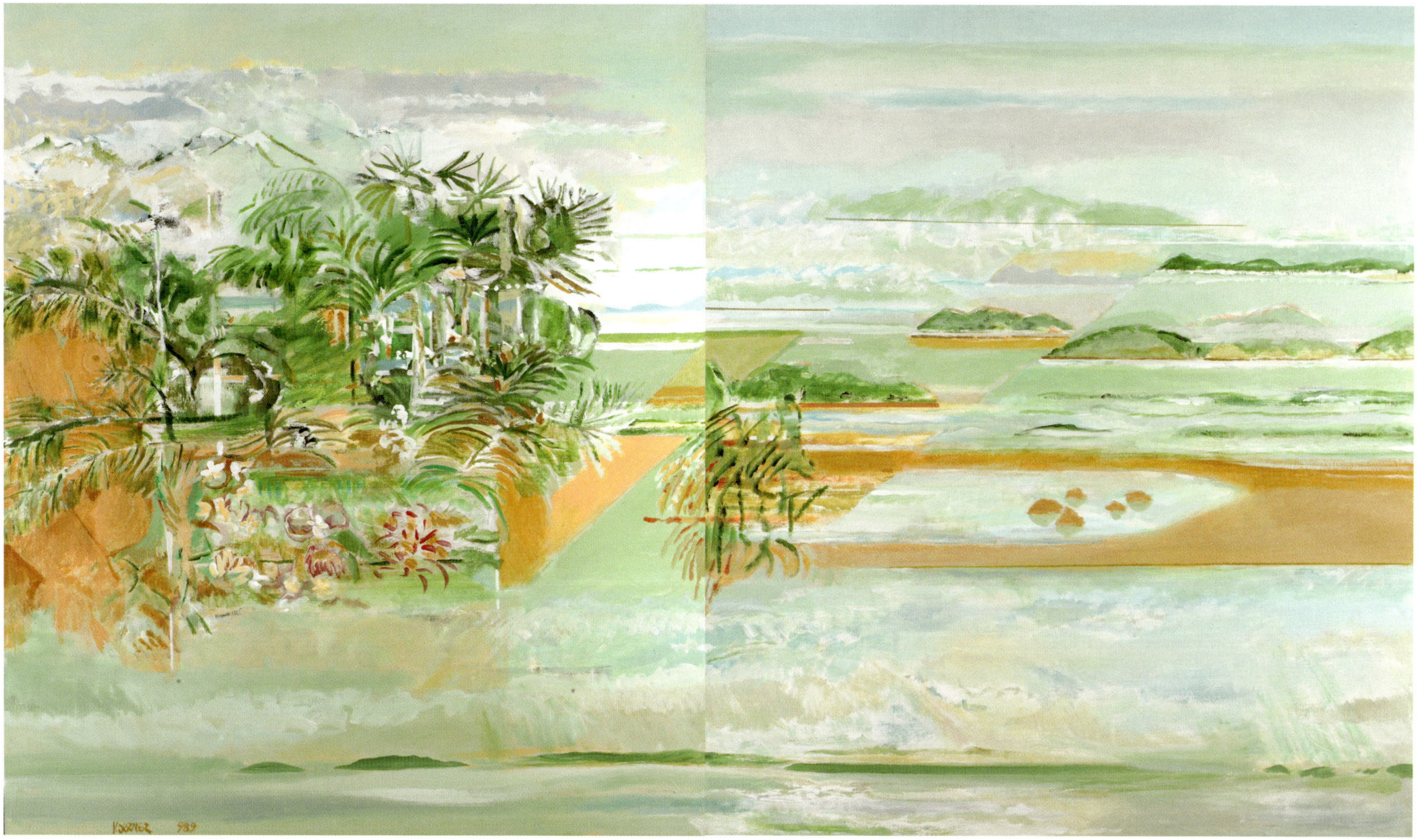

The Garden of Eden (30), acrylic on canvas, 50 x 84 inches (diptych), 2003, collection of the artist

This *Garden* is set somewhere in the Pacific Region. There are multiple horizons, alluding to the unreliability of our senses, which help to avoid tunnel effects in the picture plane.

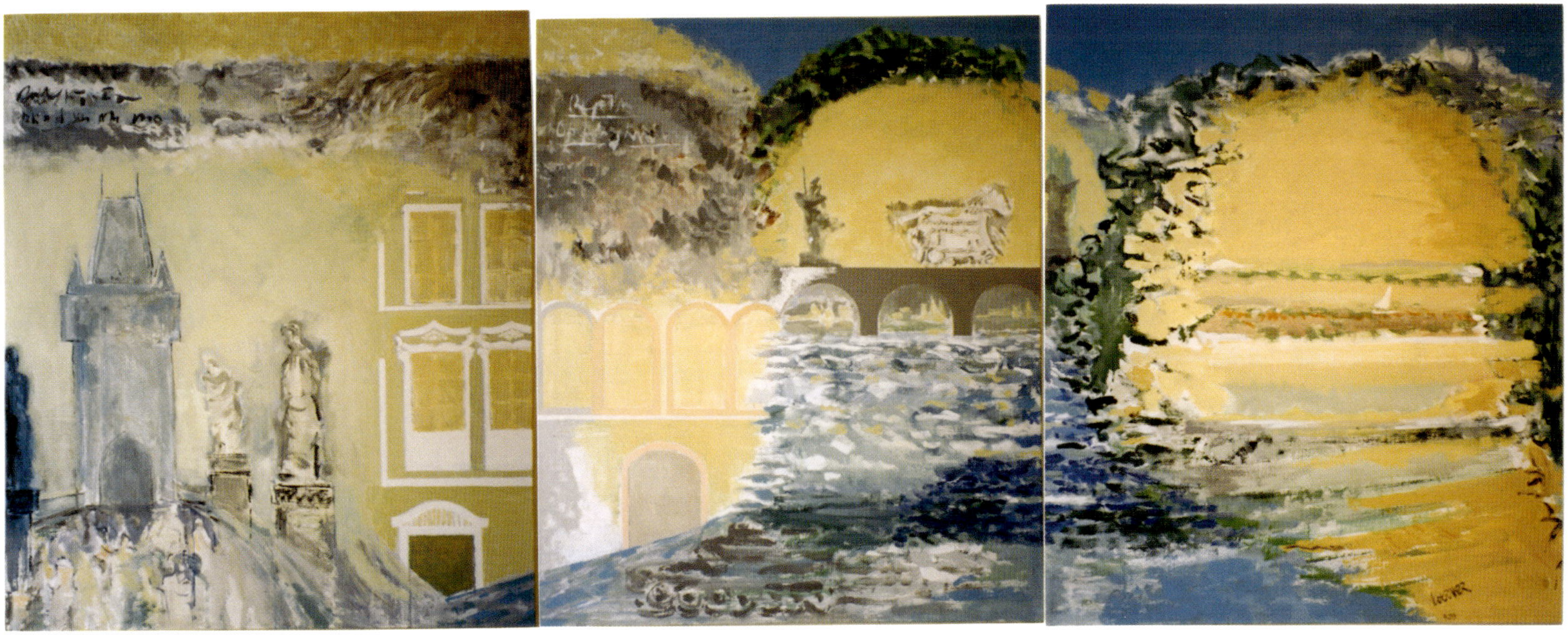

Past Presence (3), acrylic on canvas, 50 x 126 inches (triptych), 1992, collection of Count Enrico and Countess Aline de Dobrzensky

This painting was completed after my visit to Prague in 1991. It shows a variety of aspects of the city, including childhood memories from sixty years earlier.

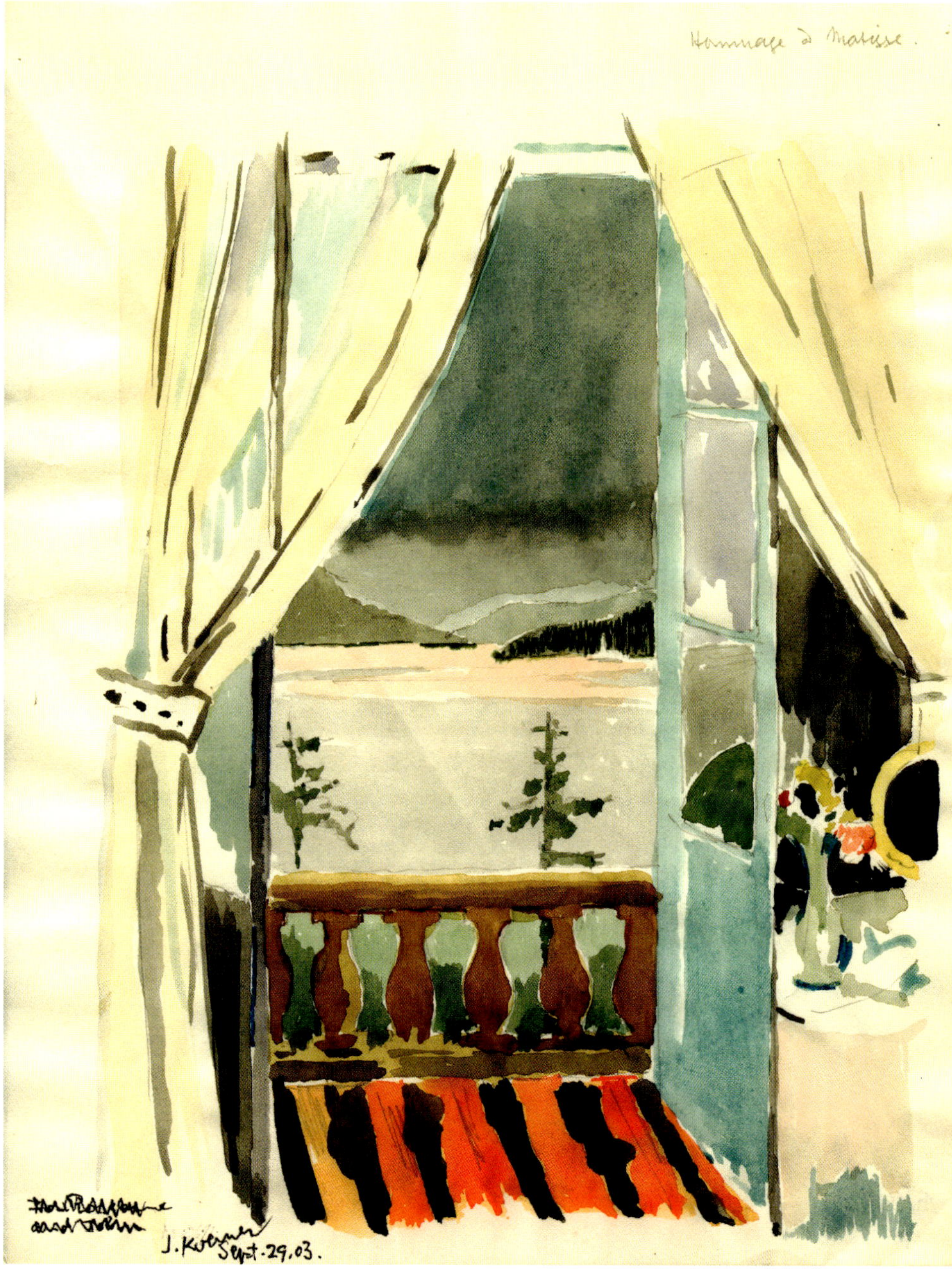

Homage to Matisse, watercolour on paper, 10.5 x 8 inches, dated September 29, 2003, collection of the artist

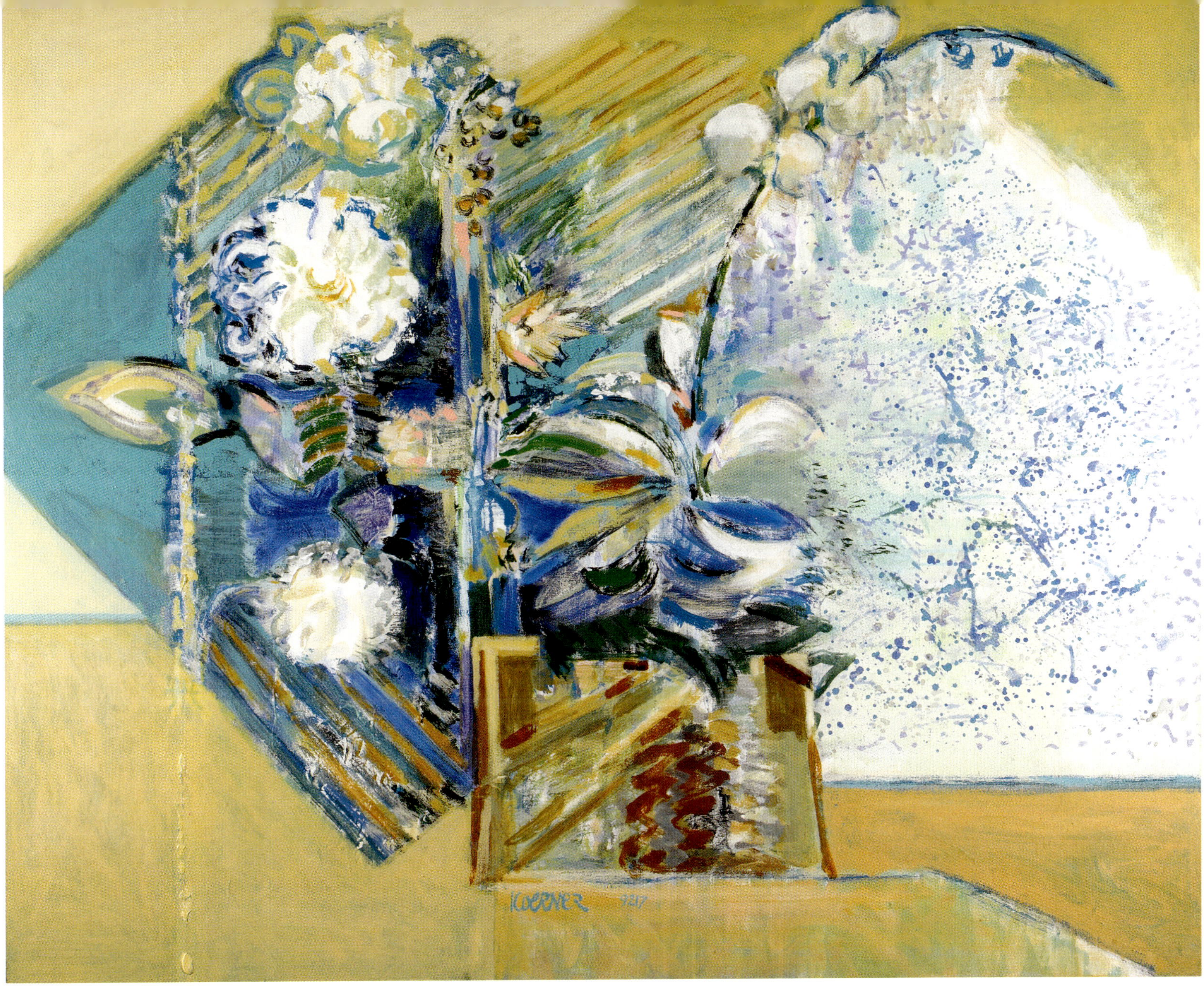

Hikari (3), acrylic on canvas, 42 x 50 inches, 1992, private collection, Vancouver, BC

The title of the series of *Hikari* paintings comes from the Japanese word for light. The concept references seventeenth-century Dutch flower still life paintings.

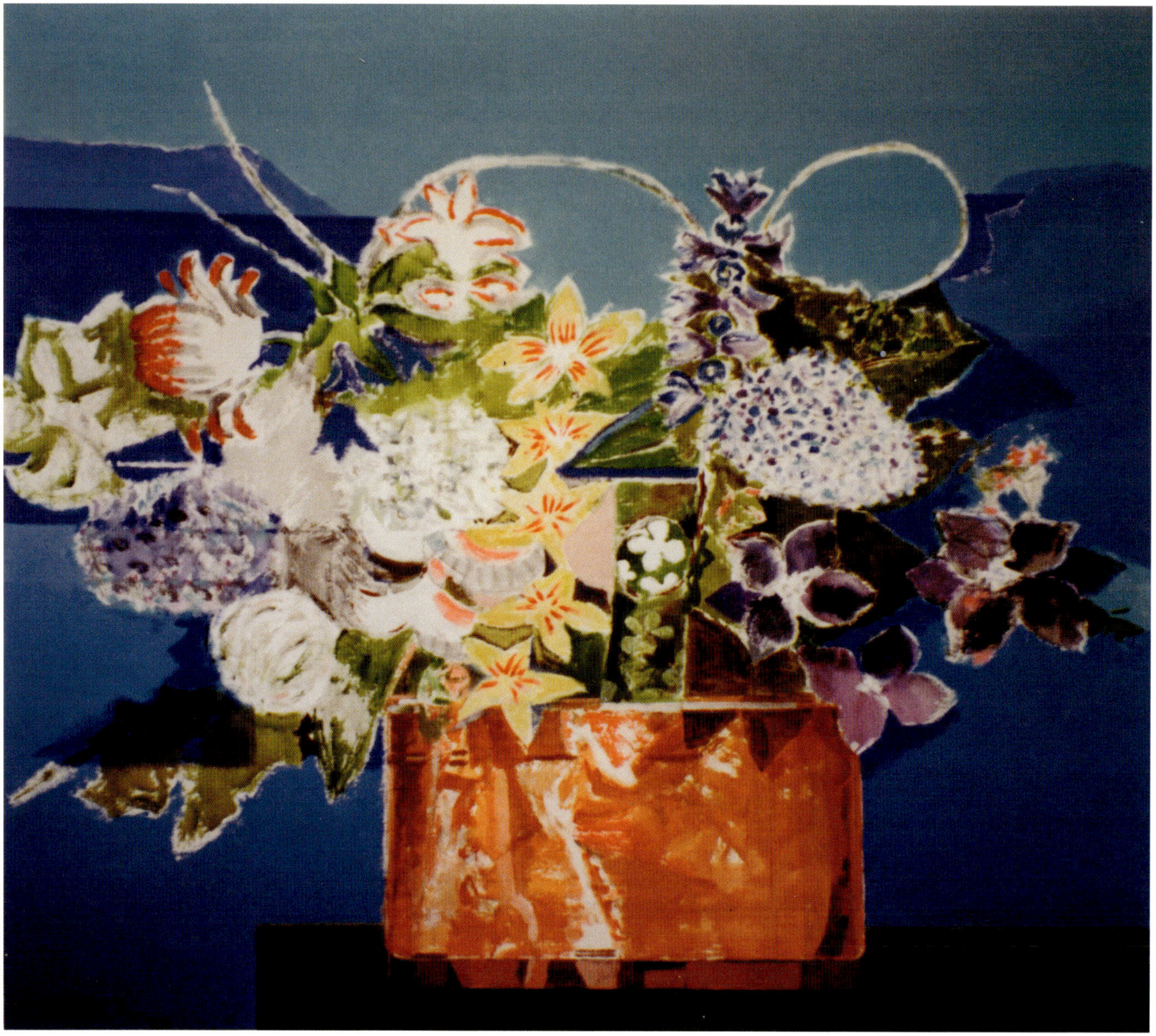

Hikari (1) Homage to D.F., acrylic on canvas, 30 x 40 inches, 1990, collection of David Lemon, Vancouver, BC

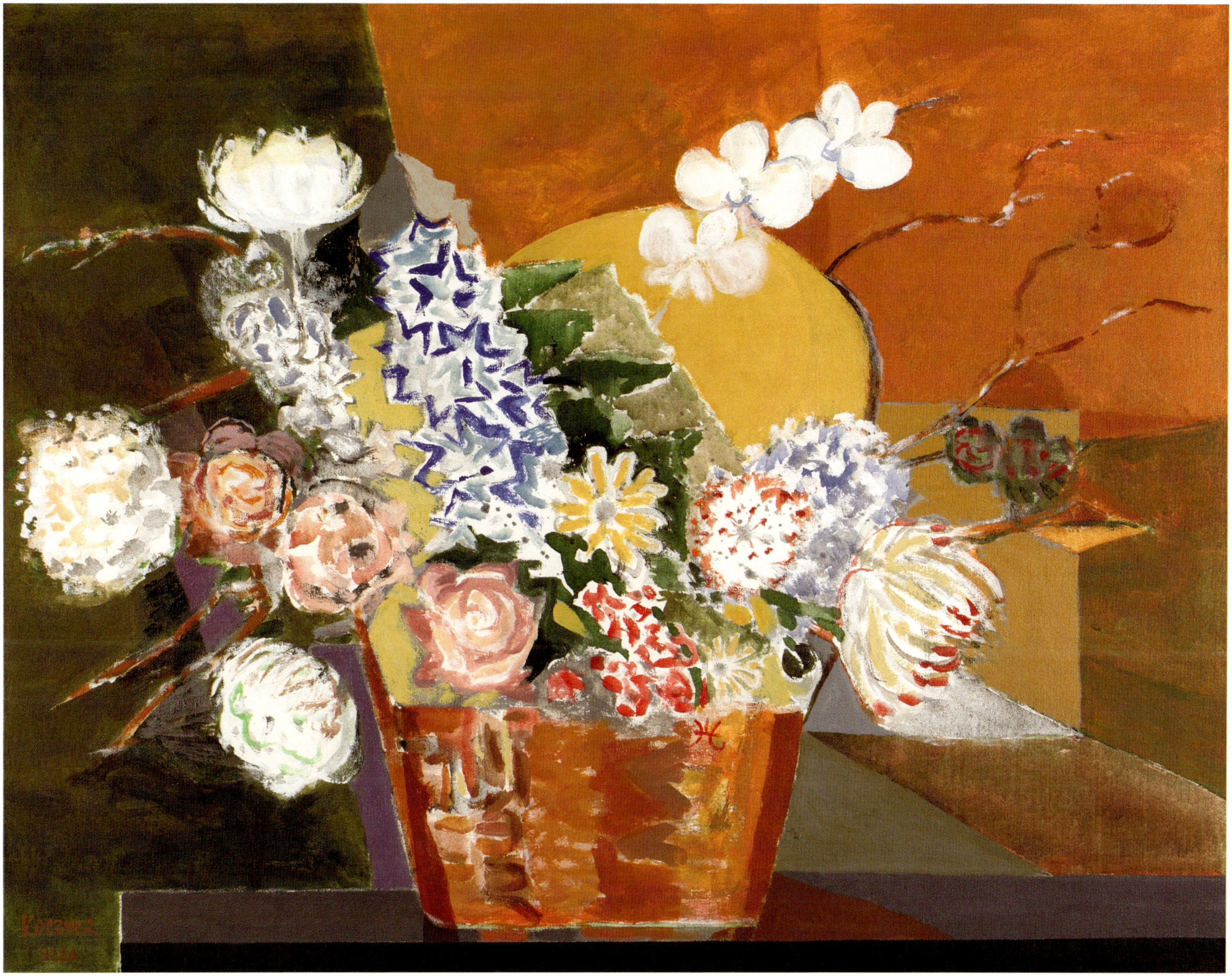

Hikari (8), acrylic on canvas, 32 x 40 inches, 1992, private collection, Vancouver, BC

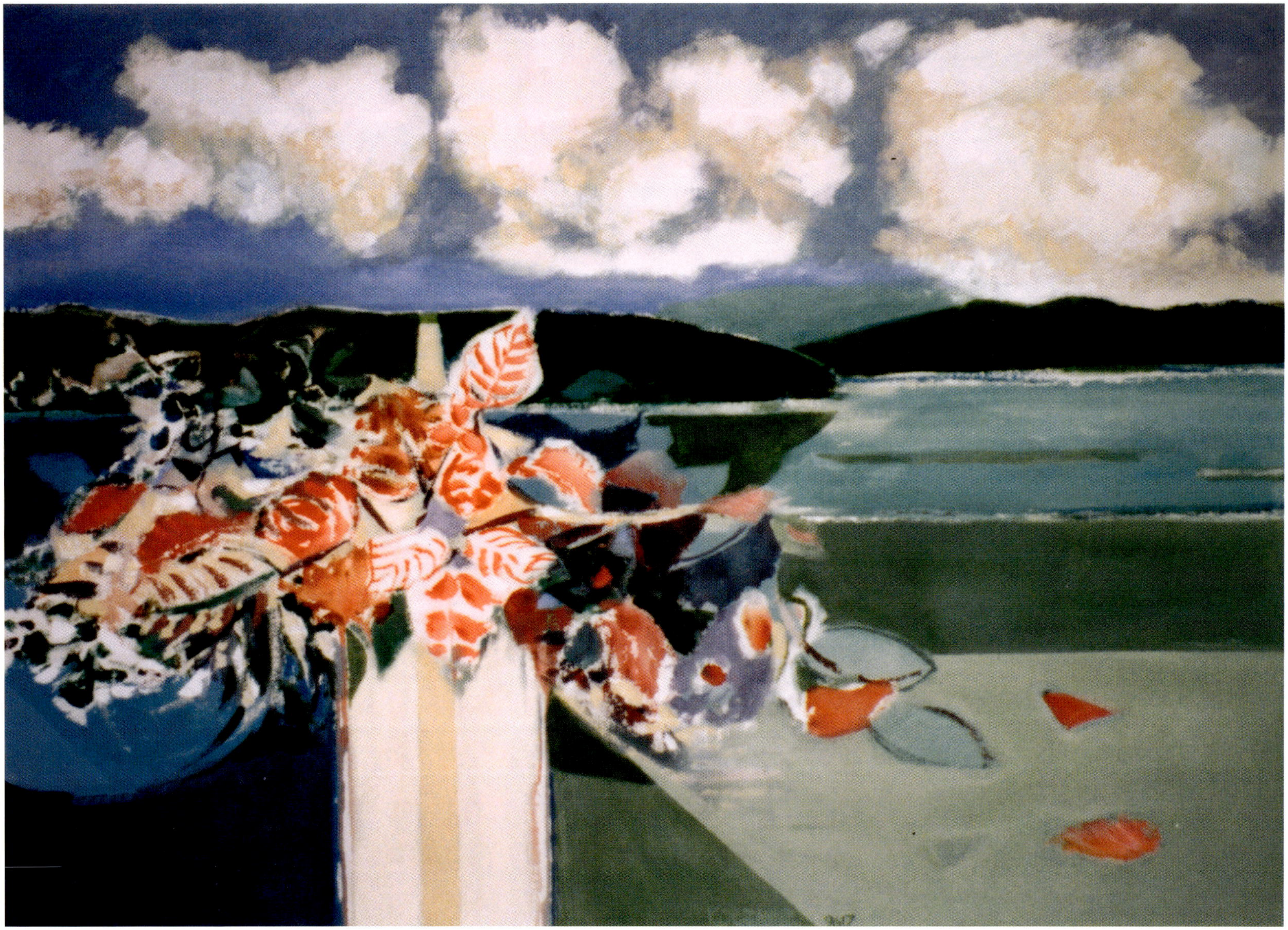

The Lighthouse with Islands (84), acrylic on canvas, 30 x 40 inches, 1996, collection of the Greater Victoria Art Gallery, Victoria, BC

This painting, like others in the *Lighthouse* series, is an homage to the fundamental light source as implied by the lighthouse.

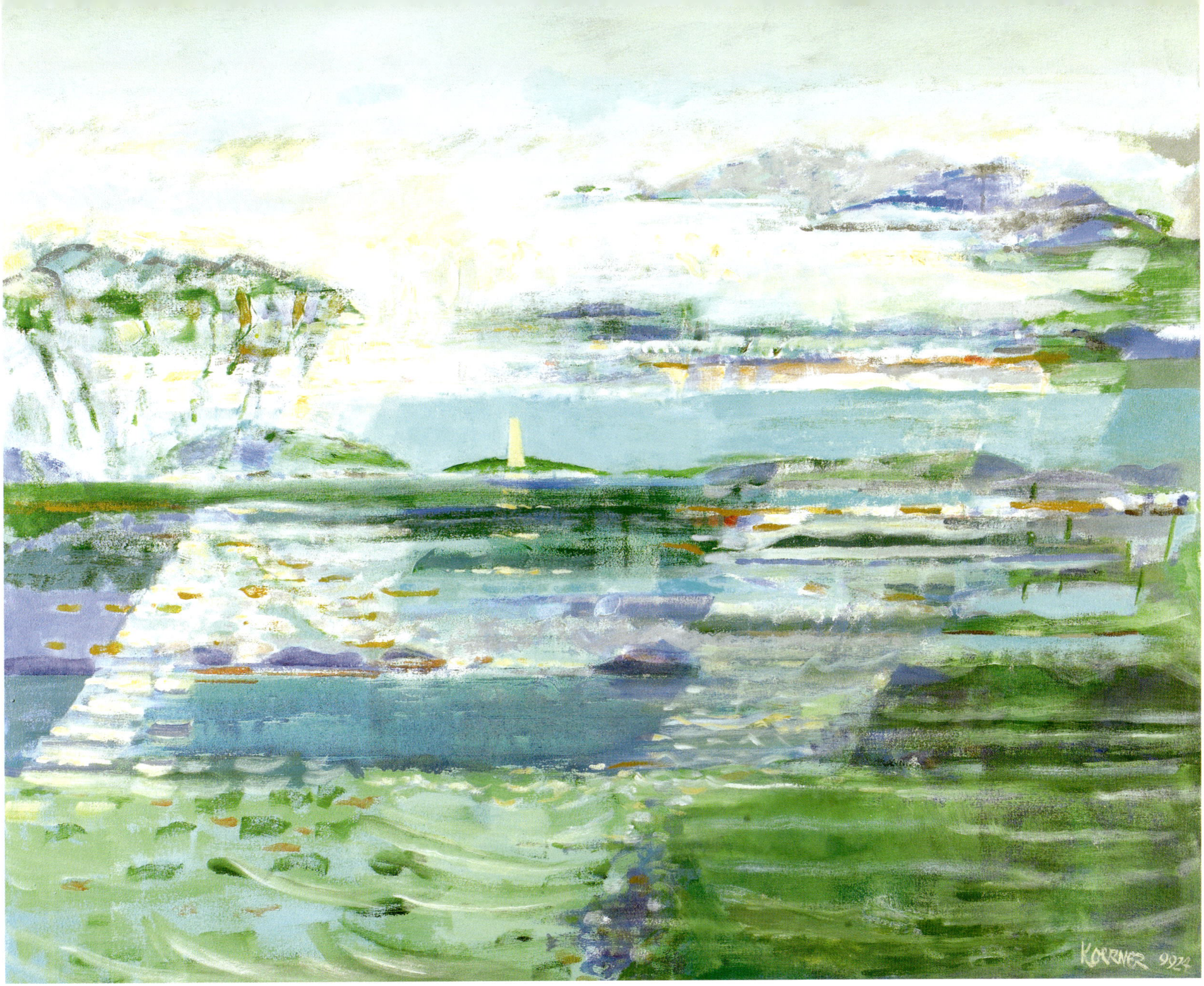

The Lighthouse (93), acrylic on canvas, 42 x 50 inches, 1991, collection of Lisa Birnie

I listened to Schubert's *Trout Quintet in A Minor* before I started this painting. It made me think that old composers never quit — they just decompose.

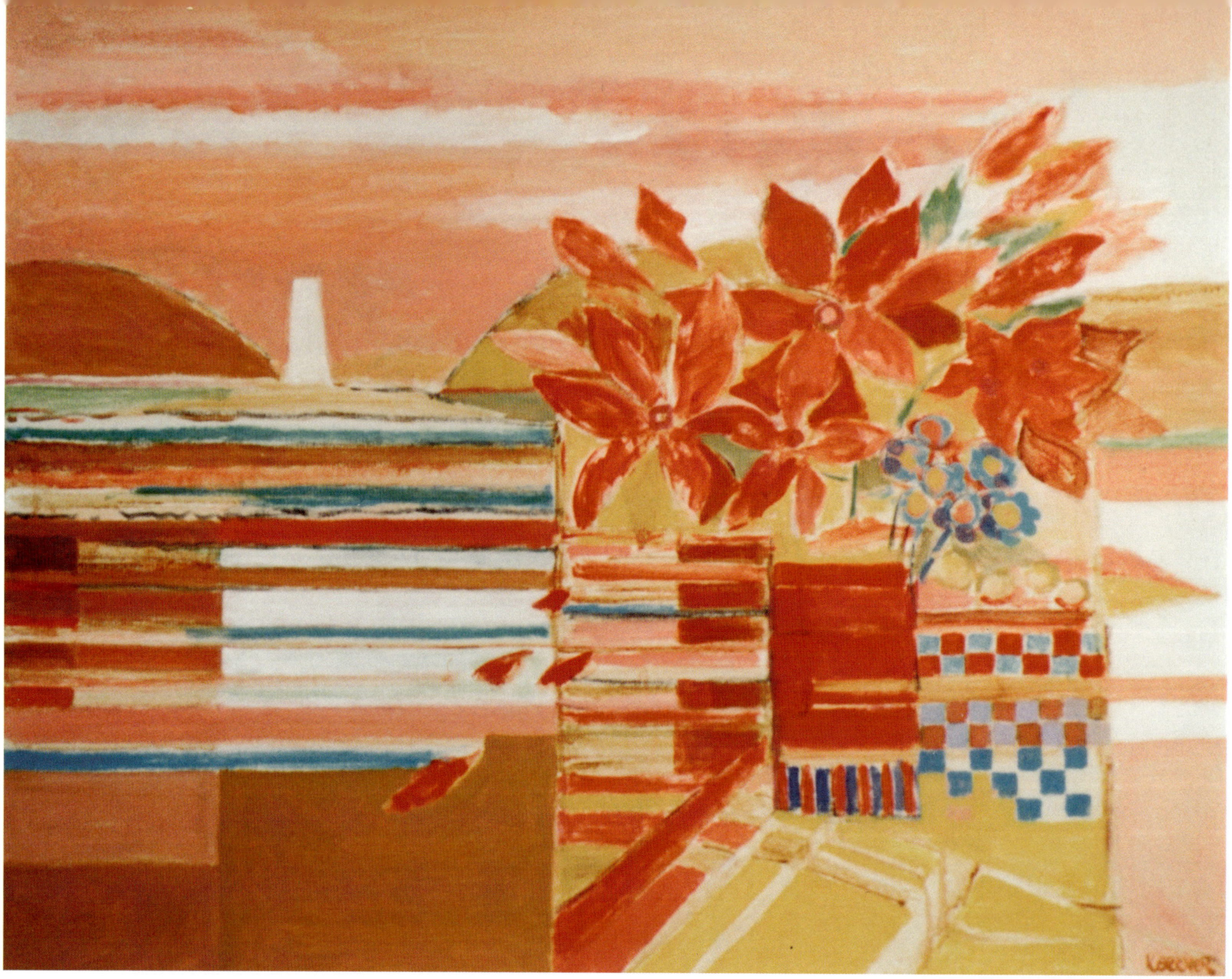

The Lighthouse (119), acrylic on canvas, 42 x 50 inches, 2004, collection of the artist

Art is a collaboration between God and the artist, and the less the artist does the better.

– André Gide

Claude Monet (1840–1926) said that his interest in the waterlilies started when he was looking through a catalogue showing pictures of garden furniture. He knew then that one day he would tackle the subject of *nympheas* and, indeed, he started to paint water lilies in 1897. Later he wrote to a friend, "I have again begun to work on something impossible to accomplish; water lilies on an undulating surface of water. It is beautiful to look at, but it drives me crazy to do it. Why do I always try for things like that?" There are over 250 paintings in Monet's *Waterlilies* series.

For me, a painting begins with an unmistakable colour or a combination of colours. In *The Lighthouse with Compass Rose,* I was thinking about Monet's *Waterlilies* palette.

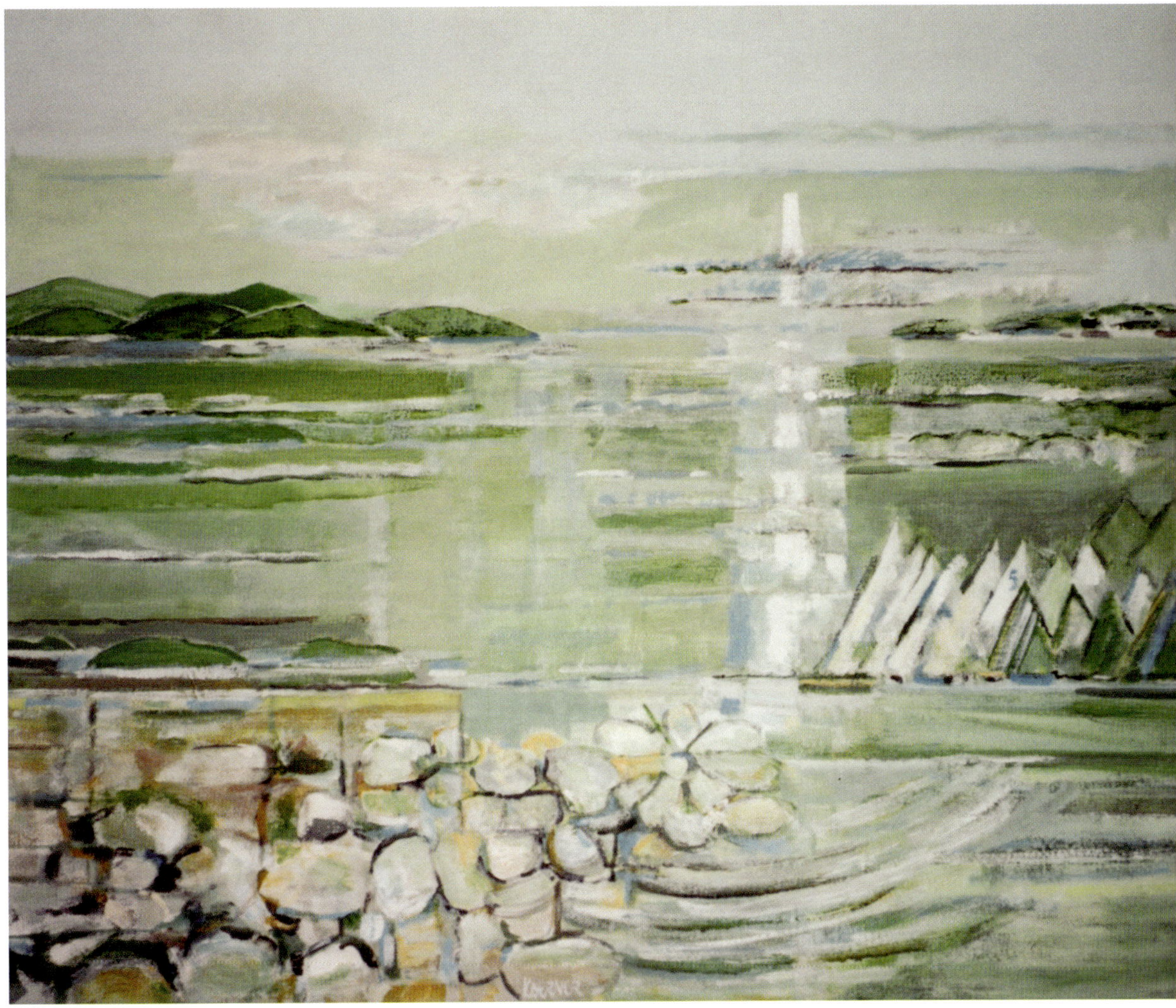

The Lighthouse with Compass Rose (1), acrylic on canvas, 42 x 50 inches, 2003, collection of the Canadiana Fund, Capital Commission, Ottawa, ON

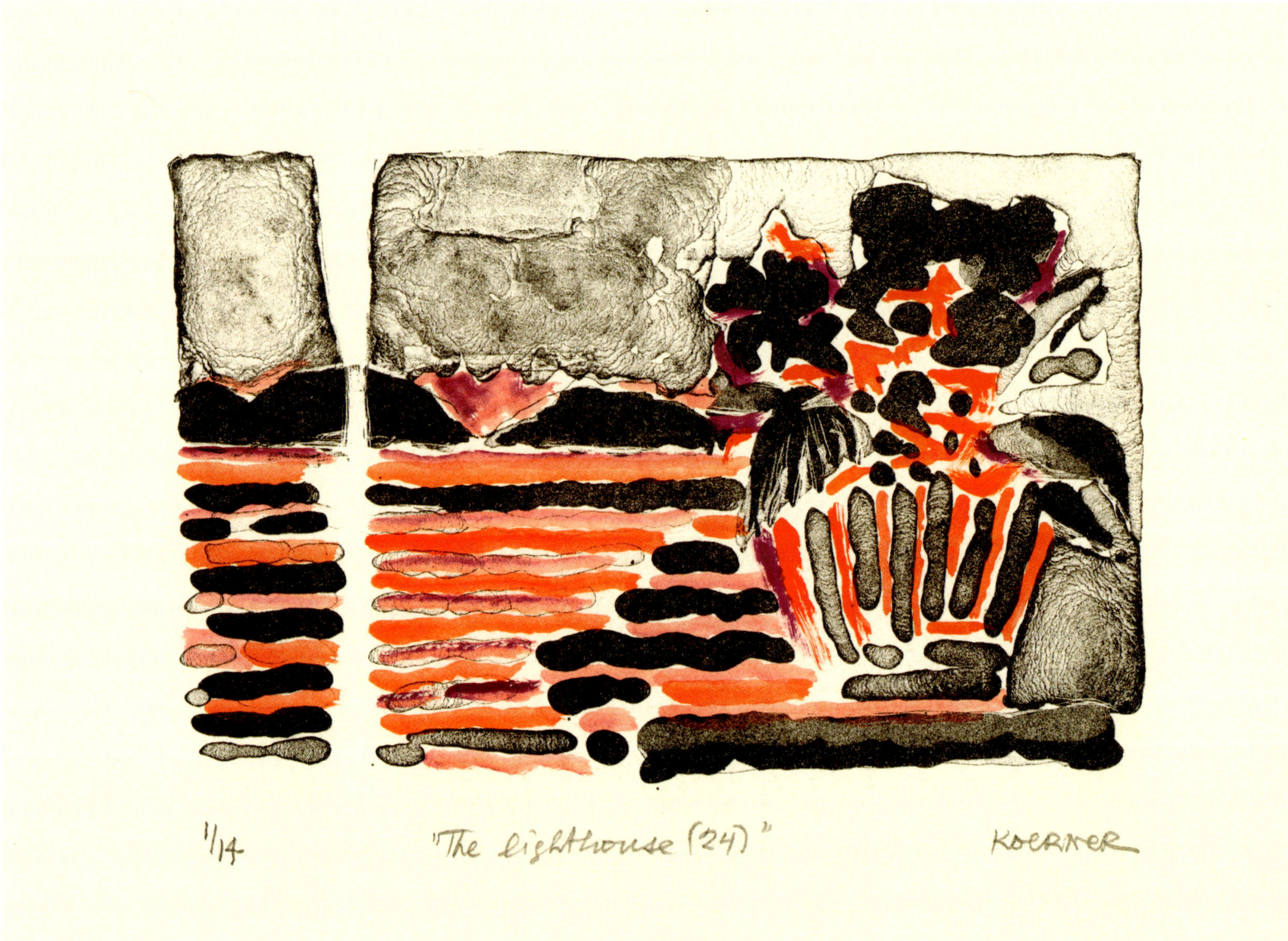

The Lighthouse (24), lithograph, 7 x 8.75 inches, edition 1/14, collection of the artist

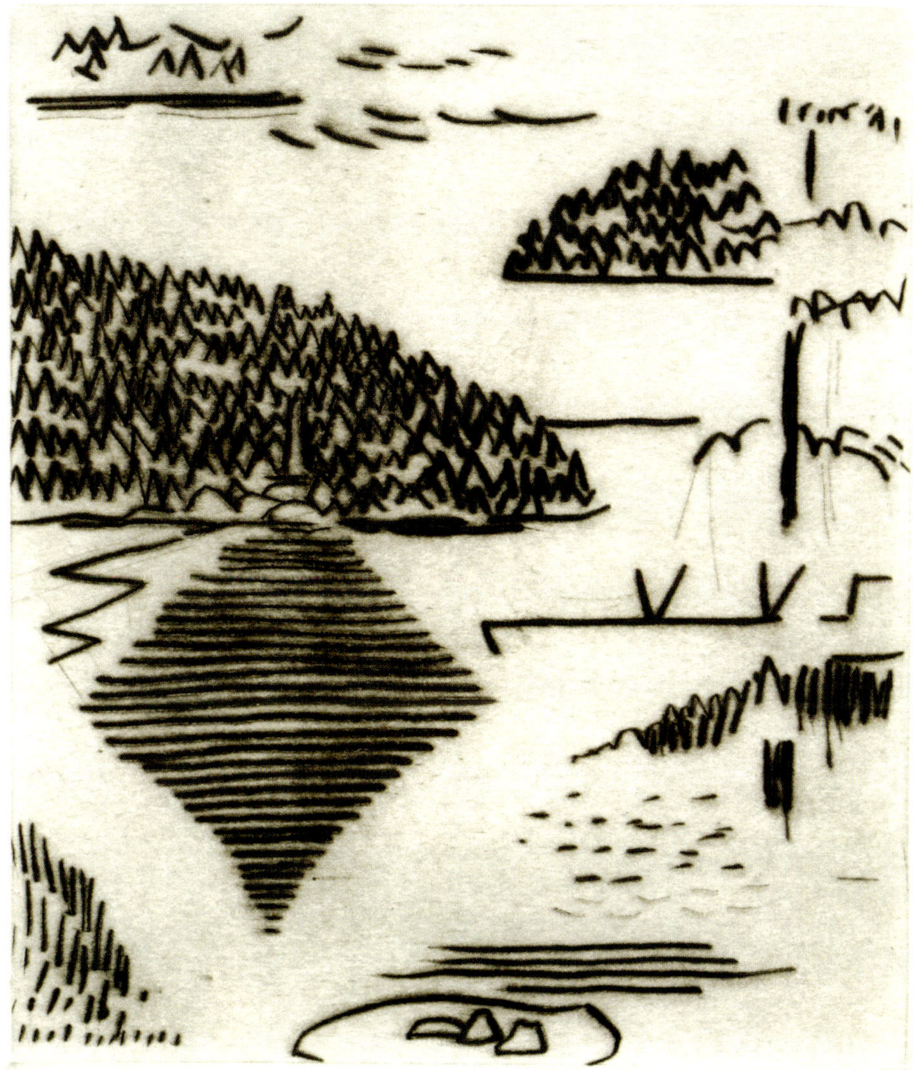

The Lighthouse (81), lithograph, 10.5 x 9.5 inches, edition 10/13, collection of the artist

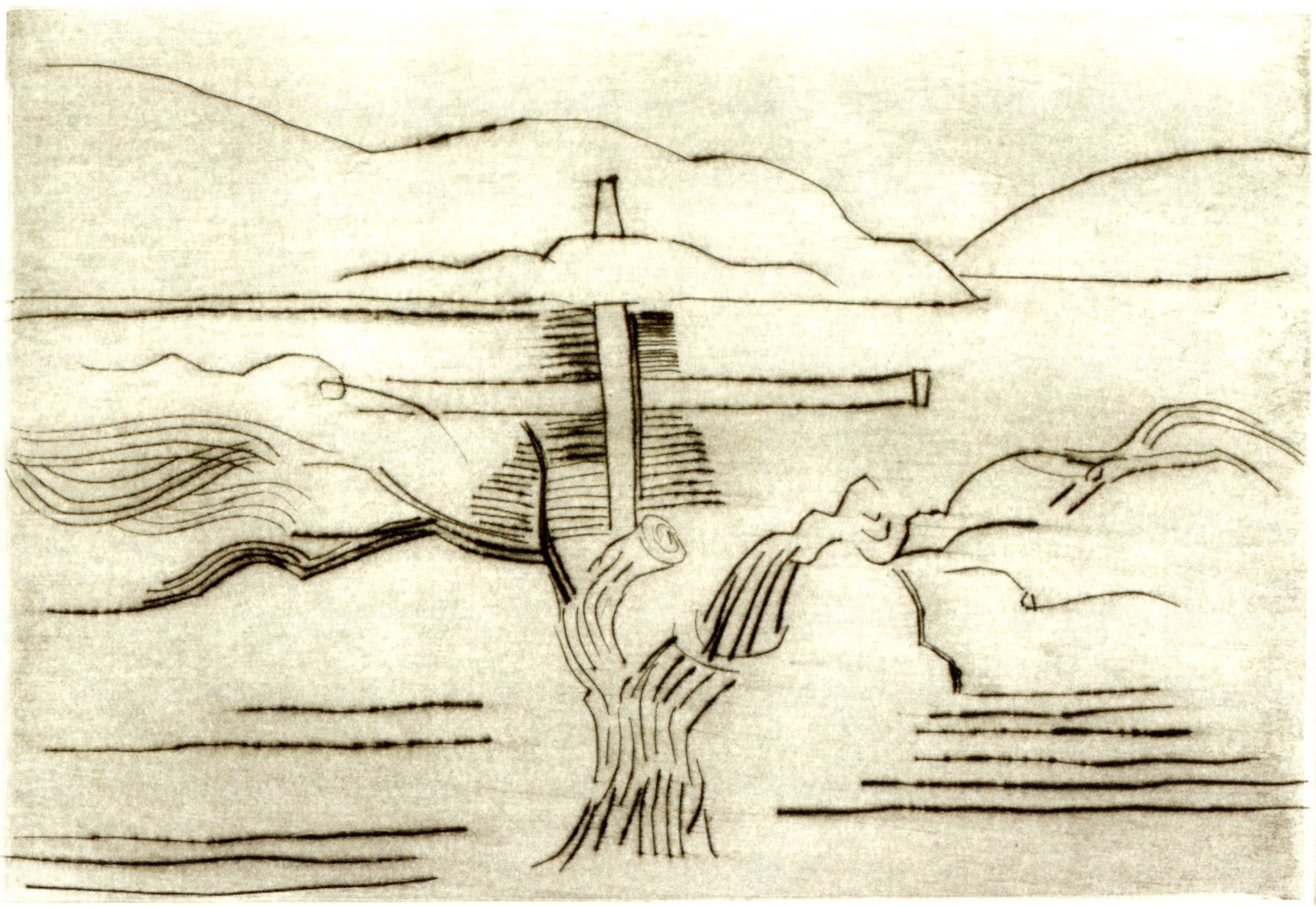

The Lighthouse (80), lithograph, 9.5 x 12 inches, artist's proof, collection of the artist

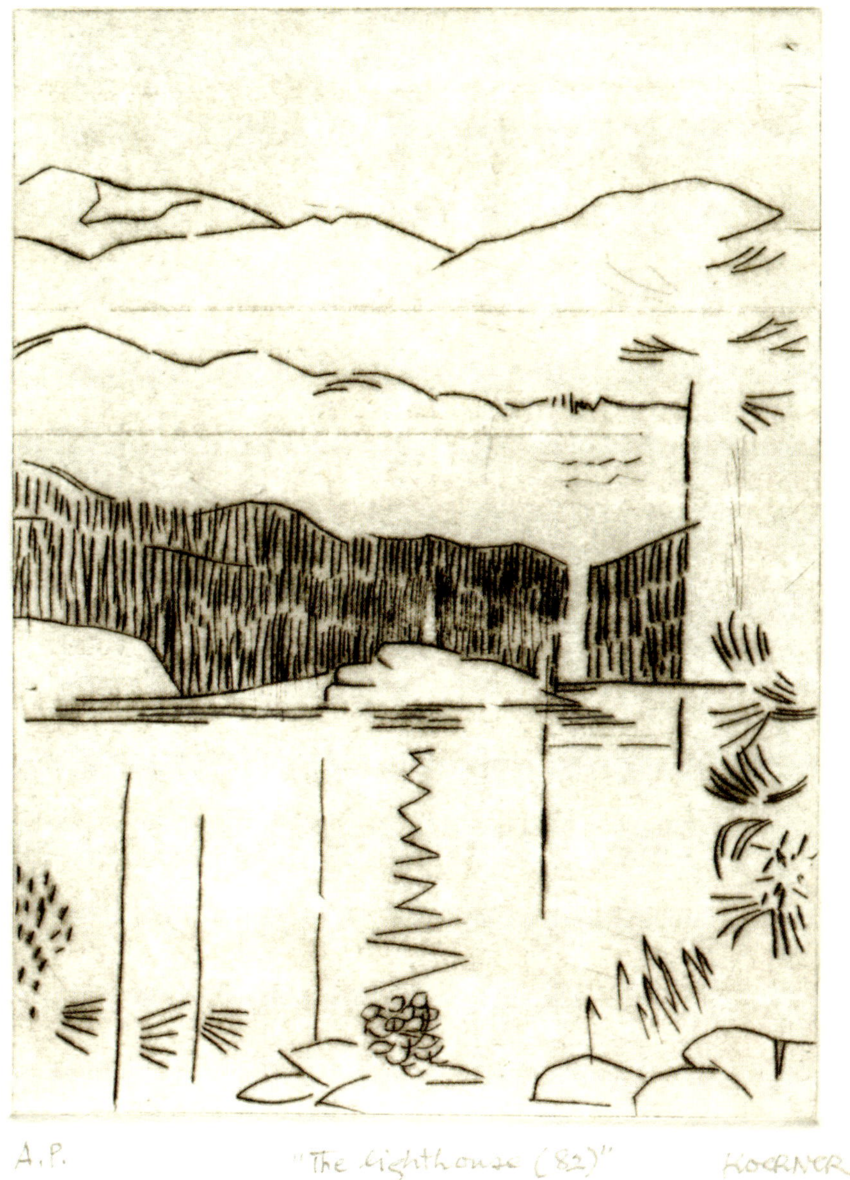

The Lighthouse (82), lithograph, 11.5 x 9.5 inches, artist's proof, collection of the artist

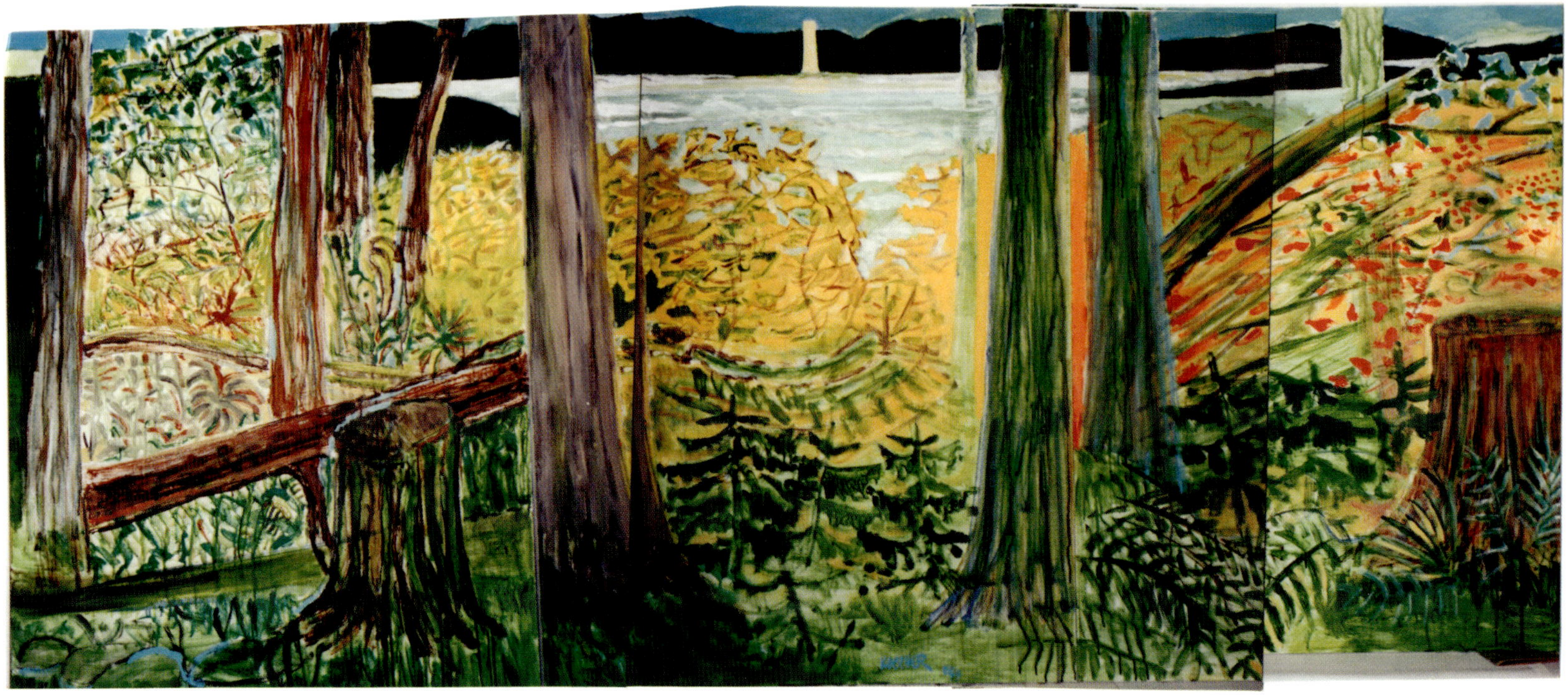

The Lighthouse (117), acrylic on canvas, 48 x 108 inches (triptych), 2004, collection of the Kay Meek Centre of the Performing Arts, West Vancouver, BC

There are now over one hundred and thirty paintings in *The Lighthouse* series. In all of them the lighthouse is a metaphor for an elemental source of light.

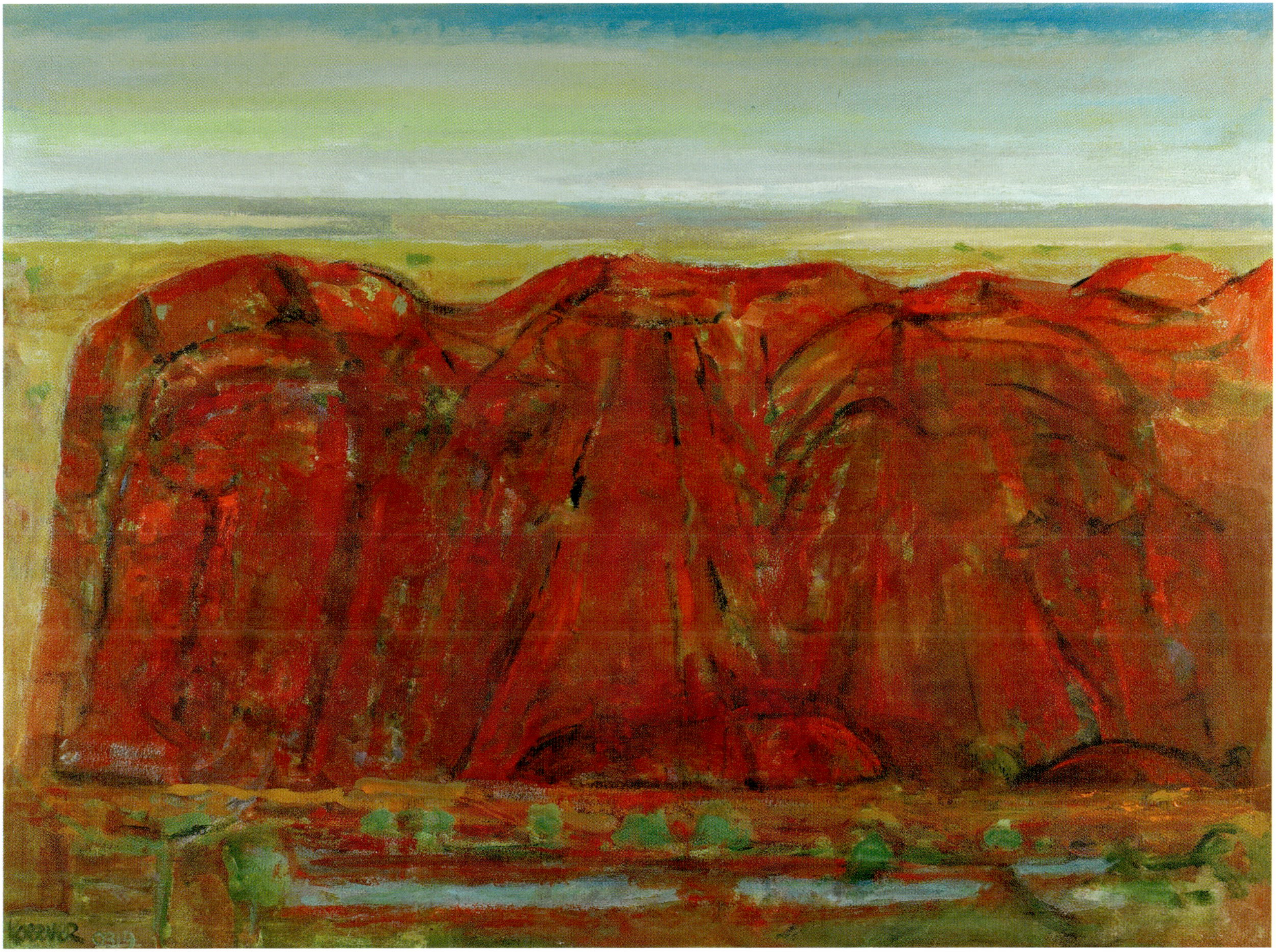

The red rock in the midst of the Australian desert. Unforgettable.

Uluru (1), acrylic on canvas, 30 x 40 inches, 2003, collection of Lisa Birnie

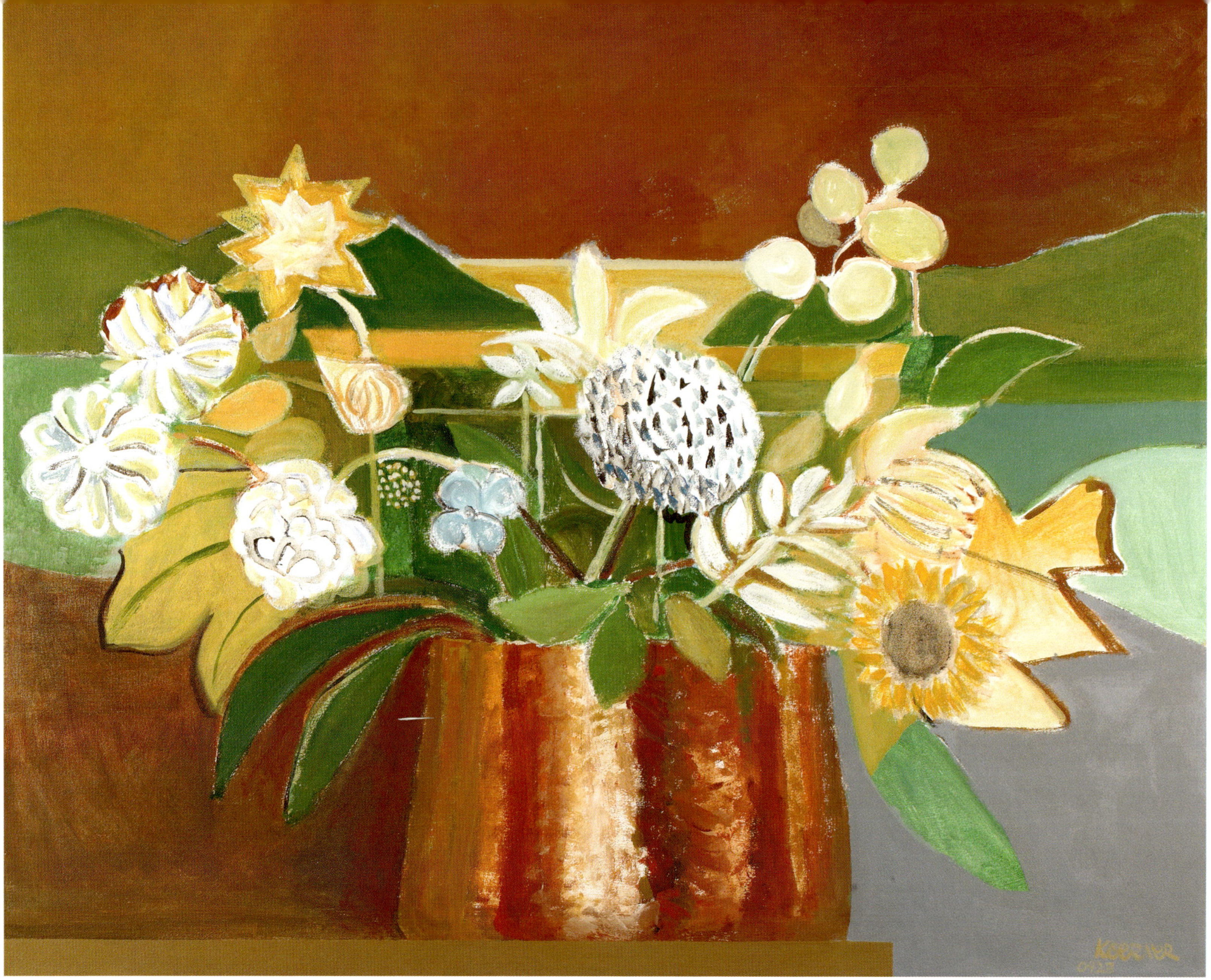

Celebration (6), acrylic on canvas, 42 x 50 inches, 2005, collection of Jerri Hass & Leon Bibb

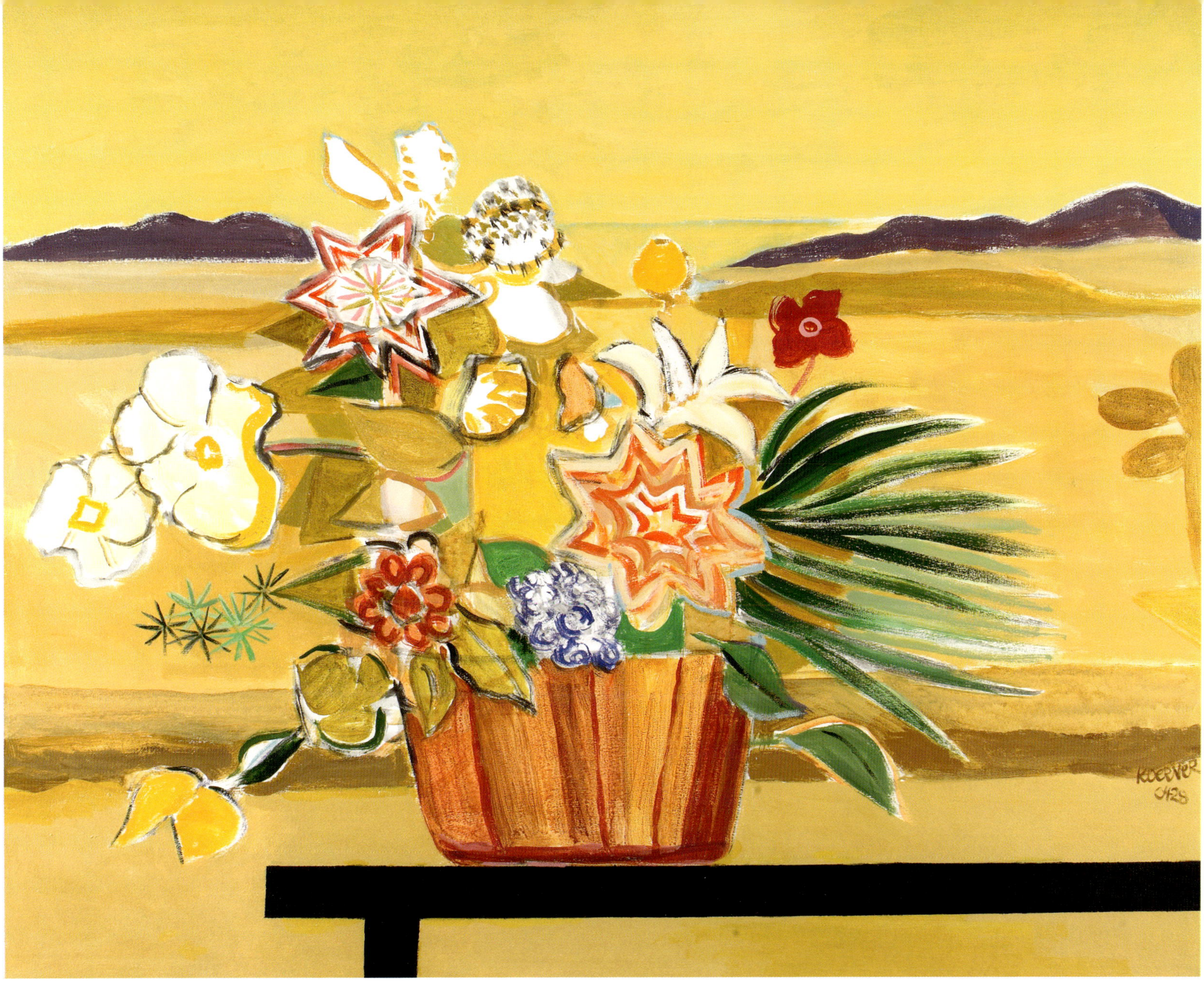

Celebration (9), acrylic on canvas, 42 x 50 inches, 2005, collection of the artist

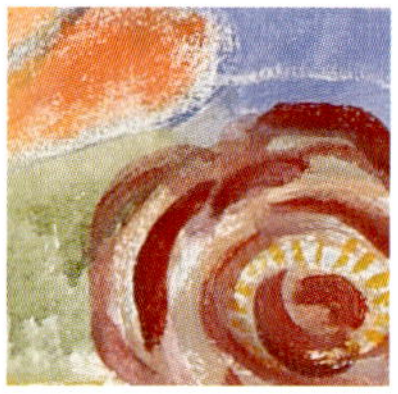

The following group of paintings had an unusual beginning. In December 2004, I fell ill with pneumonia and spent eight days in hospital. After the fever and chest pains subsided, I returned home hooked up to a noisy oxygen machine. By the end of January, I was able to get up for short periods of time and could paint for ten or fifteen minutes before returning to a horizontal position. In the past, I thought I could work successfully only if I felt completely fit, so I was elated to be able to work again and for gradually longer periods. I also felt enormously grateful for the exquisite care and support given to me by my dear wife, Lisa Birnie, and blessed by the loyal well-wishes of my daughters and some special friends. Throughout my illness, I optimistically held to my belief that life goes on, supported by inner energy.

By February, when I could venture out on short walks, crocuses and snowdrops were beginning to bloom. Spring and renewal was in the air, my work was proceeding, and my get-up-and-go was intensifying. As my health improved day by day, I felt like a magnet attracting good fortune and contributing to the positive forces that countervail against the chaos on this planet. A good reason to celebrate!

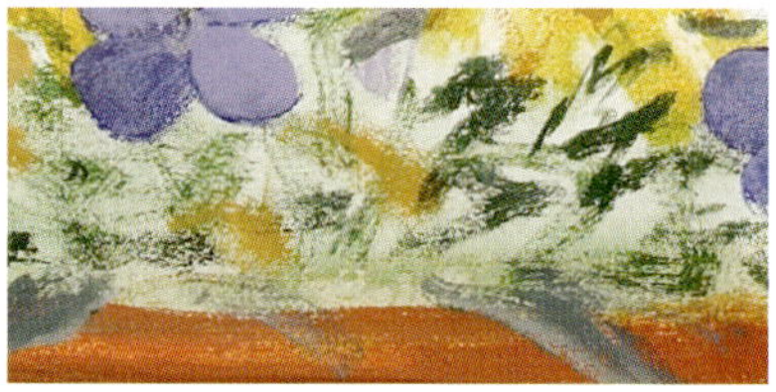

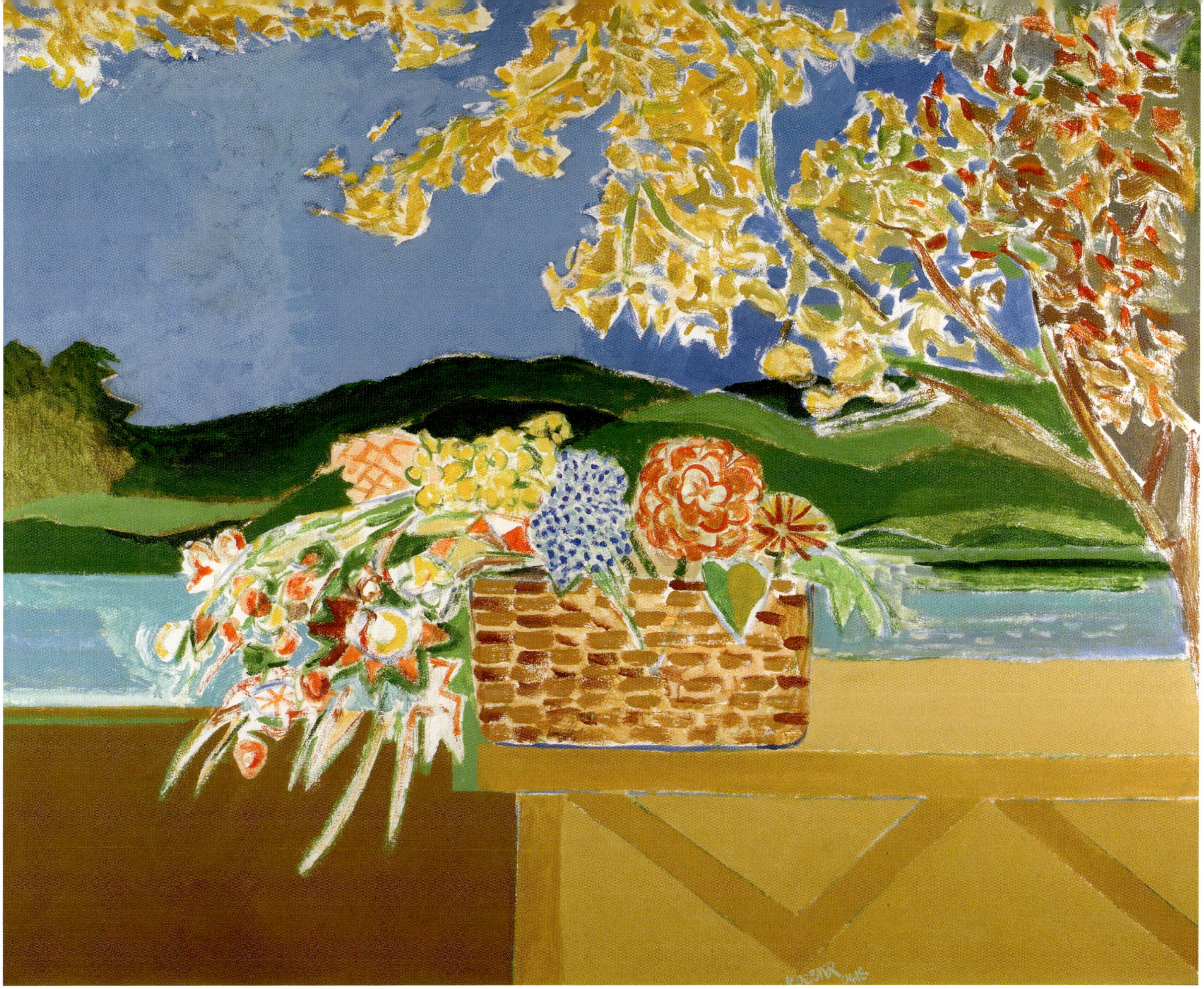

Celebration (2), acrylic on canvas, 42 x 50 inches, 2004, collection of the artist

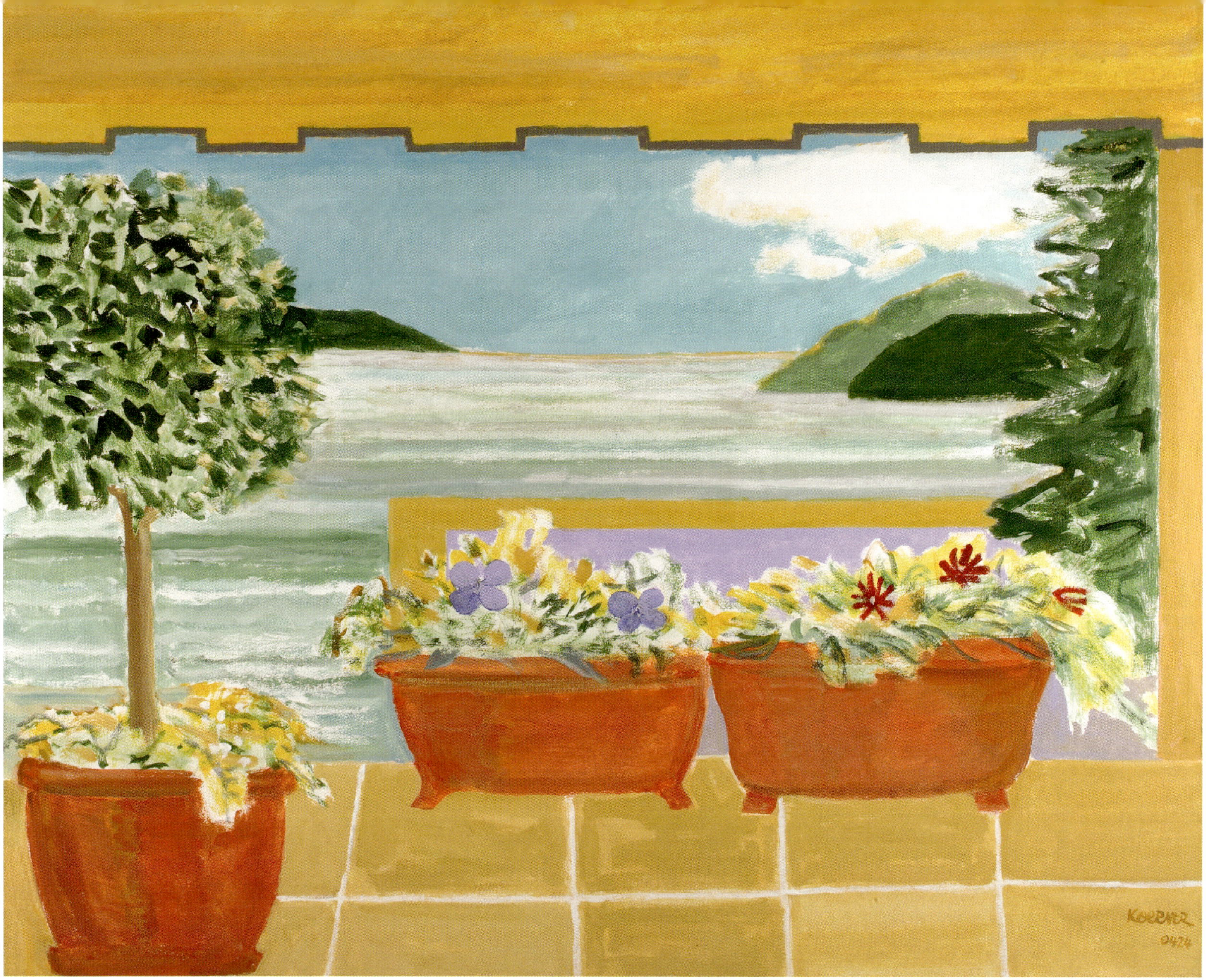

Celebration (7), acrylic on canvas, 42 x 50 inches, 2004, collection of the artist

The Message of the Shisen-Do

The Shisen-do is located just northeast of the centre of Kyoto, at the foot of the Higashiyama mountain range. The district, although part of the city now, still keeps its flavour of an old village.

Shisen-do was built in 1641 by Jozan Ishikawa (1583–1672), a samurai who was well-known as a scholar of Chinese classics and also as a landscape architect. He created Shisen-do as a place where he could live in quiet retirement.Walking up the stone path and steps, then through the spartan simplicity of the interior and suddenly encountering the vista of his garden was the highlight of my first visit to Japan.

The garden's white sand areas accentuate the trimmed azaleas and contrast with the calm surface of ponds, the textures of rocks and moss, and the surrounding greenery of trees. Everything is in relationships that lead the eye along the flow of the composition. The sound of water trickles through a bamboo pipe, intermittently punctuated by the clacking from a *sozu* as it overbalances and strikes a rock, tipping its contents of water. (In ancient times, *sozu* were used to scare away wild boars.)

Everything in the garden shows restraint, something that is almost unknown in the Western world. Shisen-do is a prototype of the aesthetic sensibility encompassing the many nuances and concepts inherent in Japanese culture. It is based on the highly regarded expression, *mono no aware*, which variously means "aesthetic sensitivity," "sense of beauty," or "sense of the beautiful."

In Western culture, scientific developments and emphasis on intellectual structures have led to a cult of consciousness through rationality at the expense of aesthetic values and intuitive feeling. As a result, conscious thinking is held to be more important than subconscious intuition. If scientific rationality is considered to be the road to truth and knowledge, by inference aesthetic intuition must be inferior to scientific understanding. Yet scientific discoveries frequently come from leaps of imagination, intuitive ideas that are afterward proven through experimental evidence. Reasoning, enquiring, and experimenting are admirable endeavours, but they are only half of the equation. The Japanese mind embraces both rational and non-rational ways of dealing with the world.

Intuitive perception also plays an important role in my working process. While I am painting I need to be completely relaxed, without any interference of critical viewing or thinking, and with no apprehension about the eventual results on the canvas. All is complete concentration and attention to the work and its needs. This meditative state of oneness with the painting, a lack of subject-object opposition, is well known in Zen. Later, of course, in a more detached mood, comes the checking, pondering, and sometimes re-working of the painting.

The concept of rising space in Japanese art has parallels in many Japanese gardens. Rising space can perhaps best be described as fluctuating, layered space ranging from wide vistas to shallow, restricted surface areas. For example, in a garden located on a hill, separate levels will appear to flow imperceptively together, creating the perception of deep space. In other gardens, diverse design elements, while organically linked, are distinguished by different patterns and textures. The intimacy of each area is preserved even though some Japanese Imperial properties are of considerable size.

All of these design elements find an affinity in my multiple horizon paintings where each unit is intended to work on its own and, at the same time, integrate into the total image. By providing more flexible layers of meaning I try to make the space more alive, more open to different interpretations. Interestingly, this duality is in accord with current scientific thinking, particularly theories about the transmission of light and quantum physics.

Nagare — flow — is the notion of space beginning inside the house and flowing in a continuous form outward. This is not only an aesthetic idea but is at the root of Japanese feeling toward the flow of life. In Western thought, life and decay are opposites. The Shinto belief is that living and dying are related and connected.

Another contrast between Western and Eastern aesthetics was articulated by Manet, Whistler, and other nineteenth-century artists in their enthusiasm for Japanese woodcut prints. They noted that the Western eye seems naturally to prefer the symmetrical while the Japanese eye appreciates the asymmetrical. The mind that thinks naturally in mathematical terms assumes that the asymmetrical is a deviation from the symmetrical, whereas the aesthetic mind might say that the symmetrical is a special, accidental arrangement—a chance

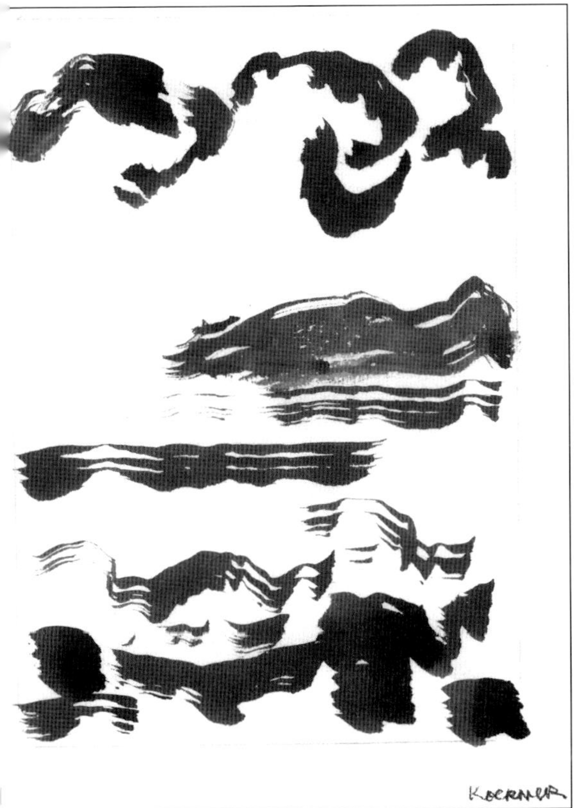

Three-Lined Haiku, ink brush on paper, 11.5 x 8 inches, 1980

The three lined haiku,
tried one evening to write one,
the day break is near.

ordering in a world that is fundamentally asymmetrical. Yet experiencing and observing nature would lead one to conclude that branches of a tree grow as they will, subject to light, nourishment, or obstructions. Similarly, flowers appear where the seeds happen to fall or are blown by the wind.

It is sometimes argued that Japanese gardens require a lot of planning and maintenance, and the forms are therefore not natural but imposed. That argument stems from a misunderstanding of what is meant by harmony with nature. Nature in a garden is not synonymous with nature gone wild. Nature's own life forms must be sensitively studied to discover how optimum beauty might be expressed. Without guidance, nature can quickly become a jungle. *Mono no aware* is recognizing an existing form and assisting it, realizing that harmony is not the application of a set of rigid calculations — such as in the mathematical layout of French gardens like Versailles — but is achieved by seeing into the heart of beauty, even into its prosaic aspects, such as the bamboo cane trestles that Japanese gardeners use to tenderly support the outstretched branches of old pine trees.

Despite the extreme ugliness of parts of Japanese cities, which very much resemble urban centres elsewhere in the world, there is evidence everywhere of appreciation for purity of form. This desire, which seems to be a national trait, appears not just in traditional architecture and design but in the attention to detail in things connected with daily life: the choice of utilitarian tableware, the placement of food on plates and trays, the care given to potted plants at the entrance to residences. A similar sensitivity is seen in contemporary designs on kimonos. They are not treated merely as decorative garments for special occasions but as continuously evolving expressions of a traditional aesthetic.

The connection between past and present Japanese sensibility toward purity of form is illustrated by the story of the Zen master Sen-no-Rikyu (1521–1591) when he instructed one of his disciples to clean the tea garden. The disciple washed the stones, the lanterns, and the steps several times, but each time he completed the cleaning he was ordered to repeat the process. Finally, in desperation, the disciple appealed to the Zen master for an explanation why the garden was still not pure. The master shook loose some autumn leaves from a branch of a maple tree, letting them fall and be carried by the breeze. "This," he said, "is purity."

Is Change Permanent?

It took an unknown expanse of time for man to develop from the most basic single-cell life form. At an unknown instant, the principal change of all changes took place — man arrived at consciousness. He became aware of his own existence. His mind became activated and gradually he became endowed with a wide range of perceptions and sensations.

It is not known how and when this change, which differentiates man from animals, took place. The cause for this change must have been determined in the spiritual sphere. It is idle speculation to try to explain or decipher this event which is one of the many mysteries of human life.

Since that moment of change, our faculties have undergone changes. Some of them have become more acute. For instance, we developed the ability to perform several complex tasks simultaneously, and to think logically, inventively, and creatively. Other faculties seem to have atrophied, such as the power of seeing or sensing objects and actions removed in space and time from ordinary observations.

More changes are likely to occur because of one significant aspect of our lives — the ever-present momentum of change. This is most noticeable in continual innovations in the various areas of technology and science. Recently, the area of communications has shown rapid advance. In medicine, while notable improvements are announced almost daily, antibiotics and other drugs used to fight contagious diseases are probably the most outstanding achievements of the last hundred years.

Change, like growth or the passage of time, is fundamentally a natural state. Change has been ongoing for millions of years. Change has formed today's creatures, their complex organs and instincts accumulating innumerable variations. Change has shaped the earth we live on, demonstrating its constancy in earthquakes and weather. Our bodies renew themselves continually, the climate changes not only with the seasons, galaxies go from birth to destruction to new creation.

Change also occurs in individuals, in a purely spiritual form, as we develop awareness of our inner selves.

Art, as a human endeavour, is an example of the liveliness that goes hand in hand with change. In earlier societies, the artist was recognized as a spokesperson for the people, a storyteller or carver, who had the vision and the proficiency to express their emotional needs. This bond between artist/poet and community existed until some time in the seventeenth century when skepticism started replacing blind faith.

Inevitably, artists belong to their time and place. Quite naturally, they will reflect its character and biases in their work. Reflections can be very perceptive and strike a chord of affirmation and enthusiastic acceptance. This was true until the end of the Renaissance. After that time, artists explored modes that were not as representational and, therefore, not as easy to read, leading to the beginning of alienation between artist and viewer.

Paul Klee complained, "*Das Volk trägt uns nicht*" — "we don't have the support of the people." Yet he was reacting to his changing world in a very legitimate and creative way. The Impressionists' landscape paintings became more and more unlike what was previously known as a landscape, and their still life paintings became even less like those of their predecessors. Suddenly there were no more velvety Chardin peaches. Cézanne's still life paintings are as far from the Dutch still life tradition as his nudes are from a Titian nude. Only much later was it generally realized that art had changed into a language peculiar to itself. Similarly, the sciences developed their own idiom, another symptom of change in a world that had become more complex.

In the visual arts the next step was a search for a means of rendering movement. There were attempts by the Italian painters Gino Severini (1883–1966) and Umberto Boccioni (1882–1916). The French artist Marcel Duchamp painted a nude descending a staircase in 1912, but movement on a picture plane was better indicated indirectly than literally. It called for more than a new method of portrayal or a new treatment; it required the development of sequence. Quite logically, this led to the motion picture which adopted the visual arts' previous aim of representing the world as closely as possible. In other words, cinema adopted representation.

If Impressionists were well aware of the changes in the study of optics, Cubists were aware of the new theories of quanta and relativity asserted by Albert Einstein. In

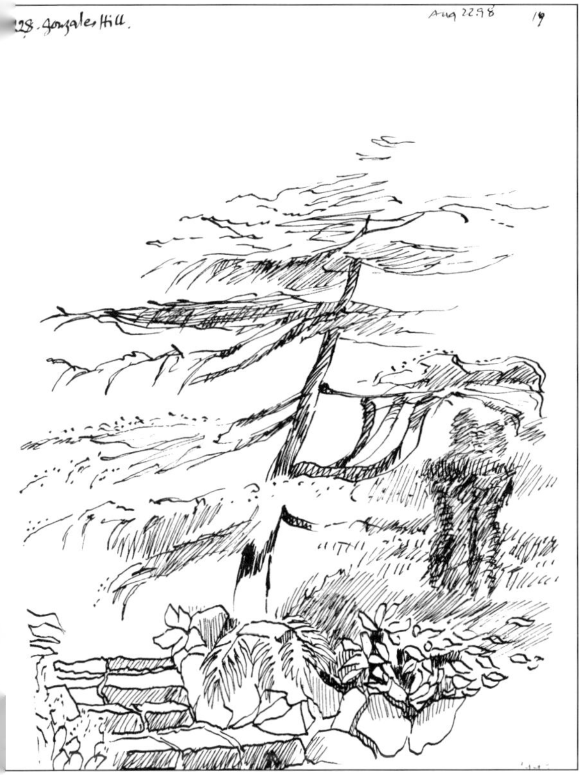

Gonzales Hill, ink on paper, 10.5 x 7.8 inches, 1998

some way, this awareness influenced their exploration and use of multiple aspects of form. Even if this did not happen deliberately, the sensitivity of the artist prepares him to react in a seismographic way to the slightest changes in his environment. Inversely, it is also possible that the momentum of change and its influence on everyday life can lead to a reaction by creative artists.

Such reaction occurred early in this century when Duchamp exhibited a urinal at the 1917 Society of Independent Artists show. Here an ordinary object, stripped of any connotation as a cultural object, drew attention to its very existence. It was also an act of showmanship, intended to attract attention. The "pure painting" of the past that all Dadaists vehemently opposed was, to them, not capable of commenting on a world badly in need of change. They saw conventional art as escapist, isolated in its aestheticism.

Duchamp was the principal leader of Dada. He put aside paints, brushes, and canvas to create an anti-art of "readymade" objects and images. His concern, and that of his colleagues, was to totally diverge from the art of his time, even to "humiliate" it, as Tristan Tzara (1896–1963) advocated, by assigning it "a subordinate place in the supreme movement measured only in terms of life."[1]

André Breton, the founder of Surrealism, went a step further by calling painting "a lamentable expedient" in a world whose "more and more necessary transformation [was] other than that which could be achieved on canvas."[2]

Dada got its name in Zurich in 1916, although it originated four years earlier. The nonsense vocabularly of Dada perfectly denoted its attitude toward nineteenth-century bourgeois values, and its logic was justified in view of the carnage of World War I. Surrealism evidenced the changes taking place in the areas of psychology and psychiatry, namely the conclusions reached by Freud and Jung, and was particularly attracted to the interpretation of dreams and expositions of the subconscious.

During the 1940s Surrealism lost its early lustre and ceased to exist. Dada, on the other hand, had a vision of the future and was suited to accommodate the irrational in human behavior. Jean Arp, one of its exponents, wrote, "Dada wishes to destroy the hoaxes of reason and to discover an unreasoned order." At the heart of Dada lay the "gratuitous act," the paradoxical, spontaneous gesture aimed at revealing the inconsistency and insanity of conventional beliefs. The senseless performances and "happenings" of the 1950s were foreshadowed by earlier acts performed at Dada *soirées* where the value of art was believed to be in the act of making it rather than in its eventual outcome.

Salvador Dali dominated the Surrealist scene for a short period of time in the 1930s. I saw his first one-man show in Paris, at the Galerie Camille Goemans in 1929, when he exhibited his famous *Persistence of Memory*. His acrobatic illusionism was stunning, although his "paranoiac-critical method" of painting, as he called it, and his hallucinatory visions, left me unconvinced. Later, his intensity and his involvement with psychological theory seemed to dissipate as his affectations and desire for publicity overtook his abilities.

The Surrealist I found most appealing was René Magritte. His art contains few of the bizarre figures of Max Ernst, and none of the paranoid fantasies of Dali. Instead, it involves irony and deadpan humour, which I thought were pleasantly surprising. Michel Foucault's *Les Mots et les Choses* (*The Order of Things*) (1966) intensely interested Magritte, as did the writings of Hegel, Heidegger, and Sartre. Magritte's fascination with the relationship of words and things became the theme of many of his paintings. His *Ceci n'est pas une pipe* (1928–29) initially met with disfavour but, in its simplicity, showed great foresight in preceding Klee and Kandinsky, who later insisted that a painting is nothing other than itself.[3] Formally, Magritte was also a precursor. His "all-over" treatment became familiar in abstract painting.

There are many different ways of looking at or approaching art. Artists and collectors, to whom art is an important part of life, often have a clear and quite specific line of interest. Other people may have a wide or diverse range of appreciation that may seem incomprehensible and which they may hope will become clearer with the passage of time. One such person in search of the unknown was the Australian, John Peter Russell, who lived and worked in Europe between 1876 and 1921. He was an able painter, although his work remained obscure until the 1970s when art historians discovered he had played a decisive role in the lives of many French artists.

In 1886 Russell met Monet on Belle Ile in Brittany and the two men painted together during that summer. Long before Van Gogh and Monet, Russell collected Japanese woodcuts and prints. He became friends with Van Gogh and owned twelve of his paintings. Many of the Van Gogh drawings in Russell's

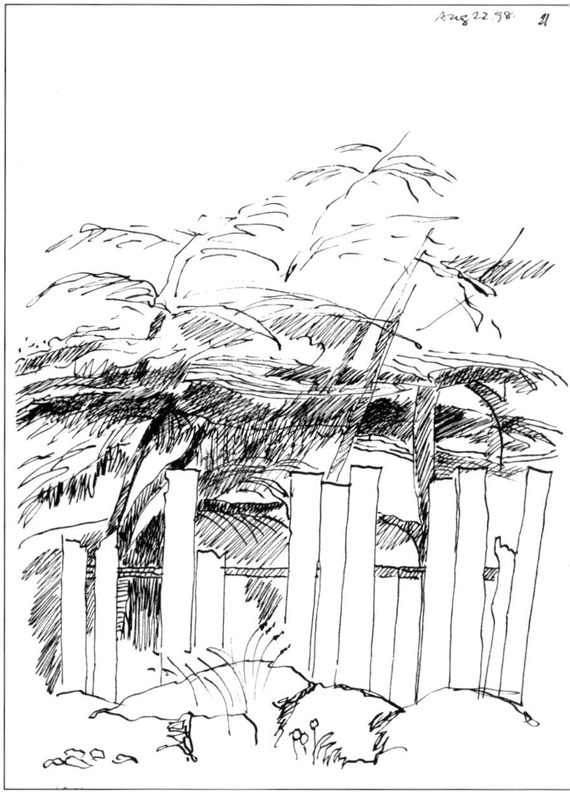

Untitled ink drawing, ink on paper, 10.5 x 7.6 inches, 1991, collection of the artist

art collection were related to major canvases painted during Van Gogh's first season in Arles, a collection that also included paintings by Monet, whom he introduced to Matisse.[4]

Many periods in history have discovered new truths and new ways of looking at things. Some periods discover, mostly in retrospect, false premises leading to fallacies and delusions. Often these deceptions contain a fragment of truth and are therefore more difficult to identify.

In 1910 Wassily Kandinsky published *On the Spiritual in Art* in which he wrote that art's force and endurance "do not lie in the external but in the deep roots of mystical inner thought." Although this statement is substantially true, it leaves enough scope for misinterpretation. That is what happened when a great number of artists in Europe and North America endorsed the idea of the primacy of intuition over analytical thinking. The American artist Marsden Hartley (1877–1943), for instance, became immensely enthusiastic about mysticism and, in his paintings, tried to suggest the universal and transcendental. He was disappointed when a visitor observed, "You have no idea of what you are doing. These pictures are full of kabbalistic signs and symbols." Hartley did not know the difference between the occult and the spiritual.

Another example of misguided intentions is Hilma af Klint. She was a Swedish artist (1862–1944) who experimented with mediumistic messages and subliminal influences, allowing herself to be led by "Higher Powers" who instructed her as to what she should paint.

A gifted painter who also experimented with the occult was František Kupka (1871–1957). His interest in the supernatural dated from his childhood in Bohemia. Although Kupka is now credited as a pioneer of abstract art, he was not shy about stating his beliefs about contacting the dead and other questionable practices.

In contrast to this flawed view of the spiritual is the work of Matisse. Here the process of change can be traced by looking at the way Matisse's work was seen by his contemporaries.

In 1905 Matisse was condemned as an apostle of ugliness, yet later he was praised for the spendour of his colour. In 1934, the critic Pierre Courthion wrote that Matisse was "a painter's painter. His work is purely visual." This reputation as an artist devoted only to visual sensation caused Matisse to be viewed as a hedonist and, indeed, he did provide intense aesthetic pleasure through his decorative organization of the picture surface. At the same time, the criticism of his work as "purely visual" was misinterpreted to suggest he was concerned with visual pleasure alone, that his luscious use of colour and seductive nude figures were mere rejoicings in the good life. Of course, Matisse's paintings are a celebration of life, but they also transcend any superficial frivolity of the shallowly pleasurable. His lightheartedness is not without a sense of profound emotion.

Matisse's work recalls Keats' assertion that poetry "is to sooth the cares, and lift the thoughts of man."[5] If Matisse's paintings were the result of his attitude toward life, they also project the immediacy of his experience and were the product of intense private imperatives. His output was awesome. In addition to hundreds of paintings and murals, he produced drawings, prints, book illustrations, tapestry and window designs, ceramics, and sculptures.

Matisse's life was filled with hardships. His father was very much opposed to his desire to become an artist. Critical reactions to his early paintings were hostile. He spent many years in abject poverty. Although he had collectors in Russia, Germany, and the United States, his achievements were not recognized by his own countrymen until he was fifty-one years old, when the Luxembourg Museum purchased one of his odalisques. Despite all this, his canvases are the happiest of all the twentieth-century French artists. His work and his life demonstrated a relentless devotion to his art.

Matisse's attitude toward dealing with reality is well expressed in his own words. "There is an inherent truth which must be disengaged from the outward appearance of the object... this is the only truth that matters." His goal was to "penetrate" the subject, going so far as to identify himself with it to bring out its essential truth. He believed that the work is not changed by the different conditions under which it is realized; "on the contrary, the expression of this truth... gives it light and even life, by the turn of the spirit of the artist whose expression it is."

The questioning of reason as the predominant criterion of art making is as justifiable today as it was in the Dada period after World War I. Duchamp's urinal and Claes Oldenburg's *Soft Typewriter* (1963) are direct forerunners of Canadian artist Kelly Wood's *Continuous Garbage* (2003), a 300-photograph documentation of

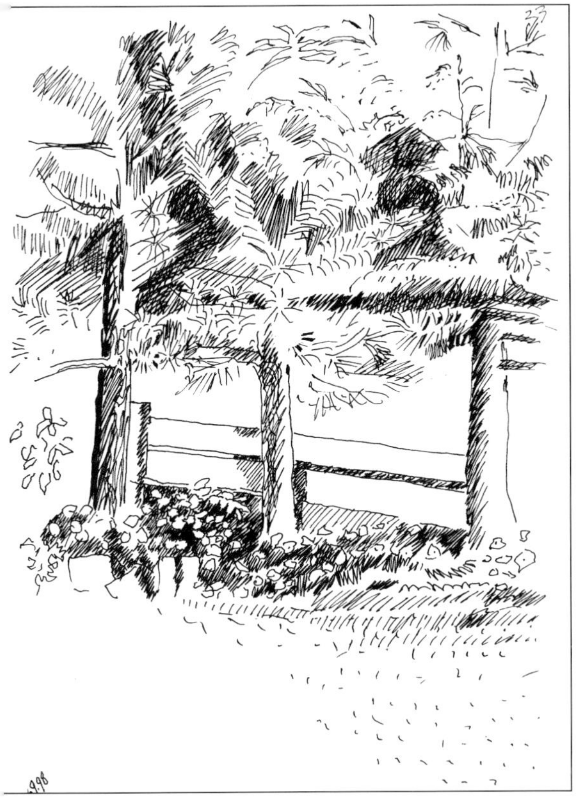

Untitled ink drawing, ink on paper, 10.5 x 7.6 inches, 1998

her personal trash, accumulated in plastic bags over a period of five years. Similarly, in *sleep patterns* (40-minute video, 1999), Canadian artist Germaine Koh documents the beds she slept in during one year, showing in a succession of stills with voice-over what abstract observation of an object may reveal or hide. In both cases, the photographic records are less than revealing.

Commentaries, in unadulterated artspeak, only add to the confusion. The following example is from a text by curator Okwui Enwezor written for the Vancouver Art Gallery's *Mirror's Edge* exhibition:

> Whether through the invocation of the city as a built environment and constructed terrain, or as a ceaselessly contingent, deterritoralized and reterritoralized space; occupied and reconstituted by the massive drift of populations travelling beyond home, nation, and identity; or the city as an emergent form of a new sociality, a node in the reworked and rerouted paths of the information autobahn, linking globalization to remote circuits of production and circulation, today it has become clear that the very discourse of the city requires new elaboration. No longer can the city, in the old situationalist mode, be read in relation to a performative event which the anonymous figure of the urban dweller can only traverse as a ghost that haunts its marginal locales, the seedy dives of the discredited immigrant quarters. The city today has acquired, through years of grime, immigration, economic and technological activity, a new density. Thus the global city sits today at a crossroads of a new imagery reconstitution.

This is the pathetic way a changing world affects some artists and their critics —a focus on the ordinary object, and a determination to give it new importance and a new but stilted context.

Looking at changes such as these can also remind us that about 150 years ago an English clergyman put forward an argument that disturbed everyone, but which has since grown ever more convincing by its sheer logic and weight of evidence. The evolution of organisms outlined by Charles Darwin in *On the Origin of Species by Means of Natural Selection* has, most recently, been confirmed in the mutations of some AIDS lineages. In his time, Darwin was the target of great opposition from theologians and the public at large. They pointed out that no one had ever seen a new species arise. Darwin claimed that nature changes not by sudden leaps but by gradual evolution. Today we know that sudden leaps are also a natural form of change. Quantum observations show that reality is incurably granular, while geology reveals that catastrophes have helped to destroy dinosaurs and promote mammals. So the Darwinian synthesis marches on, stronger than ever. New evidence continues to appear in biology, physics, geology, and cosmology. New data hints that even the most fundamental laws of nature can mutate and evolve. Scientific theories point to an ever-changing, self-organizing world that never stops diversifying. There is a natural creativity within the system, a creativity that creates more creativity and change.

Scientists now agree that even the simplest organisms cannot be broken down into a single building block, nor can a unified field theory explain and encompass the abundance of nature's transformations and diversity. There is, however, a sequence that can be discerned in the arrangement of the basic constituents which seems to point to the conclusion that the essence of life is something immaterial. In addition to the supranatural forces that effect change in the largest masses of dense matter and in the smallest particles, I believe all matter responds to a cosmic, spiritual principle. Change is a ceaseless aspect of life and, although it eludes examination, is one of the constants within our enigmatic universe.

As I look back on my sixty years of work, I can see some slight changes, but they are mostly of a technical nature. *Plus ça change plus c'est la même chose.* I have experimented with different media and different ways of painting. I have commented on Impressionism and Cubism and, of course, Abstraction. They all assisted in developing my own vocabulary, suited to what I wanted to say. They were all stages of change; however, my foremost objective has remained the same.

I remember a Sunday morning when Eileen and I were in Ryerson Church and our daughters were attending Sunday School in an adjacent building. The sun was streaming through the pseudo-Gothic windows and suddenly it came to me, unexpectedly but very clearly, that my painting must represent fully my commitment to the world view that I had been trying to absorb from the writings of Bô Yin Râ. He advises that our actions, our words, and even our "thoughts" should all be

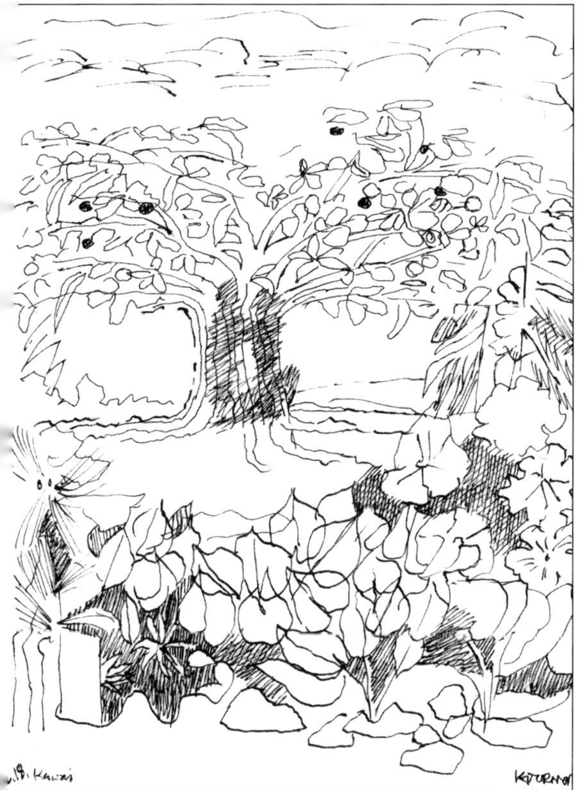

Untitled ink drawing, ink on paper, 10.5 x 7.6 inches, n.d.

ruled by the same feeling of love, a love that is disinterested, insofar as it does not try to dominate or possess.

The direction that Bô Yin Râ indicates is not an easy path, but after all these years I still believe in his advice. His books are guides to a perception of reality that neither philosophic speculation nor dogmatic faith can attain. I have attempted to produce work that would be in complete accord with this reality, a task that hasn't been too difficult as I have lived fully wrapped up in it. Throughout my life certain people have recognized my objective, but it has also been aimed at a future generation that may be more conscious of our delicate link with the spiritual world. I hope they will detect echoes of such meaning in my work.

I have always disliked the word *inspiration*, as it had an unfortunate relationship to nineteenth-century Romanticism. Then, as mentioned earlier, I realized one day that the word comes from the Latin *in spiritu*. Painting is eminently capable of metaphoric indications which provide a natural way to non-verbally communicate spiritual matters.

In several of my series of paintings, nonverbal clues begin where the title ends. The *Lighthouse* series, for instance, started with an actual view of a lighthouse but, over time, grew to incorporate other meanings — from a lighthouse to a non-lighthouse to an inner lighthouse.

Throughout the evolution of my work, the prime constants have been my commitment to our spiritual legacy and my endeavour to bear witness to it in everything I do. I believe we are born into this physical world by "falling" from the spiritual heights of the lightworld, unable to resist the attraction of the physical sphere. The lightworld remains close to us, but cannot manifest its presence unless we develop our perceptive faculties to permit us to apprehend the immaterial energy that gives that realm its substance, breath, and life. Here I am referring to the most essential change of all — apprehending the resources created by the Spirit's radiant substance in our soul. I believe that is the main objective of life, even if our minds cannot explain what we consciously perceive, and even if this aim is not recognized or followed in the noise and hustle of daily life. At times the world of light comes close to us. It happens at moments when we are moved by a work of art, a beautiful landscape, or a piece of music; each is brought about unknowingly by inner contact with a world we cannot see. The experience can be put aside and forgotten, yet it would be wise to heed these moments as important indications of change within us, leading eventually to the most far-reaching change of all — knowledge of our inmost self. The first step toward this goal is the fulfillment of all our duties and obligations (so that our conscience is clear). Only then is it possible to be in a state of inner peace, and only then can there be further progress along the path to where change becomes permanent.

Endnotes:

1. H. Matarasso Librairie, *Surrealism: Poésie et art contemporain*, Paris, 1949.
2. *Le Surrealism et la Peinture*, Paris: Gallimard, 1928.
3. Michel Foucault's monograph about Magritte's *Ceci n'est pas une pipe* was published in 1973.
4. Hilary Spurling, *The Unknown Matisse*, Hamish Hamilton, 1998.
5. John Keats, "Sleep and Poetry," December 1816.

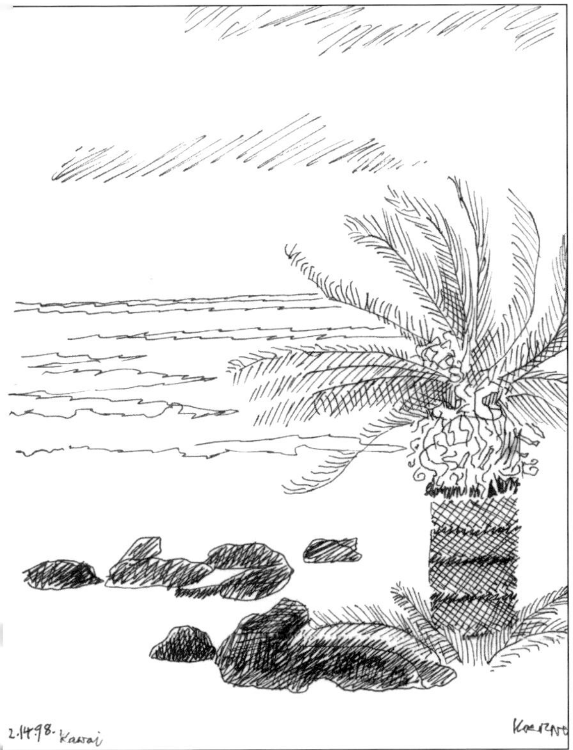

Untitled ink drawing, ink on paper, 10.5 x 7.6 inches, 1998

From the Book on the Living God by Bô Yin Râ

The forces of the universe are causes generating effects. This has been misunderstood, leading to the quest for an imagined first or primal cause. There has never been a first cause. God eternally brings forth himself/herself, rising from the chaos of the unformed elements of Being. Nothing here is cause, nor anything effect. There is alone the Spirit's free, self-knowing will, which manifests its very being, for itself, as God.

At their very source, where they are hurled forth from the ground of Being, the unformed elements of Being manifest themselves as chaos, as the profoundest, most prolific forces of eternal nature. Here they assert themselves as purely driven needs and urges, neither aware of their being nor of the consequences they effect. Here they still are opposed to one another and every element asserts itself alone.

From the self-assertion of opposing elements will result polarity and thus reciprocal attraction. Such attraction will prepare, in time not countable in human terms, the gradual accumulation of the scattered elements.

In the dimension of the soul of mortal man the elements arising from the ground of Being will then become united once again, if human will aspires to attain that goal. The turmoil in our hearts that seeks expression, the inner restlessness that keeps us constantly in motion, the driving need of having to achieve a certain goal, herein we may perceive the influence effected by the elements of Being, which seek to unify themselves again in us, now in a specific, individuated form.

As to the universe, it exists because the elements of Being cause it to exist; not, however, of itself.

We still speak of a God whom we consider the creator of all things; a God who brought forth and sustains an everlasting world in His own honour, declaring His own glory. Yet such a vision of God and of creation's origin could only be excused in ages past that possessed no knowledge of the countless ways in which the elements of Being manifest themselves; today, knowledge should be sufficient for a thinking mind to put away the old ideas.

God is the creator of only His own Self in all things that exist. Everything that truly *is* embodies Being that is God's. God brings forth Himself alone, and He did not, as some believe, create the human being (starting with Adam) and the world. The *perpetuum mobile*, which fools and sages have endeavoured to invent, always has existed and cannot be invented a second time. Those who laboured to invent it merely sensed within themselves the essence of the boundless All; the truth of that which is in being through itself — without beginning, without end — Eternal Life proceeding through its cosmic cycles.

The forces that give shape to all the suns and worlds within creation are aspects of the Spirit — elements that form the Ground of Being — and as they manifest themselves in time and space, they generate phenomena within these limitations; things existing only for a time, and always subject to the laws of space. Forever altering their effect, the elements that form the Ground of Being at times will manifest themselves as forces that create, at other times they will destroy what they have created. They themselves are simply *in being*, from eternity to eternity, and they were not created by anyone.

There never has been a beginning of this everlasting life, nor can it ever have an end. The whole, unfathomable universe with its immeasurable wealth of forms, with all its visible and unseen dimensions, is but the ever restless surface of an eternal spiritual sea from which arises, through its own inherent power, the radiant cloud of the Godhead.

Except for God, there would exist no universe, and if there were no universe, there would exist no God.

Bô Yin Râ's teachings are published by
Kober Press
2534 Chilton Way, Berkeley CA 94704 USA.
www.kober.com
koberpress@mindspring.com

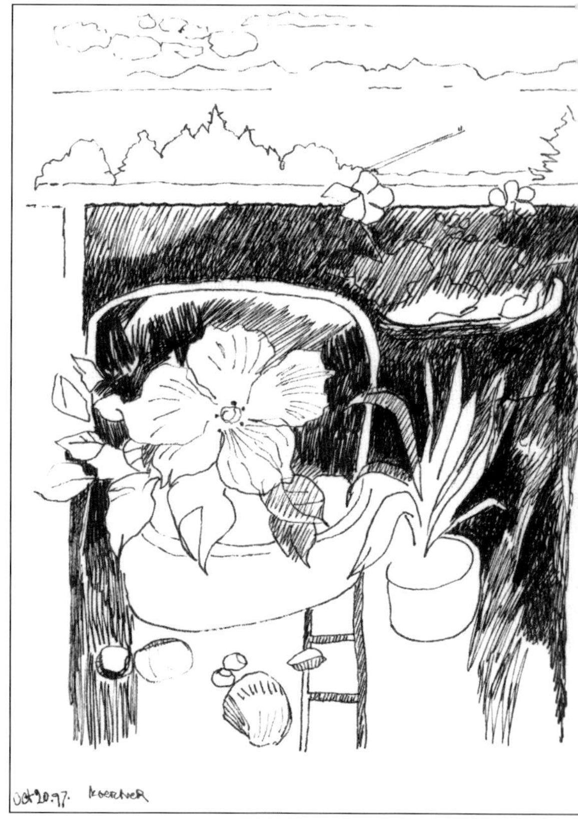

Untitled ink drawing, ink on paper, 10.5 x 7.6 inches, 1997

*John Michael Anthony Koerner**

1913 –

painter, printmaker, muralist

1913	born September 29, 1913, in Nový Jičín, Czechoslovakia
1939	arrived in Canada, settled in Vancouver BC
	Canadian citizen since 1944
1953–1958	teacher of drawing and painting, Vancouver School of Art
1958–1962	teacher of drawing and painting, University of British Columbia
1962–	living and painting in Vancouver BC

EDUCATION

studied painting with Fritz Kausek in Prague 1931–1934;
with Victor Tischler, Othon Friesz, Paul Colin, Paris, 1938–1939;
studied philosophy and history of art at the Sorbonne, Paris

*The family name Körner was officially changed to Koerner in 1971. Some early works were signed John Körner.

Exhibitions

SOLO EXHIBITIONS

2005	*Celebration Series*, Diane Farris Gallery, Vancouver BC
2000	*From Balcony to Compass Rose*, John Ramsay Gallery, Vancouver BC
1999	*New Paintings on an Ancient Theme*, John Ramsay Gallery, Vancouver BC
1998	*The Garden of Eden Series*, John Ramsay Gallery, Vancouver BC
1997	*Variations on the Lighthouse*, John Ramsay Gallery, Vancouver BC
1996	*Pacific Gateway Series*, Diane Farris Gallery, Vancouver BC
1995	Yongen Gallery, Ginza, Tokyo, Japan
	Kisshodo Gallery, Kyoto, Japan
	Awanosato Art Forum, Tokushima, Japan
	Diane Farris Gallery, Vancouver BC
1994	Fran Willis Gallery, Victoria BC
	Variations on a Theme, Diane Farris Gallery, Vancouver BC
1993	Clare Hall, Cambridge University, Cambridge UK
	Diane Farris Gallery, Vancouver BC
1992	Regent College, University of British Columbia
	retrospective: Art Gallery of Greater Victoria, Victoria BC
	Trinity Western University, Vancouver BC
1988	Robertson Gallery, Toronto ON
1986–1991	Diane Farris Gallery, Vancouver BC
1983	Annenberg Centre, Rancho Mirage CA
1976–1985	Bau-Xi Gallery, Vancouver BC and Toronto ON
1977	*African Series*, Bau-Xi Gallery, Vancouver BC
1970	Palm Springs Desert Museum, Palm Springs CA
	Galerie Lefort-Godard, Montréal QC
1967–1975	Bau-Xi Gallery, Vancouver BC
1966–1968	Dresdnere Gallery, Toronto ON
1965	Galerie Agnès Lefort, Montréal QC
1965–1968	Douglas Gallery, Vancouver BC
1964	Fraser Gallery, Vancouver BC
1963	Galerie Agnès Lefort, Montréal QC
1963–1965	Morris Gallery, Toronto ON
1960–1967	Galerie Mira Godard, Montréal QC
1959–1962	Laing Gallery, Toronto ON
1959–1967	Seligman Gallery, Seattle WA
1958–1960	Galerie Agnès Lefort, Montréal QC
1955–1963	New Design Gallery, Vancouver BC

SELECTED GROUP EXHIBITIONS

1993	National Gallery of Canada travelling exhibitions (Australia, Africa, India, England)
1992	National Gallery of Canada Biennial
1991	Prague, Czech Republic

SELECTED COMMISSIONS

1993	mural, The Magic Flute, Vancouver BC now in the collection of Vancouver General Hospital
1986	mural, Queen Elizabeth Theatre, Vancouver BC
1972	mural, Douglas Simpson residence, West Vancouver BC
1967	sculptural light mural, Duncan Hospital, Duncan BC
1967	mural, R.J. Young residence, West Vancouver BC

AWARDS

1967	Centennial Medal

AFFILIATIONS

associate British Columbia Society of Artists 1954, member 1955, president 1956–1958; Canadian Group of Painters 1957; associate Royal Canadian Academy of Arts 1960–1966; Federation of Canadian Artists 1960–1970.

PUBLICATIONS

Unseen Dimensions, John Koerner, Sono Nis Press, Victoria BC, 1997; twelve essays disclosing glimpses into the artist's creative process, illustrated.

Public Collections

Agnes Etherington Gallery, Queen's University, Kingston, Ontario
Alma Mater Society Art Gallery, University of British Columbia
Art Gallery of Greater Victoria, Victoria, British Columbia
Art Gallery of Ontario, Toronto, Ontario
Beaverbrook Gallery, Fredericton, New Brunswick
Burnaby Art Gallery, Burnaby, British Columbia
Centre for Dialogue, Simon Fraser University, Vancouver, British Columbia
Canadian Catholic Conference, Ottawa, Ontario
City of Vancouver, Queen Elizabeth Theatre, Vancouver, British Columbia
Clare Hall, Cambridge University, Cambridge, United Kingdom
Confederation Art Centre Gallery, Charlottetown, Prince Edward Island
Department of External Affairs, Government of Canada, Ottawa, Ontario
Desert Museum, Palm Springs, California
Edmonton Art Gallery, Edmonton, Alberta
Faculty Club, University of British Columbia
Government House, Victoria, British Columbia
Graduate Centre, University of British Columbia
Hart House, University of Toronto, Toronto, Ontario
Joseph Hirshhorn Museum, Washington D.C.
Justice Building, Ottawa, Ontario
London Public Library and Art Museum, London, United Kingdom
McMichael Collection, Kleinburg, Ontario
Musée des Beaux Arts, Montréal, Québec
Musée des Arts Contemporain, Montréal, Québec
National Gallery of Canada, Ottawa, Ontario
Palliative Care Unit, Health Sciences Centre, University of British Columbia
Palm Springs Museum, Palm Springs, California
Seattle Art Museum, Seattle, Washington
Sir George Williams Art Gallery, Concordia University, Montreal, Québec
Skin Care Centre, Vancouver General Hospital, Vancouver, British Columbia
The Tate Gallery, London, United Kingdom
Waterfront Hotel, Vancouver, British Columbia
Tokushima Museum, Japan
Willistead Art Gallery, Windsor, Ontario
Winnipeg Art Gallery, Winnipeg, Manitoba
Vancouver Art Gallery, Vancouver, British Columbia
Vancouver General Hospital, Vancouver, British Columbia

Corporate Collections

BC Gas Inc.
Bank of America
Burns Fry Ltd.
Canadian Forest Products Ltd.
Esso Resources
Royal Bank of Canada
Teleglobe Canada
Toronto Dominion Bank
Imperial Oil

Index

A

B

C

D

E

F

G

H

I

J

N

O

P

Q

R

S